IRELAND'S ECONOMIC HISTORY

Ireland's Economic History

Crisis and Development
in the North and South

Gerard McCann

PlutoPress
www.plutobooks.com

First published 2011 by Pluto Press
345 Archway Road, London N6 5AA
www.plutobooks.com

Distributed in the United States of America exclusively by
Palgrave Macmillan, a division of St. Martin's Press LLC,
175 Fifth Avenue, New York, NY 10010

Distributed in the Republic of Ireland and Northern Ireland by
Gill & Macmillan Distribution, Hume Avenue, Park West, Dublin 12, Ireland. Phone +353 1
500 9500. Fax +353 1 500 9599. E-Mail: sales@gillmacmillan.ie

British Library Cataloguing in Publication Data
A catalogue record for this book is available from the British Library

ISBN 978 0 7453 3031 0 Hardback
ISBN 978 0 7453 3030 3 Paperback

Library of Congress Cataloging in Publication Data applied for

This book is printed on paper suitable for recycling and made from fully managed and
sustained forest sources. Logging, pulping and manufacturing processes are expected to
conform to the environmental standards of the country of origin.

10 9 8 7 6 5 4 3 2 1

Designed and produced for Pluto Press by Curran Publishing Services, Norwich

Simultaneously printed digitally by CPI Antony Rowe, Chippenham, UK and
Edwards Bros in the United States of America

CONTENTS

ACKNOWLEDGEMENTS

This book is the product of a search through Irish economic history for ideas that could shed light on why the island has been so unfortunate in its progress and development. Tragedies have been recurrent and solutions have been elusive. In order to get some appreciation of the complexities of this turbulent history, I have trawled through primary and secondary documents which have marked the understanding of this topic. This research is built upon the platform created by a long list of economic historians, and hopefully a clearer overview of Irish economic history has resulted. In terms of acknowledgements, I would like to thank Roger van Zwanenberg for the initial idea and the encouragement to undertake such a task. Likewise, I would like to offer my appreciation to the Pluto staff and associates for their patience: Robert, Chris, Susan, Alec and Conor. For comments on the points made or reading drafts, I would like to acknowledge the help of Stephen McCloskey, Ciaran Crossey, Eoin Ó Broin, Charlie Fisher, Andy Storey, Peter Collins, Denis O'Hearn, Paul Hainsworth, Karen, Feilim, Doug, Angela and Birgit. Ba mhaith liom aitheantas a thabhairt do ról mo chomhghleacaithe ar an Fhóram Eacnamaíochta Iarthar Bhéal Feirtse as a ndíograis agus as an treoir a thug siad dom thar na blianta. Thanks are also due to the helpful librarians in St Mary's University College, Queen's University, Trinity College, Krosno College, Cork University, the Ulster Folk Museum, and the wonderful Linen Hall Library. Faults and flaws, neglect and oversights are due, in total, to the author.

INTRODUCTION

The collapse of the Irish economy in 2010 signalled the end of a particularly difficult period in Ireland's economic history. As with the cessation of the conflict in the 1990s, the recent economic crisis has created a moment for reflection on the history of a troubled island. Typified by extremes and crises, the advanced neoliberal economy that became the Celtic Tiger did not leave a legacy of social enhancement or sustainability, but one of perversity, squander and poverty in equal measure. The greed that fixated the beneficiaries of this economic model contorted Irish society to leave a sense of victimhood for those caught in the fall-out of this type of economic development. Through it Irish society changed, as did the economy, but the neoliberal method of forcing a society into an artificial, eminently destructive economic process should be seen as not new to Irish history. Its patterns of development have been familiar, involving land deals, corrupt politicians, cronyism, monopolies, financial scandals and an ideology that has placed profit for a few above the needs of the rest. The disastrous outcomes have been similar across a number of moments in Irish economic history.

The collapse not only revealed the extent to which the Irish economy had become integrated into the broader European and global economic systems, it served to highlight the vacillating and diverging processes that have destabilized its economic base. Often against conventional economic wisdom, the various political gambles that have been taken have had a tendency to accentuate the peripheral position of the island, warp commercial activity, aggravate divisions across the island, and arguably frustrate social and economic development. The underlying problems are arguably a result of policy management and governance. Within the context of the European Union, the Republic of Ireland and Northern Ireland have remained anomalies, committed to the principles of European integration with its freedom of movement, integrated social market and dissolving borders, yet they have been divided against the general spirit of the treaties that were intended to bring Europe's peoples closer together. Economic divergence on the island of Ireland has been endemic to its social and political make-up, leaving a system that has created one of the largest gaps between rich and poor in Europe and one of the most polarized and conflict-prone communities in the world.

Apart from rare social market interventions, the economic manage-ment of the island has remained steadfastly conservative, monetarist and divisive, against the prevailing social democratic and democratic socialist trends prevalent on the continent.

An ideological understanding provides one answer to the question of why Ireland has suffered such a prolonged disloca-tion process. The disintegration of key financial, indigenous and public sectors in the southern economy with the end of the Celtic Tiger, and the entrenched dependency of the north on the British Treasury, have highlighted fault lines across the Irish economy. Ideological extremes have become systemic, not only affecting the political economy of the island, but also shaping a long and difficult economic history that has evolved out of colonial engagement, imbalanced industrial development, dependence on an agricultural base, a structural deficit, and disjointed strategies that have led to shocks and crises on a regular basis. The trauma that has been Irish economic history has to a large extent been a product of unsustainable development and a continual failure to overcome divergence across the island. Arguably, it has been a result of mismanagement by successive administrations throughout its modern history.

The Irish economy has conventionally been portrayed as a product of the island's political history, divided and analysed as distinct entities, north and south, with each taking differing paths to development. Commentators and government agencies alike have looked at the two regions on the island in terms of absolutes, without adequately acknowledging the interactive nature of these border economies. From a policy perspective, the respective juris-dictions have been studied as separate, occasionally connecting, political entities while at a macroeconomic level the various points of interaction (particularly in Belfast and Dublin) have been evaluated from differing UK or EU perspectives. This skewed approach to Irish economic history suggests the need for analysis that circumvents the conventional policy bias, to investigate crises and change from a more integrated economic and ideological basis. One of the primary aims of this book is to highlight the systemic shocks that have come to shape these respective economic bases, north and south, and discuss the uneven patterns of development that have led to often volatile, often extreme, systems of economic management.

As an overview of the development of the economy on the island of Ireland, this polemic aims to search for policy links in an otherwise uneven process. In order to do this a chronological approach has been taken. To clarify the points being presented and to give the analysis a framework, the text has been arranged into successive periods of economic development: the colonial economy, famine, industrialization and militarization, partition, the war economies, the modernization process, the conflict economy, the role of the border, peace and reconciliation, neoliberal Ireland and the recession. Because of the scale of the undertaking, the research draws from both primary and secondary sources, with deference to the authoritative commentators who have specialized in the various periods covered. This study is built on their work. From this reading of modern Irish economic history three distinct features emerge: first, the conservative and often fundamentalist nature of economic theory as it has been applied to the Irish economy; second, the destructive implications of the forced divergence of the northern and southern economies; and third, conflict as a disintegrating factor, which evolved into an economic process in its own right.

The book also aims to provide an analysis of economic development on the island of Ireland with respect to issues pertinent to the causes of regional conflict, marginalization, dependency, inequality and economic injustice, marking key staging posts for the Irish economy as it has evolved. It looks at the influence of classical liberalism, and its hybrid neoliberalism, in the development of the island's economy; assesses partition as a facet in the volatile nature of the economy; highlights the patterns of development on the island in respect to co-joined border economic systems; and, finally, examines the possibilities of cohesion and harmonization within the context of an island economy. The study explores the processes that have underpinned economic development on the island to date, suggesting that the base motivations that drove the bankers, property developers and politicians into the recent cycle of exploitation have the same ideological stem as those who exploited the land and its people during the famine, carried the island into the sectarian carve-up of partition and profited from the forced emigration of literally millions of Irish people, generation after generation. The intention is to draw upon expertise and informed perspectives to present a comprehensive overview of the patterns of development, starting with the structural adjustment of the pre-famine years, with all its sociological implications, and finishing with the breakdown of the recent depression. Its scope is wide and its analysis is an introduction to the various topics. Many points are included to provoke reflection on the historical management of the Irish economy. Ultimately, its objective is to explore the contention that the political economy of the island of Ireland and its dominant ideological form – emanating from classical liberalism through to neoliberalism – has been *a*, if not *the*, cause of this turbulent history.

1 THE COLONIAL ECONOMY (1831–1860)

The Act of Union between England and Ireland came into effect on 1 January 1801. From that point onward economic activity in Ireland was to change radically, with the ubiquitous and indigenous economic system – as it had evolved on the island until that period – being forced into a larger, more centralized laissez-faire trading system dominated by London. The shock that this brought to the island's economic base could be sourced to article six of the Act, which introduced a mechanism to abolish tariff protection for Irish produce, abolish the Irish exchequer and merge the currencies:

> That, from the first day of january one thousand eight hundred and one, all prohibitions and bounties on the exports of articles, the growth, produce, or manufacture of either country, to the other, shall cease .... That all articles, the growth, produce, or manufacture of either country ... shall from thenceforth be imported into each country from the other, free from duty. (Act of Union, 1 August 1800; available at www.statutelaw.gov.uk)

Not only did the Act introduce the Union Jack as a symbol of political intent, with the dissolution of the Irish Parliament it removed Irish stewardship over indigenous economic destiny. The relative autonomy of the Irish Parliament in Dublin and its economy was subsumed by London's commercial weight under the auspices of a compliant Anglo-Irish landed ascendancy. From their perspective, free trade between the two countries would assist in opening up the Irish market to commercial activity within the context of a larger system. One hundred Irish members of the Westminster Parliament would be able to platform Irish affairs and ensure that the adjustment to free trade would permit access for the Irish commercial and landed classes to the growing imperial and industrial market. The pay-off to the ascendancy for supporting the Union was obvious – 28 new Irish peerages were created and a further 20 peers were elevated within the ranks of the Lords (Kee 1976a: 158).

From another perspective, the Act was to usurp the commercial potential of the island in a colonial relationship that would change the Irish economic base in a manner that would destabilize the society for generations to come. The first act of resistance came as early as 23 July 1803 when the United Irishmen, inspired by the French revolution, staged a failed rebellion. Led by Robert Emmet, Thomas Emmet and Thomas Russell, their Proclamation of the Provisional Government introduced the first statement of independence for the island and a call to arms: 'You are now called upon to show the world that you are competent to take your place among the nations; that you have a right to claim their cognizance of you as an independent country' (Kee 1976a: 166). In its list of decrees it proposed a republic that would revoke the Union, abolish tithes, transfer all Church land to the new nation, introduce universal suffrage, and suspend all transfers of land and financial securities. The rebellion was suppressed within weeks and Robert Emmet was hung, drawn and quartered as a lesson to would-be resistants to the Union. R. R. Madden, in his homage to the 1798–1803 radicals and their attempts to decolonize Ireland (in *The United Irishmen*), considered the Anglo-Irish union prophetically:

> Whether we contemplate past or present rule in Ireland every thing offers a warning against dangers, and woe betide the people, in such circumstances as ours, by whom it would be despised .... God made the land, and all his works are good, Man made the laws, and all they breath'd was blood; Unhallowed annals of six hundred years, A code of blood – a history of tears! (Madden 1846: xi)

The economic changes that the Union brought were caught in the maelstrom of the times. Overshadowing the Act was an ongoing war with republican France and London's urgent priority to defend England against invasion. Westminster continued to fear a Jacobin rebellion in Ireland and believed that it needed to subdue an Irish population which was increasingly politicized, conscious of economic exploitation and resistant to military repression. This suspicion of the Irish by the English establishment and the ascendancy affected all 32 counties of the island. Edmund Curtis, in his *History of Ireland*, noted that an estimated 100,000 troops were stationed in Ireland going into the Act of Union to fortify it against external *and* internal subversion (Curtis 1952: 349). The Napoleonic wars had projected Ireland to a new level of threat for the Tory establishment under William Pitt, with the Act being seen as a means of controlling a volatile and exposed region. In the aftermath of the republican uprisings and the 30,000 deaths that their suppression cost, Ireland was constantly and vigorously monitored.

The state's reaction was to reinforce the garrisons and its military networks across the island, to create a rearguard defence – and to keep the economy of the island linked as closely as possible to the English supply chain. In the restructuring, Irish produce was put to new ends: wool, rope, uniforms, armaments, ceramics and agricultural production were adapted to support military demands. Consequently, in the aftermath of war with republican France the Irish economy suffered a major depression and the diversifying markets that had created prominent hubs of activity around Galway, Westport and Belfast contracted. Beyond its role as an island fortress, where significant aspects of economic life were integrated into the defensive complex, Ireland retained its primary role as a colonial supply route. Indeed, by the time of the famine in 1845 it was the barracks for more troops than were stationed in imperial India, with one British soldier for every 80 Irish people. Their role was straightforward – controlling the population, repressing resistance and assisting in the extraction of whatever was commercially viable.

The implications of article six of the Act were pervasive. The free trade 'partnership' that was mooted at the outset of Union dissolved rapidly into a colonial relationship, with Ireland as a dependent economy. Cecil Woodham-Smith reflected on the effects in *The Great Hunger*:

> The hope of investment proved a delusion. Free Trade between the two countries enabled England to use Ireland as a market for surplus English goods; Irish industry collapsed, unemployment was widespread, and Dublin, now that an Irish Parliament sat no longer in College Green became a half-dead city. (Woodham-Smith 1991: 16)

The imposition of the Union forced change in commercial activity across the island – with the north-east acting to strengthen its cotton and linen manufacture, while the south and west underwent a coerced diversification process to become a supplier of agricultural products such as barley, livestock, wheat and potatoes. While profit gravitated towards the financial hubs of London and Dublin, prosperity was increasingly being distributed on the basis of location, family heritage, faith and loyalty. For the vast majority of the population of the island, however, the new order meant socio-cultural subjugation matched with grinding poverty. It brought reaction and comment.

The Select Committee into the Disturbances in Ireland in 1824 cited a resident magistrate in Cork who stated: 'I have seen several countries and I never saw any peasantry so badly off' (House of Commons, *Hansard*, 1824: 300). On a visit to Ireland in 1825, Sir Walter Scott commented on the lives of the rural Irish: 'Their poverty has not been exaggerated: it is on the extreme verge of human misery' (quoted in Pomfret 1930: 8).

Contemporary observations on the extent of economic degradation in the early 1800s give some indication of the intensity of the adjustment process that took place post-union. The warping of production and market forces, and the elevation of the export side to make it more compliant to the demands of the larger neighbour, left a large proportion of the population vulnerable to change. Woodham-Smith pointed out that between 1801 and 1845 warnings about the volatile state of the Irish economy were noted by no fewer than 114 commissions and 61 special committees, each referring to impending crises (Woodham-Smith 1964: 31). Beyond *Hansard* and newsprint, there were also a number of key governmental reports, each cataloguing economic activity and poverty in Ireland in the years preceding the 1845 famine: the 'Poor Inquiry' of 1835–6, the Census of 1841 and the report of the 'Devon Commission' in February 1845. There were also a series of period observations which, together with the state's evidence, provided an intimate portrait of conditions on the colony. In sequence, they were Edward Wakefield's *An Account of Ireland, Statistical and Political* (1812), James Ebenezer Bicheno's *Ireland and its Economy* (1830), Henry Inglis's *A Journey Through Ireland* (1834), Alexis de Tocqueville's *Journeys to England and Ireland* (1837), Gustave de Beaumont's *L'Ireland: sociale, politique et religieuse* (1839), William Makepeace Thackeray's *The Irish Sketchbook* (1843) and J.G. Kohl's *Travels in Ireland* (1844). Collectively, they presented a distressing view of a society and an economy on the verge of collapse. Thackeray presented a pen-picture of life in the Irish townlands at this juncture:

> The houses have a battered rakish look, and seem going to ruin before their time. As seamen of all nations come hither who have made no vow of temperance, there are plenty of liquor-shops still, and shabby cigar-shops, and shabby milliners' and tailors' with fly-blown prints of old fashions. The bakers and apothecaries make a great brag of their calling, and you see MEDICAL HALL, or PUBLIC BAKERY, BALLYRAGGET FOUR-STORE (or whatever the name may be) pompously inscribed over very humble tenements. Some comfortable grocers' and butchers'

shops, and numbers of shabby sauntering people, the younger part of whom are barelegged and bareheaded, make up the rest of the picture which the stranger sees as his car goes jingling through the street. (Thackeray 1843: 12; also see the www.dippam.com repository)

The psychological imposition of colonial Ireland proved to be as pervasive as the economic. 'A Child of the Dust Must Not Be Proud', written repeatedly on slates by children in pre-famine Ireland, was one of the most common National School punishments for minor misdemeanours. It is quite a complex statement, but it says more about the system that formed a population into the colonial mindset of the period than about the impoverished children late for school. The Copy Book punishments mirrored the political economy of the day – structured, hierarchical and repressive (Scally 1995: 158). Social positions were asserted clearly in a popular Irish hymn of the time: 'The rich man in his castle, the poor man at his gate, God made them high and lowly and ordered their estate. All things bright and beautiful, all creatures great and small ....' The structure and composition of Irish society resembled a jigsaw of economic and cultural activity dominated by agricultural production for export, emigration and shipping between the island and the neighbouring industrializing cities of Liverpool, Manchester and Bristol. The island's east–west divide was also cemented at this period, as Dublin's powerful economic interests recoiled from the hinterland of the west.

The gaelic areas of the island had changed little since the Huguenots arrived in the early 1700s, while the east of the island – increasingly concentrating around Dublin and Belfast – had bustling trading links shipping wheat, barley, tobacco, cotton cloth, whiskey and labour to and from competing English and Scottish ports. Liverpool in particular saw a trade flow from Ireland that gave it a unique position in the development of the island. Built on the profits of the African slave trade and its proximity to the expanse of agricultural land and to the Atlantic Ocean, Liverpool was elevated to become a trading hub in the way that London had become the financial and political powerbase of the two islands. A feature that was to become significant for the evolution of the Irish economy was the role of shipping labour to and from Liverpool docks throughout the 1800s. Liverpool's century began with 'cargoes' of slaves from Africa to the Caribbean and ended with the freighted Irish peasantry in all its desperation at the height of the mill system.

The era just prior to the famine saw a society on the verge of catastrophe, with an agricultural economy strained and exploited, residing uncomfortably with a nascent modernity, yet seeking dependence on British commercial and imperial power. The economic culture that was prevalent in English society – dominated by an utilitarian mix of capital appreciation, surplus value, labour and its division, manufacturing and ultimately profit – brought an alien economic culture to the Irish. For the English commercial managers Irish economic culture was antiquated, backward and unprofitable. Their target was the informal economy and means of exchange that would have been commonplace in Irish communities, notably in the rural west, and seemed incompatible with the regulated monetary system that accompanied free trade. Indeed, as Robert Scally pointed out in *The End of Hidden Ireland*, two distinct economic cultures were present in Ireland in the 1830s, one looking eastward to the commercial 'sophistication' of London and the other to a communitarian and indigenous form. The social and economic differences were profound:

> emigration from the townlands before the famine was restrained by a culture and worldview consonant with this seclusion, deeply suspicious of outsiders, secretive in its dealings with them, and scornful of those who strove to become like them, whether in regard to property, social station, or personal ambition. (Scally 1995: 7)

While the management of the state's economy was bureaucratic, with dealings often documented in an assiduously methodical manner, the social economy of Ireland retained many of the *mores* pertinent to more flexible methods of commercial activity. This indigenous culture would repeatedly frustrate the establishment of what was ostensibly a London-focused market system. By holding on to the obstinate economic culture of rural Ireland the Irish showed themselves to have more akin with other colonial economic cultures than the disciplining laissez-faire culture of the south-east of England.

For most of Ireland in the pre-famine economy, activity was not geographically centralized or monetarily fixed. The dominant commercial centres outside the ports were the village markets which served tenant cottages and small farming communities. The centres of Irish society were the *bailia* (ballys), clusters of smallholdings dotted throughout the landscape where families and immediate communities would have resided for centuries. Its patchwork form remained its strength, giving a sense of collectivity and local identity, self-sustaining when permitted to harvest its own resources. The jigsaw-like pattern of this gaelic model of settlement can be seen in the Ordnance Survey records of the 1830s, with communities often described as *baile fearann* (home towns) representing the link between townland communities and extended families. One of the most insightful pre-famine investigations of the nature and form of the *bailia* (and the *clachan*, Irish village) came from the federalist philosopher Alexis de Tocqueville. Tocqueville's observations were taken in the summer of 1835 and referred to various aspects of Irish life and economic activity at this crucial juncture (Tocqueville 1968: 154–5). The picture he painted of rural Ireland in *Journey's to England and Ireland* was of a pre-industrial world of lime-whited thatched cottages, grouped occasionally into small communities and focusing on local and often isolated market towns. This was the environment where most Irish lived, with barefooted poverty, sociological complexes respectful of gaelic heritage and folklore, resistant to the recently repealed penal laws, with historical patterns of worship, knowledgeable of a European diaspora, and of the French and American revolutions.

For the rural population in general the short lives that they lived were wretched and impoverished, yet their resilience featured in both social interaction and economic survival. In the social memory of this society – comprising an estimated 62,205 *bailia* throughout the island – the rebellions and wars of the late 1700s still resonated (Evans 1949: 90; also see Canavan 1991). Their existence had no legal personality under British law. It was a society that referenced a pre-colonial world. With the 'granting' of status from London to specific Irish towns, two distinct maps were effectively rolled out over the island – one communitarian, clannish, culturally aware; the other paternalistic and exploitative. As with other colonial systems, the legal imposition with all its Whig formality accentuated the socio-economic divisions that already existed, rural and urban, landlords and tenants, county to county, political and religious. One testing corollary of this divided society was the common pre-famine adherence to *brehon* law, the uncoded conventions that were recognizable to the indigenous population and which ran parallel to the Crown's legal system with its ceremony and foreignness. *Brehon* rule was as prominent in many areas as the emerging state formation, with a set of conventions that could deal with perceived injustices. Compensation, for example, was an aspect of *brehon* law that was unrecognizable in the Crown's judicial system, where debt could be repaid in alternative ways. Unjustified rises in food prices at markets could be resisted by community protest; the 'boycott' and the fast – whereby individuals or the community could resist what was perceived to be an injustice – were acknowledged as legitimate means of negotiation. Disputes commonly dealt with by *brehon* law included unauthorized land exchanges, intra-family disputes, lifestock confusion and pricing disagreements. If disputes were not resolved, the community itself, or local clergy, would seek consensus to close the issue. Crucially, arbitrary violence and eviction from cottages were not punishments recognizable under this community-sourced system of justice.

Joel Mokyr, in *Why Ireland Starved*, gives perhaps the most insightful breakdown of the demographic mix that constituted Irish society prior to the 1841 Census. The rural population was by and large made up of small tenant farming families who were unable to produce much more than a subsistence living. Three distinct classes were defined in this Census. 'Class I', the professional and landowning class, comprised 2.6 per cent of the population. This amounted to 1.9 per cent of the rural population and 6.6 per cent of the urban population. 'Class II' included 'skilled artisans and farmers holding fewer than 50 acres'. This represented 31.8 per cent of the Irish population: 28.3 per cent of the rural population and 49.9 per cent of the urban population. 'Class III' was made up of labourers and smallholders, 'persons without capital, in either money, land, or acquired knowledge [education]' (Mokyr 1983: 18–19). This category included 65.6 per cent of the population of the island: 69.8 per cent of the rural population and 43.5 per cent of the urban population. In total 81 per cent of the population of the island tilled less than 15 acres of land, with 55 per cent living off less than ten acres. With families often exceeding eight people, subsistence living was the norm.

In the conventional economy there remained a right to barter, outside the strictures of 'legitimate' commercial activity which had been brought in with the Act of Union and its monetary system. The attempts to regulate non-monetary economic activity intro-duced additional complications for community market activity. This imposed form of commerce had a tendency to inflate prices and devalue indigenous produce, while facilitating comparative values from across the empire. By adding a new layer to the traditional economy the circulation of sterling pushed market prices up. The competitive advantage in most cases went against Irish traders. The economic theory behind this disciplining of commerce was that of classical liberalism, which presented enterprising profitable interaction as the primary motivation in human society. But it needed sound management. Its foremost advocate, Adam Smith, was to consider informal commercial exchange – such as barter – unenlightened and ultimately unprofitable. The two economies lived uneasily together until the vital systemic break of the 1840s.

LAND AND LAISSEZ-FAIRE

The 1841 Census of Ireland categorizes most of the 8 million Irish as 'smallholders' and 'labourers', revealing a society where the vast majority of the population lived in rural communities. Land, its use-value and sale, was central to socio-economic activity. In this pre-famine economy land was used as a means of exchange, even for small tenants, through dividing and sub-dividing. The rural economy was built around leaseholding farmers and cottier labourers who could lease land, often on an annual basis. Consequently, the overuse of land was an ongoing, intractable problem. This complicated economic quilt was to become very evident in the run-up to famine, as the surveyor John Kelly noted with reference to the midlands in 1834:

> It is subdivided into very minute holdings, occupied generally by cottier labourers; and consequently the population settled in it is excessively numerous, their dwellings of a miserable description, and the Lands more or less worn out by continued burning of the soil for tillage. (quoted in Scally 1995: 25)

The land question would become more desperate as the population grew and as fields were sub-divided for sons or leased off in times of need.

The source of mass disaffection began, however, with the changing tenancy system enforced throughout the 1830s as an attempt by large landowners to open up the land market. Increasingly, absentee landlords were utilizing the powers of rent collectors to manage Irish properties, enforce rent collections and evict non-compliant households. An initial wave of evictions came in the mid-1830s with inevitable consequences. Within Irish society there remained an obstinate popular political culture. It was manifested through a disdain for authority, a habitual rejection of class structures and a willingness to resist imposed changes (Clark 1979: 66). A legacy of the penal times, the *rebelliousness* across Irish society was instinctive, community based and informed by a social memory that was drawn from long-past atrocities and engagements. With the evictions that accompanied the changes to tenancy regulations the new society was again confronting the old. Scally makes an important comment on the tensions that had come between these two worlds:

> Just as acquisitiveness or hoarding were still generally held by subsistence tenants as violations of traditional moral proprieties, private immodesty in dress, discordant pretensions of manner or speech or personal vanities in a man or woman could bring sharp rebuke or ridicule down on individuals or entire families. The townland strove to maintain its covert economy with an internal moral and even aesthetic code that was equally at odds with that emerging all around it. (Scally 1995: 34)

In many townlands the tenancy regulations were as alien as the monetary economy or the English language that came with it, restricting it mainly to the cities and larger towns. Barter would have been a common means of exchanging goods, with many families relying on a 'potato wage' – where tenants would be paid in potatoes or labour merely for food (Ó Gráda 1994: 194). Any breakdown of this form of pre-industrial economic activity was important in this context due to the sheer numbers who were vulnerable to market fluctuations. Large farmers often acted as intermediaries in collecting rent, levying additional pressure on the tenant population in times of economic stress. Changing macroeconomic circumstances would impact on tenants also, and while the larger farmers could diversify their produce to engage with broader market circum-stances, the smallholders lived precariously dependent existences. With shifts towards food production for export, monoculture for subsistence became widespread. Furthermore, scarce resources and the dependency on weather cycles give a harshness to life in Ireland. A culmination of all these factors meant that for the smallholders and their families, shortages and hunger were a way of life – and they represented the bulk of Irish society.

The economy of the 1830s is an important marker in the develop-ment of the island, because it gives an insight into a colonial society prior to the dislocation of famine, a snapshot of a unique world at the point of breaking. As the 1841 Census and the contempo-rary observers showed, pressures were building on this population in its struggle to sustain itself. The forms of contract for tenant leasing and the aggravated division of smallholdings, together with economic depression and the corresponding drop in the prices of agricultural produce, all provided early evidence of stress. The colonial economic framework had compelled the country towards crisis and this would inevitably reveal itself to be rural in form. The urban and rural divide contorted economic relationships across the island, with resistance to modernization and urbanization forcing rural communities to withdraw further into the microeconomies that had sustained these communities in the past against similar external pressures. Culturally they carried a general disdain for the urbanized centres of the east coast and a political ambivalence that would be common to rural Irish society. In 1840 a Repeal Association was formed, led by the celebrated 'emancipator' of Irish Catholics, Daniel O'Connell. It called for the repeal of the Union and the establishment of a native Irish Parliament. Crucially, its popularity and that of O'Connell depended on an engagement with the land question:

> Though always inclined to use 'Repeal' as an emotive inspiration, and careful not to commit himself in much detail to the practical measures required to change society, he did definitely commit himself to the general principle of fixity of tenure for the tenant, making it clear that he was prepared to interfere with the basic structure of the landlord–tenant relationship. (Kee 1976a: 193)

In Cork in May 1843 half a million came to hear O'Connell call for Repeal and the economic appendages of fair rent, free sales and fixity of tenure, all of which would have revolutionized land relations on the island.

While economic activity was predominantly restricted for most to a limited exchange of produce – such as wheat, livestock, barley and potatoes – other more luxurious goods would have been commonplace in certain circles. Commodities being brought in from the colonies were making it through to the upper echelons of Irish society. Remembering that slavery in the colonies was not abolished until 1834 and carried on in many regions throughout the world for decades after – including most of America – imports were often slave sourced. Tobacco, sugar, cotton and tea were to be found across the island, becoming features of Anglo-Irish patrician society. The recipients of laissez-faire commerce, the richer farmers and the emerging legal and commercial professions, revelled in the exotic ornamentation that bedecked their homes and lifestyles. Whereas the tenants lived in their austere world of church and poverty, without furniture or sufficient apparel, the landlords' families benefited from both the exploitation of the smallholders and a myriad of colonial spoils.

The rituals and couture of these Irish landowners often puzzled and amused onlookers. Indeed, they were often seen as vulgar profiteers in English circles, whereas in Irish society their fixation with exploiting the tenants brought them disdain and occasional violent reaction. While forging control over the workings of the Irish economy and government, this class mimicked across the island the libertine chaos that they were exposed to in London. Marx and Engels made the point cynically:

> Their country-seats are surrounded by enormous, amazingly beautiful parks, but all around is waste land .... These fellows are droll enough to make your sides burst with laughing. Of mixed blood, mostly tall, strong handsome chaps, they all wear enormous moustaches under colossal Roman noses, give themselves the false military airs of retired colonels, travel around the country after all sorts of pleasures, and if one makes an inquiry, they haven't a penny, are laden with debts, and live in dread of the Encumbered Estates Court. (Marx and Engels 1971: 85)

Resplendent in brightly coloured cotton clothes courtesy of the slave plantations in the southern American states, sugar from the Caribbean, cosmetics and ivory ornaments from East Africa, the landlord lifestyle was paid for by tenant labour and rent. Even the cultural highlights of the pre-famine years were steeped in the economy of exploitation: the pianos, African woods and jewellery that decorated many of the middle and upper-class houses were by-products of the ebony and ivory trades, and slavery in East Africa. Poignantly, the Irish tenants with their lime-whited turf walls and thatch, their beads and rituals, language, regional cultures, hunger and conflict, could be seen to have more in common with the slave communities of Mississippi or the villages of Guinea than with the individualized, anglicized rich of Dublin, Cork or Belfast.

The members of the Anglo-Irish ascendancy, along with increasing numbers of Irish Catholic landowners, were to oversee the agricultural modernization process and evictions for farm extensions. Together with representatives of the absentee landlords and of the Crown they constituted an establishment. It was recognizable as a distinct hegemony on the island. At times of scarcity they were the purveyors of hardship. Conflict with tenants, and the brutality that came with it, evolved through the 1800s as an aspect of commercial activity. Evictions created space for a change of land use, while depressing the price of local produce ensured that agricultural goods could be purchased at a fraction of previous costs. The more the landowners and merchants could squeeze the tenants, the more market expansion could be facilitated. They even accounted for resistance. For them, periodic and sporadic protest was interpreted not as a response to grievances, but as potential insurrection, anti-state activity which necessitated suppression.

Land exploitation and the oppressive methods of this landowning class deliberately targeted the poor and, while the tenants struggled for survival, the profiteering of the landowners undermined sustainable farming practices. Furthermore, the agents, who had the task of managing tenants and their payments, aggravated the conditions by often violent methods of rent collection. The divisions within the society were obvious to the population. Cathal Póirtéir, in *The Great Irish Famine*, commented that between the years 1832 and 1859, 70 per cent of members of parliament and peers from Ireland were from this landowning stock (1995). Unlike the process of industrialization evident across England, which involved certain rights and obligations by many owners, Ireland had been cynically and systematically underdeveloped (Thompson 1991: 83–96).

The Devon Commission, the Royal Commission which was set up to look at the state of the country in 1843, commented on the: 'strong sense of the patient endurance which the labouring classes have exhibited under sufferings greater, we believe, than the people of any other country in Europe have to sustain' (Woodham-Smith 1964: 24). The fragile nature of the society was becoming increasingly evident on a number of fronts. Discontent was rife and confrontation occasionally erupted between tenants, agents and the militias who were assisting in enforcing rent collections and evictions. The Commission, chaired by the Earl of Devon and reporting in February 1845, was categorical in its condemnation of governance on the island of Ireland. Its brief was: 'to inquire into the law and practice with regard to the occupation of land in Ireland' (Woodham-Smith 1964: 21). Even though all of the members who sat on the Commission were landowners, they could not conceal the scale of the dispossession, anticipating economic meltdown. The inquiry estimated that in 1842 alone £6 million in remittances had been extracted from the Irish tenants by agents. The beneficiaries were the estates of the ascendancy and the landlords of London. There was no pretence of loyalty to tenant or land in this crude exploitation of natural and human resources. This was intensified by the 'middleman' system, where the agents employed to manage land were sub-letting plots. The landowners received their remittance, while the agent could extract a further toll from the tenants. It led to the sub-dividing of plots, with the agents getting additional profit through the continual segmentation of farms. This *conacre* system created the familiar patchwork division of the Irish landmass.

Historically there had been agreed conventions on tenant rights, which had been customary in form and which included the acceptance of improvements in the holdings by tenants and security of tenure. These rights continued to be practised in parts of Ulster and ensured the adaptation of, or investment in, the holdings. There was also the assurance that eviction would not be arbitrary. More often than not, however, across other parts of the island 'improvement' – trying to enhance a property by, for example, replacing a door – could be used as an excuse for eviction. Similarly, lack of financial security or the introduction of leasing papers could be seen as opportunities to extract rent to the point of eviction. The insecurity of tenants was accentuated further by the seasonal urgency of producing goods for sale or having to labour for the agent or landlord.

With the cash economy being a state and largely urban phenomenon, and the rural economy often working from an 'in kind' basis, tenants spent much of their lives working to pay off debt. Indebted tenants would often be left with rent arrears 'hanging' until the next season provided the opportunity for payment through bonded labour. It was used as a means of keeping tenants perpetually vulnerable to eviction and dependent. Edward Wakefield noted this system of rent collection to be: 'one of the greatest levers of oppression ... the lower classes are kept in a kind of perpetual bondage ... this debt hangs over their heads ... and keeps them in a continual state of anxiety and terror' (quoted in Woodham-Smith 1964: 23). The social philosopher John Stuart Mill, in his contemporary study *England and Ireland,* commented:

> In Ireland alone the whole agricultural population can be evicted by the mere will of the landlord, either at the expiration of a lease or, in the far more common case of their having no lease, at six months' notice. In Ireland alone, the bulk of a population wholly dependent on the land cannot look forward to a single year's occupation of it. (Mill 1886: 16)

By 1841 two-thirds of the Irish population, which numbered over

8 million people, were caught in this rural economy, their plight aggravated by the monoculture that had evolved since the Act of Union where large numbers of families – being tied to smallholdings of less than one to 15 acres – were dependent on the high-yielding potato crop for survival.

As with the maize that slave ships brought back to Africa from the American plantations, so too the potato was brought from the Americas to become the food of the Irish poor. Together with dairy produce, curd and milk, by the first two decades of the nineteenth century the potato had become the principal diet of the Irish population. Other crops were produced for export to supply English industrial cities, but potatoes provided Irish tenant families with a basic subsistence and rapidly became identified with the lives of the Irish poor. This identification can be seen from one emigrant's experience going from Cork to North America in 1823:

> The children during sickness called constantly for potatoes, refusing arrowroot or any other aliment more congenial to their situation, and nothing could prevail on man, woman, or child to eat plumb pudding which as is usual on ships board was part of the Sunday dinner. (quoted in Ó Gráda 1994: 14)

The monoculture and the lack of a cash economy left the west of Ireland particularly vulnerable. Furthermore, potato crop failures were recurrent, with an estimated 24 crop failures between 1728 and 1882, the most destructive in 1739, 1740, 1770 and 1880. Indeed, extensive crop failures occurred in a sequence of years up until 1844. There was a general understanding of the disparate yield of the crop, yet there remained dependence for a significant proportion of the population. When *phytophthora infestans* blighted the 1844 yield it signalled something catastrophic. The rot was to take full effect the following year (Donnelly 2005: 40).

Christine Kinealy, in *This Great Calamity*, looked at the reaction to the arrival of the potato blight, noting that the Mansion House, Dublin Castle and Westminster – including British prime minister William Gladstone – were well aware of the impending crisis (1994: 32–33). On 13 September 1845 the *Gardeners' Chronicle and Horticultural Gazette*, edited by the professor of botany at the University of London, John Lindley, warned of blight: 'We stop the Press with very great regret to announce that the potato Murrain has unequivocally declared itself in Ireland ... where will Ireland be in the event of a universal potato rot?' (quoted in Woodham-Smith

1964: 40). In the event the outcome was mass starvation made worse by a sequence of incompetent attempts to address the situation. The catastrophe was fuelled by establishment inaction and a fundamentalism that contained a lethal mix of classical liberalism, ideas of population management and racism.

Ideological zeal for the market in the early 1800s had brought the customary form of the Irish economy into stark conflict with classical liberal perceptions of what should suffice for freeing commercial enterprise and releasing market forces on all aspects of society. Advocating deregulated, unfettered free trade became the passion of classical liberalism, the dominant ideology of the Whig establishment. Arguing for laissez-faire within the economy, the supposed natural evolution of the economic system could, in theory, bring prosperity with profit for those engaged in commercial activities. Popularized by James Mill in the 1824 edition of *Encyclopaedia Britannica*, the term resonated among pioneers of free trade across the British Isles. While they did not overtly engage with the French term itself, a generic form of laissez-faire could be read in the economic theories of Adam Smith, Thomas Malthus and David Ricardo, each presenting a case for the freeing of the market and the necessity of 'natural' competitive renewal within economies. For Smith the 'invisible hand' of the market system was the life force which compelled society forward. It was only individual commercial enterprise that could unlock this energy:

> Every individual ... neither intends to promote the public interest, nor knows how much he is promoting it ... he intends only his own security; and by directing that industry in such a manner as its produce may be of the greatest value, he intends only his own gain, and he is in this, as in many other cases, led by an invisible hand to promote an end which was no part of his intention. (Smith 1776, Book IV, Chapter II: 456)

While never visiting Ireland, Smith was a fervent supporter of the Act of Union as a means of market expansion, and colonization as a rich source of profit generation.

Laissez-faire as a doctrine galvanized Dublin's elite and those in London who saw property management and private enterprise as primary social activities. Excessive government, as perceived by Adam Smith and the classical liberals, was a hindrance to profitability and therefore it should be restricted from intervening in the economy. From this perspective it was not prudent for the government to overtly manage economic activity – this should be the role of enterprising individuals. Liberty for the elite, property ownership and the right to profit, were synonymous. Transferred to the Irish context this ideology meant limiting governmental intervention that would subdue market activity. If the market was to falter, classical liberals argued, it should be left up to market forces to readjust it. Interference was seen to be disruptive to this natural process and ultimately, whatever the circumstances, the market must take its course.

One of the most influential books of the period pertains to this ideology while introducing presumed laws of nature, 'natural law' that brings consequences to those who are perceived as not having the faculties or enlightened acumen to live in what was interpreted as the civilized world. George Combe's *The Constitution of Man and its Relations to External Objects* sold 350,000 copies between 1828 and 1900, outselling Charles Darwin's *On the Origin of Species* (1859) by seven to one. Combe's comments on the Irish people provide an insight into the mentality of the governing and academic classes at the time of the famine:

> By reckless marriages they have increased their numbers far beyond their capital, means of employment, and of subsistence; and abject poverty, occasionally destitution and famine, with the fearful ravages of disease, stalk through the land, appalling the beholder, and leading feeble minds to question the sway of a benevolent Providence in Irish affairs. The oppressors and the oppressed stand equally rebuked. A great calamity presses upon both; and it reads an instructive lesson concerning the practical evils of teaching religious doctrines irrespective of natural science and its applications. (Combe 1847 edn: 434)

The idea that famine was a natural form of social adjustment became a contemporary rebuke which could also be read into Charles Darwin's theory of natural selection, later termed 'the survival of the fittest'. The concept was defined initially in 1838 and, as *the* scientific revelation of the day, was feverishly applied to economics, population and dependency during the Irish famine (Desmond and Moore 1991: 263–74). The starving Irish were to become the live experiment for this theory. One of the most influential interpretations of the philosophy came from the Reverend Thomas Robert Malthus, who had been influential in the development of Darwin's theories. In his *Essay on the Principle of Population* (1798), Malthus

elaborated on the idea of natural selection. It was his observation that in nature plants and animals produce far more offspring than can survive. His theory was that humans were also capable of 'over-producing' if left unchecked. Malthus concluded that unless family sizes were regulated, the misery of famine would become an epidemic that would eventually devastate humanity. For him population levels needed to be occasionally checked with food supplies managed in an arithmetical manner; poverty and famine were logical, natural outcomes of population growth.

Although Malthus thought of famine and poverty as natural processes, as a man of the Church he saw the ultimate force behind these outcomes as divine intervention. He believed that famine was God's way of preventing humans from becoming feckless. Furthermore, charity towards the poor could be seen to be self-defeating in that it created a situation where dependency thrived and the numbers of those in need would exponentially increase – putting more pressure on food supplies. The solution was that the poor needed to be disciplined into 'improving' their own conditions. The first major test of his theory came with the Irish poor:

> Here, then, under our own eyes and on a large scale, a process is revealed, than which nothing more excellent could be wished for by orthodox economy for the support of its dogma: that misery springs from absolute surplus-population, and that equilibrium is re-established by depopulation. This is a far more important exper-iment than was the plague in the middle of the 14th century so belauded of Malthusians …. The Irish famine of 1846 killed more than 1,000,000 people, but it killed poor devils only. To the wealth of the country it did not the slightest damage. (Marx 1867: 658)

The most stringent application of the Malthusian system came with the introduction of the Irish Poor Relief (Ireland) Act of 1838 – 'An Act for the More Effectual Relief of the Destitute Poor in Ireland' – which extended the 1834 British poor relief system to Ireland. The country was divided up into a number of Poor Law Unions with the task of overseeing the establishment of and manage-ment of workhouses. The obligation of the Unions was to force the poor into becoming more compliant contributors to the general economy. The workhouse was the punishment for those who were not 'improving'.

LVIII. And be it enacted, That every Person who shall refuse to

be lodged and maintained in the Workhouse of any Union, or abscond out of such Workhouse while his Wife, or any Child whom he may be liable to maintain, shall be relieved therein, and every Person maintained in a Workhouse who shall refuse to be set to work ... contrary to the Orders of the Commissioners, shall, on Conviction ... be committed to the Common Gaol or House of Correction, there to be kept to hard Labour for any Time. (Poor Relief (Ireland) Act 1838, www.workhouses.org.uk)

The poor were to be disciplined into productivity and servitude until such time as they were deemed capable of inclusion within commercial society at large. The architects of this system did not, however, envisage demand for relief outside the workhouse. Nor did those who designed the system, instituted just seven years before the famine, anticipate such a complete breakdown that the workhouse would become a refuge from starvation. The blight of the 1845 potato crop left millions in this struggle to survive. When the situation across Ireland became apparent, theories of racial superiority were introduced to explain a malfunction in this natural scientific system – where ideological dehumanization could be utilized to relieve the conscience of the establishment. The 'inferior' Irish, as with other colonial peoples, were just not 'evolved' enough or capable of civilized social engineering.

Nineteenth century theorists divided humanity into 'races' on the basis of external physical features .... Needless to say, the Teutons, who included the Anglo-Saxons, were placed at the top. Black people ... were at the bottom, with Celts (Irish) and Jews somewhere in between. (New Jersey Commission on Holocaust Education 1998: 56–7)

THE FAMINE ECONOMY

In the early years of the Union, ongoing change to the agricultural base brought with it investment in marketable crops while encouraging sustenance farming which could keep the farming families alive and producing. In this economy the importance of the potato cannot be overestimated for rural life, as it was used to sustain life as a basic diet, as a fertilizer, for animal feed and even distilled down for poteen. Unlike anywhere else in Europe, in Ireland even bread was a luxury, as life rotated precariously around one crop. The sequence of events which caused the collapse of the domestic economy was thus tied to potato production, and its severity was largely a consequence of excessive profiteering and mismanagement on a monumental scale by landlords, Dublin Castle and Westminster. As Robert Kee pointed out in *The Most Distressful Country*: 'Everyone knew that Ireland was short only of the potato and otherwise full of food in the form of oats, wheat, butter, eggs, sheep and pigs, all of which continued to be exported to England on a considerable scale' (Kee 1976a: 244). The blight first spread its way through the land in 1845 and led to the partial destruction of that year's crop. This was followed by the complete failure of the 1846 crop and subsequently no seeds to sow for the 1847 crop. With an estimated 3 million Irish people totally dependent on a single crop for survival, famine was inevitable (Kennedy et al. 1999: 69). A further blight in 1848 was the final devastating blow to the society, its population and the conventional way of life.

The ongoing and forced changes to the economic base magnified the difficulties faced by the population, where instead of intervention and structural support, the market was left to extract profit where it could be located – within decreasing and contorted economic activity. As the communities struggled to provide food they were forced to consume what remained on the smallholdings, their livestock and less profitable vegetables. Confusingly, livestock production contorted the agricultural market by showing profitability throughout this period, resulting from land clearances for cattle and sheep rearing and returns on animal produce such as leathers. Consequently, agricultural practices and employment warped in reaction to the malfunctioning economic system: 'tillage output was down 21.3 per cent, potato output was down 75 per cent' but 'the volume of animal products was up 30.8 per cent' (O'Rourke 1994: 310). Robert Kee recounted Daniel O'Connell's rebuke to the House of Commons:

> More wheat, barley and wheat meal flour, he pointed out, had in fact been imported into Great Britain from Ireland in 1845 than in any other of the three previous years, and between 10 October 1845 and 5 January 1846 over 30,000 oxen, bulls and cows, over 30,000 sheep and lambs, and over 100,000 pigs had sailed from Ireland to English ports. (Kee 1976a: 247)

O'Connell died of a brain haemorrhage in Lyons on 15 May 1847.

As with all famines, the poor and weakest were to suffer the most. A letter to the *Evening Freeman* on 9 December 1847 conveyed the commonplace misery of the famine years:

The infamous and inhuman cruelties which were wantonly and unnecessarily exercised against a tenantry, whose feelings were already wound up to woeful and vengeful exasperation by the loss of their exiled relatives, as well as by hunger and pestilence, which swept so many victims to an untimely grave – in my opinion may be assigned as the sole exciting cause of the disastrous event which has occurred. I saw no necessity for the idle display of such a large force of military and police, carrying outside so many rounds of ball cartridge, and inside some substantial rounds of whiskey, bacon and baker's bread, surrounding the poor man's cabin, setting fire to the roof while the half-starved, half-naked children were hastening away from the flames with yells of despair, while the mother lay prostrate on the threshold writhing in agony, and the heartbroken father remained supplicating on his knees. I saw no need for this demonstration of physical force, nor did I see any need for brutal triumph and exultation when returning after these feats were nobly performed. Nor can I conceive that feelings of humanity should permit any man to send his bailiffs to revisit these scenes of horror and conflagration, with an order, if they found a hut built or a fire lighted in the murky ruins, to demolish the one and extinguish the other, thus leaving the wretched outcasts no alternative but to perish in a ditch. (quoted in Scally 1995: 83)

The effects were devastating for the population across the island. More than 20 years after the famine, on 16 December 1867 in a speech to the German Workers' Educational Association on 'The Irish question', Karl Marx made an insightful comment: 'A million people died of starvation. The potato blight resulted from the exhaustion of the soil … Over 1,100,000 people have been replaced with 9,600,000 sheep. This is a thing unheard of in Europe' (Marx and Engels 1971: 141–2). Marx was alluding to the fact that market forces, in the midst of famine, were continuing to adapt to adversity and extreme market conditions. Three particularly forceful interventions reverberated throughout Irish society during the famine period: mass eviction, used to adjust the agri-economy and causing the expansion of the workhouse system; forced emigration moved onto an industrial scale; and the adjustment of free market practices, bringing about the repeal of laws restricting imports and trade.

Eviction had enabled new markets as well as the possibilities that came with clearing communities from the land. During the famine the systematic extraction of rent from tenants led to eviction being treated as a commercial opportunity in its own right by landlords. Eviction left few options for the impoverished tenants, and out of the desperation a new market emerged which was to prove to be one of the most profitable enterprises of the period – that of shipping Irish emigrants. The shipping companies had suffered ill fortune with the demise of the slave trade, but the acceleration of evictions and famine gave the companies a reason to refit their vessels to revive this lucrative trade in people. The crude shift from one market to another, however, left many of the old practices in place, including the hellish treatment of the 'cargo', the sorry state of the ships and the brutality of the mariners. Nevertheless many prominent members of Anglo-Irish society were to find the shipping of the starving Irish more acceptable than shipping African slaves, and it was immensely profitable. Even Lord Palmerston, at the pinnacle of the British establishment, ventured into the business by chartering craft for the shipment of Irish to North America. As a result of the business, the 'coffin ship' was to become synonymous with the plight of the poor rural communities trying to escape the hunger.

> In the decade 1845–55 two million emigrants left Ireland, around 1.5 of them going to the United States. In Black 1847 the mortality rates on ships from Liverpool stood at 1 in 14, and from Cork at 1 in 9. Of the 97,000 Irish, who sailed for Canada in that year, a third died at sea or shortly after landing. (Rogers 2009: 291)

Rumours and anger at atrocities were not only voiced in the political circles of Dublin and London, but reverberated fearfully throughout Irish society itself, provoking attacks and reprisals – and a demand by landowners for the government to enforce military rule in many rural areas.

Emigrating Irish labour helped resuscitate the shipping market. The key figure that jumps out in regard to this resurgence of shipping is that just before slavery was abolished in Britain and Ireland in 1806 there were fewer than 100 ships going from Ireland to the northern states of America, yet in the worst years of the famine there were 2000 ships in operation. In the earlier years of passage, berths were built into the ships, many of which had been adapted for wood carriage also, with the passengers providing their own food for the journey. The volume of ships and the frequency of the journeys meant that prices remained relatively affordable. This market expansion led to the emergence of licensed agents in Irish towns and cities, 'passage-brokers' who could arrange transportation. Known for opportunistic, fraudulent and exploitative behaviour, they nevertheless provided a way out for those who had nothing left but the workhouse between them and starvation.

While comfort and support during the voyage varied immensely, from the coffin ships to more salubrious vessels, the consensus between the government and the shipping magnates was to keep the fares as affordable as possible. In 1842 for a man to travel with his wife and four children to New York cost £21; to go to Quebec in 'British North America' would cost £6. To avoid paying the bond to enter US ports, emigrants would often make the transatlantic journey to Quebec and then cross the border to settle in Boston, New York or other developing northern cities. Tellingly, the United States Consul in Derry wrote:

> To the United States go the people of good character and in comfortable circumstances ... to British North America the evil and ill disposed. They go to Canada either because the fare is cheap or their landlords are getting rid of them. (quoted in Woodham-Smith 1964: 212)

Ellis Island, the importation centre off Manhattan, holds an unusual statistic in relation to disembarkation. Its halls received more Irish people through their doors – they estimate 12 million – than indigenous Irish living on the island of Ireland itself. Indeed, Paul-Dubois called the American Republic 'Greater Ireland', and Karl Marx noted that 'emigration forms one of the most lucrative branches of its [Ireland's] export trade' (1867: 659; www.dippam.com). The United States and Canada were to become mass workhouses for Irish people, as the population of the four provinces decreased year after year with poverty and famine driving millions to seek better lives elsewhere.

There was forced emigration across the island where landlords such as the Honourable Mr Wandesford (Kilkenny) or Colonel Wyndham (Clare) cleared hundreds of their tenants overseas. Over 85,000 people left for the United States in 1847 alone, and an estimated 109,000 for British North America. Starving and exposed typically to typhus – 'ocean plague' – and other fevers, the migrants endured a passage across the Atlantic that was often as hazardous as remaining in the townlands. Cecil Woodham-Smith chronicled the worst of these journeys of which there is evidence:

The *Larch*, from Sligo, for instance, sailed with 440 passengers, of whom 108 died at sea, and 150 arrived with fever; the *Virginius* left Liverpool for Quebec with 476 passengers, of whom 158 died on the voyage and 106 were landed sick. (Woodham-Smith 1964: 225–6)

The *Virginius* came to represent the brutality of the trade of moving emigrants through the quarantine island of Grosse Île in Canada. On arrival only half a dozen were fit enough to walk from the ship; beyond those who died during the journey, the remaining emigrants were subjected to the imprisonment that came with the process of quarantine. In two months alone in 1847, 5000 Irish died in transit on the Atlantic.

The numbers taking the eight-week journey to America could be adequately monitored, whereas other migrant flows could not be easily quantified. The largely unrecorded human movement from the east coast of Ireland to Britain can reveal only approximate numbers, but the social and economic influence of the Irish diaspora on cities such as Glasgow, Liverpool and London itself has been immense. The full extent of depopulation of the island could be seen generations later when, it is estimated, over ten times the population of the island could claim Irish descent worldwide (80 million, 41 million in the United States alone) (Fitzpatrick 1989: 569). The sociological aspects of the diaspora's experience are symptomatic; emigration found a predictable pattern where the men initially moved to find work and the women and children were sent for to follow. This was compounded by young adults continuing the outward trek looking for better opportunities. What was tragic in the experience of the Irish diaspora was their inability to return to the island, engendering a culture of separation. The diaspora experience was to become perhaps the most prominent theme in Irish popular culture, playing on the melancholy of loss. Another aspect of the separation was the remittance, the sending of funds back to the family in Ireland. These remittances were to become a feature of Irish society and its economy: 'Assuming a figure of £3 million from all sources implies an inflow equivalent to 2 to 3 per cent of national income before the First World War' (Ó Gráda 1994: 228).

Within the famine economy the role of the workhouse also became formative, buildings where the surplus labour could be concentrated for incarceration and productivity. Between 1838 and 1843, 112 workhouses were built and a further 18 were under construction. These 130 workhouses were intended to cater for 94,010 'guests', the authorities believing that this would be adequate provision.

During and for some time after the famine years Irish workhouses were severely overcrowded. By 1849, some 250,000 people were being accommodated. In June 1850, there were 264,048. Even though the death rate in these institutions remained high – 283,765 died between the years 1841 and 1851 (of whom 138,576 were of children under the age of 15) – so many destitute people clamoured to be admitted that soup kitchens had to be set up beside the houses to keep the starving from rioting (PRONI, n.d.). Skibbereen workhouse in County Cork had been built for 800, yet by 1847 was holding 1300 with queues encamped waiting for deaths in the institution to secure a place. With the government concerned about widespread looting and theft, the queen's speech of that year called for tougher measures to deal with crime in Ireland (Kee 1976a: 259).

The workhouse system was but one of a number of mechanisms that were to be put in place by the authorities in Dublin and Westminster to address what was universally acknowledged to be a catastrophe of unprecedented proportions. Others included sending in troops to further suppress the starving, free transport off the island, and pseudo-scientific solutions – such as recommending the boiling of grass to eat. One of the most contentious attempts to engage with the crisis was the return to the ideological safeguard of 'freeing up' trade, and in particular the freeing of the corn trade. This market solution had been recommended by a committee of Dublin Corporation, which included notaries such as Lord Cloncurry and the Duke of Leinster. Their suggestions for confronting famine-stricken Ireland, were that ports should permit the importation of Indian corn and other foods – particularly grain from the British colonies; that the railway network should be extended; that a relief system be put in place; and that public work schemes should be set up (Woodham-Smith 1964: 49).

In response the prime minister, Robert Peel, took on the 'cause' of repealing the Corn Laws which had protected British and Irish produce against the importation of cheap corn from the colonies. As a result of this patronage and with the backdrop of famine, Westminster went into political convulsions over the fundamentals of free trade. Famine in Ireland had given the advocates of releasing the 'invisible hand' of the market the opportunity to shift the macroeconomic base away from agricultural protectionism and towards liberalization based on importation. 'The remedy is the removal of all impediments to the import of all kinds of human food – that is, the total and absolute repeal forever of all duties on all articles of subsistence' (Woodham-Smith 1964: 50). This stance pushed the question of food security in Ireland into a Tory-versus-Whig ideo-logical tussle, with a long and bitter debate about trade practices taking precedence over famine relief.

According to John Mitchel, in *The Last Conquest of Ireland* (1861), Belfast Corporation also appealed for relief, and specifically looked for support to enhance the public works schemes which they believed could provide work and revenue for the large numbers of people who were moving into the city from famine-stricken areas. This would relieve the pressures on the city and create opportuni-ties for an increasingly desperate population. Interestingly, Mitchel alluded to other examples from Europe where governments were having to dealing with this crisis of potato blight, including the government of Belgium's plan to restrict food exports yet free up the ports for imports in order to flood the local market with available and affordable produce (Mitchel 1861: 69). This type of initiative had been permitted during the 1782–3 Irish famine with relative success and was known to be effective.

In the event, among the Irish establishment, land reform was to become the limit of governmental relief. Beyond this and particularly with the debate around the Irish Coercion Bill throughout 1846 (which advocated oppressive measures as a response to famine-related unrest), the Act of Union itself and its repeal were to emerge as political rallying calls by more progressive forces in Ireland. Before being sentenced under the Treason Felony Act and deported to Bermuda, and a subsequent questionable role in the American Civil War, Mitchel etched two comments that have resonated through generations of Irish. First, that there were 'heavy-laden ships, freighted with the yellow corn their own hands have sown and reaped, spreading all sail for England'; and second, that 'the Almighty, indeed, sent the potato blight, but the English created the Famine'. The Young Ireland movement's attempted rebellion in 1848 was prosecuted in the context of the famine, and throughout these years, as noted by Cecil Woodham-Smith in *The Great Hunger*, there remained the fact that 'the poverty of the Irish peasant, the backward state of his country and the power of his landlord prevented him from benefiting from home-grown food did not mitigate his burning sense of injustice' (1964: 76).

As the years of famine went on, the establishments in London and Dublin showed little interest in countering the principal griev-ances that had incited the revolutionary movement within Ireland. Charles Trevelyan, Treasury under-secretary and free trade funda-mentalist, argued that the processes of famine should be left to 'take their natural course'. His personal objective was to export as much oatmeal from the island as possible, to adjust its natural market as a means of overcoming economic shortfalls. Charles Wood, the chancellor of the Exchequer, relayed to Russell that they should be: 'ready to give as near nothing as may be'. James Wilson, in the *Economist*, commented that 'it is no man's business to provide from [sic] another' (quoted in Ó Gráda 1994: 192). Throughout the famine the price of bread remained high, and while corn – 'Peel's brimstone' – began arriving after the repeal of the Corn Laws on 15 May 1846, the relief of those subjected to famine was wholly inadequate and contributed to the crisis.

The succession of the Whig administration of John Russell in July 1846 brought the economy and people into the heart of the famine years. Public work schemes and workhouses marked their utilitarian ad hoc approach to the alleviation of hunger, and the exploitation of the economy continued unabated. The Poor Law was amended in June 1847 to incorporate an 'improvement' measure which aimed to transfer the costs of dealing with Irish poverty to Irish resources. This attempted to shift the burden of the collapse of the Irish markets back onto the Irish economy, putting further pressures on the population through eviction and forced emigration. One severe way in which government policies were causing further degradation for the poor was detailed by F. S. L. Lyons in *Ireland Since the Famine* (1963). This was the prohibition that became known as the 'Gregory clause', a law which restricted relief (government support) to anyone who retained over a quarter of an acre of land. After spending everything on alternative food sources, rent and taxes, if the family could no longer sustain the rent they could be evicted. Lyons detailed a number of years where the clause was particularly oppressive, most notably 1849 and 1850, when (respectively) 90,000 and 104,000 people were subjected to this law (1963: 43–5).

The famine was without doubt one of the biggest humanitarian crises of the 1800s. It was to resonate as an archetypal experiment in repressive government and mismanagement. Its influence on Victorian society was unprecedented and can be seen in the manner in which Karl Marx, in *Capital*, used it as the primary contemporary example of the logical outcome of a laissez-faire political economy:

The population of Ireland had, in 1841, reached 8,222,664; in 1851, it had dwindled to 6,623,985; in 1861, to 5,850,309; in 1866, to 5½ millions, nearly to its level in 1801. The diminution began with the famine year, 1846, so that Ireland, in less than twenty years, lost more than 5/16 ths of its people. Its total emigration from May, 1851, to July, 1865, numbered 1,591,487: the emigration during the years 1861–1865 was more than half-a-million. The number of inhabited houses fell, from 1851–1861, by 52,990. From 1851–1861, the number of holdings of 15 to 30 acres increased 61,000, that of holdings over 30 acres, 109,000, whilst the total number of all farms fell 120,000, a fall, therefore, solely due to the suppression of farms under 15 acres – *i.e.*, to their centralization. (Marx 1867: 652)

In 1841, when the Census was taken, the population of the island of Ireland stood at 8,175,124. Shifts in population and the principle of natural law had brought the Anglo-Irish establishment to the vulgar Malthusian conclusion that Ireland was overpopulated, resulting in not enough food to sustain such a population. Indeed, Benjamin Disraeli stated that the island was 'the most densely-populated country in Europe'. Musing over population growth served as a convenient distraction. By the end of the famine in 1849: 'In the four provinces of Ireland the smallest loss of population was in Leinster, 15.5 per cent., then Ulster, 16 per cent., Connaught's loss was greatest, 28.6 per cent., and Munster lost 23.5 per cent' (Woodham-Smith 1964: 31, 412). This represented 20.9 per cent (1,708,600) of the Irish population. An estimated 2 million emigrated. The Irish population did not return to its pre-famine numbers until 2001.

Beyond the violence inflicted by famine at the behest of the middlemen, landlords, free traders, economists and the establishments in both Ireland and England, acts of solidarity were also evident throughout the catastrophe. Relief of the starving Irish became the *cause célèbre* for many in the middle of the 1800s. One of the most substantial contributions came from the British Relief Association, which – from its inauguration in 1847 – raised an estimated £200,000. Support came from other colonies and from as far afield as India, and even Sultan Abdülmecid of the Ottoman empire, who contributed both funding (an estimated £1000) and ships loaded with food (Kinealy 1994: 161).

Perhaps the most poignant act of solidarity and aid came from the Choctaw Indians in North America who, after suffering enforced evictions from their own lands, collected $710 for famine relief in Ireland in 1847. In the years after they too were to be subjected to a similar genocidal grab for land through the racist policy of 'manifest destiny' that was to decimate native American communities. What is nauseating to contemplate is that irrespective of the collective prostration that was famine, the Irish economy – when calculated through the prism of Smithian economics – was better off in terms of per capita income and economic growth because of the famine:

> Astonishingly, between 1840 and 1913 per capita incomes in Ireland rose at 1.6 per cent per year, faster than any other country in Europe. Where Irish incomes averaged 40 per cent of the British level in 1840, this proportion had risen to 60 per cent by 1913. (O'Hagan 2000: 20)

The shock of famine and the process of market adjustment in the years after brought economic reconstruction, but perpetuated emigration in a manner that was to redefine the geo-economic map of the island. Whereas the west of Ireland had been devastated and would never fully recover, the east of the island – and particularly the economic hubs of Dublin and the emerging industrial port of Belfast – reacted in a manner that framed recovery. Belfast's population rose from 20,000 in 1803 to 100,000 in 1851 (Moody and Beckett 1954: 34). Industrialization, the adaptation of the agri-economy, and the emergence of the linen, rope and shipping trades were to reshape the Irish economy. This also coincided with a political realignment which was to take the north and south in different directions within one generation of the famine.

The immediate effect of the famine on the Irish economy was on the utility of land and the collapse of the conventional economy. The long-term effects were to be seen in the north–south divide and a rationalized socio-economic make-up of post-famine Ireland. As Ó Gráda pointed out in *Ireland: A New Economic History: 1780–1939*, public schemes eventually came to replace farm labour as the principal means of income. At the height of the famine in 1847 the Board of Works had a labour force of over 700,000 on schemes, most of who would have come out of an agricultural background. After sustained emigration and evictions, the male agricultural labour force post-famine continued to decline (Ó Gráda 1994: 195). This imbalance in the general economic form of the island would, as a consequence, lead to years of contortion and depopulation. Furthermore, economic and business activity continued to be corrupted by nepotism and a survival instinct that would be carried into the political psyche of the Irish population. As early as 1868, the movement and radicalization of a whole generation of Irish people was to become a topical focus of study, as can be seen in J.F. Maguire's exploration of Irish political organizations in *The Irish in America* (1868), or the debate from the previous year in Marx's *Capital*. Maguire noted that: 'The mass came because they had no option but to come, because hunger and want were at their heels, and flight was their only chance of safety.' Marx put it in more colourful terms: 'With the accumulation of rent in Ireland, the accumulation of the Irish in America keeps pace. The Irishman, banished by sheep and ox, re-appears on the other side of the ocean as a Fenian' (Marx 1867: 666).

2 POST-FAMINE ADJUSTMENT AND INDUSTRIALIZATION (1861–1921)

The Irish experience of industrialization was activated by economic shock and the chaos of famine as much as by innovation and investment. The years immediately after the worst years of the famine saw a flux in the labour supply, changes to manufacturing production, increased land acquisition, and output going down across the main sectors of the pre-famine economy. With the population's decline there was a corresponding fall in the labour force of 29 per cent between 1861 and 1911. New production techniques had been introduced, and while the legacy of famine remained obvious for agriculture productivity across the industrial sectors went up dramatically, as did the concentration of labour in the industrializing port cities across the island. The effects of this readjustment process from the 1850s onwards were to shape the Irish economic landscape for a century. The most notable changes were to the agricultural base and rural life:

> The Famine almost halved the number of holdings under 15 acres. The proportion of farms of less than 5 acres continued to decline thereafter, from 24 per cent in 1841 to 12 per cent by 1901, although these tiny farms by no means disappeared. The number of cottiers fell from 300,000 in 1845 to 62,000 by 1910 .... In 1841 1.3 million classified themselves as 'farm servants and labourers'; by 1911 the number had fallen to 0.3 million. (O'Hagan 2000: 24)

Marx's analysis of the crises of post-famine Ireland, knowledgably presented in *Capital*, gave evidence of rural depression and unproductive farming methods. He noticed that in the agri-economy the prices of goods had been reduced and production was down, and there was a direct correlation to the emigration of agricultural labour. Furthermore, as his 1867 reflection on the condition of labouring families in Ireland shows, the years after the famine continued to bring hardship. Quoting the official inspectors' report on the experiences and living standards of the rural population, he noted:

Though living with the strictest frugality, his own wages are barely sufficient to provide food for an ordinary family and pay his rent, and he depends upon other sources for the means of clothing himself, his wife, and children .... The atmosphere of these cabins, combined with the other privations they are subjected to, has made this class particularly susceptible to low fever and pulmonary consumption. (Marx 1867: 663)

Between 1841 and 1861 the number of agricultural labourers – those actually in employment – went down from 1.2 million to 0.7 million. Employment decreased by 45 per cent by the 1870s. This decline, not surprisingly, led to a reduction by 50 per cent in the yield per acre of potatoes (Ó Gráda 1994: 205–6; O'Rourke 1991: 464–6). Furthermore, the rural population continued to be forced into impossible circumstances through acute poverty, often leading to the desperation of petty crime and resulting in thousands being transported off the island for theft and minor crimes to Australia and New Zealand. These victims of the criminalization of poverty merely added to the depopulation process.

Corresponding to the demographic changes through forced emigration and the depopulation of townlands, there was also a growth in various commercial activities in reaction to changing patterns of production. Apart from the clearance of agricultural areas, the 'success' of the Land Laws, the adjustment from intensive grain and potato production towards livestock signified the most visible aspect of market adaptation. By the 1890s the productive yield of the large farms would be ten times what it was in the immediate post-famine years. This increasing yield went to feed the expanding industrial working class in Belfast, Dublin and other expanding towns across the country, or was shipped out to the British market to service the demands of its burgeoning factory labour. Industrial development could be recognized throughout this period as a two-way process, where land was being appropriated and manufacturing to export was changing to support the expansion of profitable industries. Whereas the south of the island struggled to adapt to the residual agricultural market, what emerged in the north was to become a veritable 'linen rush':

Between 1862 and 1868 the number of power-looms in Ulster's linen industry rocketed from almost nil to 4108, the majority of them in small towns or hamlets. In the same period the number of linen operatives in Ireland increased from 33,500 to 57,000. (Rogers 2009: 310)

The economy of the north-east had survived the worst years of the famine and, with its proximity to Glasgow, Liverpool and Manchester, had been able to create an industrial base around linen and rope production, tobacco packaging and eventually shipbuilding.

With the collapse of the cotton trade after 1861 and the onset of the American Civil War, linen rapidly replaced cotton as the manufactured textile of choice for the mid-Victorian period. Due to these exports, from the stark indicator of economic growth rates, by 1870 Ireland was the seventh richest country in the world, the eleventh richest by 1911 (Burns 2002: 9). Within this revived market, Ulster was to adapt particularly well and innovatively to the macro-economic circumstances that had arisen.

> Between 1850 and 1875 employment in linen mills and factories rose from 21,000 to 60,000 of which about 70 per cent were women and children .... Belfast benefited from 'external economies of foreign trade' – regular trade links with markets and suppliers .... As a result the population of Belfast, which had reached 70,000 by 1841, rose so fast that by 1901 it rivalled Dublin, with about 400,000 inhabitants. (O'Hagan 2000: 21)

Post-famine Ireland remained susceptible to environmental influences as well as erratic regional commercial activity and political instability. Periodic rises in emigration and political unrest mirrored patterns of underdevelopment, a lack of effective political control, pitted with a volatile economy and food scarcity. There were crop failures in 1860–3, 1877–80, 1883–7, 1891–2, 1896–8 and 1904–5, and with each bout there were corresponding 'synchronous downturns' in land transactions and commercial activity yet, interestingly, increased monetary circulation. The numbers submitting to the workhouses were an indication of the continued stress on the townlands and their communities throughout these years. In February 1863, 67,000 were forced into the workhouses, 59,000 in 1867 (Ó Gráda 1994: 250–1). As a result of the 1879 collapse of the harvest there was widespread privation stretching the length and breadth of the island. It was evidence that it was still a population living on the cusp of starvation, with hunger in regions as diverse as the Glens of Antrim and the Burren in County Clare. Significantly, although registered deaths by starvation were not common, the government's actions in response to the 1879 crop failure contradicted Charles Trevelyan's and his ilk's market fundamentalist response that resulted in the Great Famine. In this instance the Gladstone administration from mid-1880 onwards addressed such crises with significant state involvement and £2.6 million was directed towards Irish relief. As Ó Gráda noted in *Ireland: A New Economic History 1780–1939*:

> Though the sharp rise in the numbers relieved in workhouses – 1.1 million in 1874–8, 1.7 million in 1879–83 – reflects acute distress, workhouse deaths rose less (from 55,554 to 62,277). Mass emigration relieved the pressure on those who stayed. Also, important, the Gregory Clause of 1847, which at the height of the Famine had excluded from relief entitlement those holding over 0.25 acres of land, was set aside, and never applied in time of crises. (Ó Gráda 1994: 253)

Improvements in the railway network out as far as Donegal and Westport, restrictions on the movement of the population being relaxed, and the availability of alternative food supplies, all helped steer the country through a succession of harvest failures. Island-wide rail networks created a lifeline for supplies as well as troops. As Joseph Lee observed: 'before 1850 economic development had been hindered by an underdeveloped transport network. Since 1850 Ireland has been an underdeveloped economy with a highly developed transport system' (Lee, in Cullen 1964: 87). By the 1870s over half the workforce in Ulster was engaged in industrial activity of some sort, yet across the island the numbers employed in industry did not rise above a quarter of the population. Industrial growth was, however, a definable shift in the evolution of the economy going into the twentieth century. The goods that dominated its emergence – and mostly linked to the rural and agri-economy – were linen, wool, rope-making, biscuit production, brewing, shoe production, cotton, alcohol production and the building of ships in Cork and Belfast.

Linen had been manufactured successfully in Ireland from the establishment of the Irish Linen Board in 1711. Its importance could be seen in the Board's composition and the fact that it contained 80 Irish parliamentarians. Linen production had historically been organized in its pre-industrialized form, employing weaving clusters in cottage industries, an outlet for farming communities beyond the sustenance produce of the smallholdings. When the Irish Linen Hall was erected in Dublin in 1728 it was one of the most formidable buildings in the British Isles, modelled on the royal palaces of Hamburg and Blackwell, and containing 550 rooms. It fell victim to the Act of Union, with the Board being dissolved as land exploitation and the drive for food production for the English market evolved. Outside Ulster, therefore, the infrastructure which had supported the supply of flax and production of linen had been transferred for different uses, or abandoned as a legacy of another commercial era. The famine decided the fate of the linen trade in the south, as noted in the *Irish Linen Directory* of 1876:

> The consequences of the famine were disastrous to the trade of the country. The poor were unable to do more than provide themselves with food; the small shop-keepers in the country towns lost their trade …. The agricultural and manufacturing industry was paralyzed and the want of employment added greatly to the universal distress, which in a greater or lesser degree, affected every rank and class. (Smith, *Irish Linen Trade Hand-Book and Directory*, 1876: 82; quoted in Smiley 1955: 106)

One aspect of the land laws that gave Ulster linen additional credence in its productive drive was the 'Ulster custom'. This convention meant that tenants had basic rights of tenure. Across the east of the province, tenants were afforded a position where they could improve farmland and work towards market trading and cottage production. The difference between the landlords of Ulster and the other three provinces was their belief that linen production could generate an independent and viable economy. Under the tenure of the Conway family, Lisburn in County Down was to become an administrative and trading centre for the produce; in its proximity Lord Hillsborough supported his tenants into the production of flax; in Lurgan a dedicated linen market was established; and Belfast was to benefit from substantial investment to become a supply route for the selling-on of manufactured linen. Across the north the rural and urban communities responded to the spasmodic international demand for the product. The importance of the product in this region reflected two events that provided further evidence of the switch of productive capacity from south to north. The first was the building of the Belfast Linen Hall and the second was the running down and eventual transfer of the magnificent Irish Linen Hall in Dublin to the Dublin Fusiliers to serve as a military barracks.

The onset of the American Civil War and the collapse of raw cotton supplies from the Confederate states provided the linen industry with an unprecedented opportunity to supplant the cotton trade from the 1860s until the recovery of the US market. Irish involvement was instrumental, with an estimated 150,000 fighting for the Union's

government and 40,000 for the Confederacy. Who the Irish fought
for depended on where an individual's ship landed after the famine
– New York or New Orleans. Exploiting the circumstances of the
war, the trajectory for the Irish linen trade saw the collapse of the
regional cotton trade. It was not the first time in the history of the
Irish economy that war brought benefits to industrial production,
while conversely relative peace seemed to bring with it depression.
The Crimean War (October 1853 to February 1856) had brought
opportunities for supplying the demands of the British military and
navy. At its end the profits were reinvested in the mill network across
Ulster. Indeed, William Ross, proprietor of Ross's Mill in the Clonard
area of Belfast, was so enriched by supplying linen uniforms to the
British army that he rented out to mill workers newly built two-up,
two-down terraced housing in rows of streets celebrating the battles
and characters of the Crimean War. Balaclava, Sevastopol, Odessa,
Servia, Omar and Bosnia were among the many streets in the city
that were named after battles and cities of the Empire, all celebrating
colonialism. Other imperial street names included Royal Avenue,
Great Victoria, Albert, Palestine, Jerusalem and India – all evidence
of where the new wealth of Ulster was coming from. Furthermore, the
advent of concentrated production methods and the building of mills
across the north, and to a lesser extent in parts of the south, brought
about labour relations similar to the factory system in England. It
also brought with it working conditions that were similar to those
surveyed in Engels's sociological study *The Condition of the Working
Class in England*, conditions that were to become the narrative for
Dickensian life in the late 1800s. Indeed, the organization that Charles
Dickens called 'The Association for the Mangling of Operatives', the
National Association of Factory Occupiers, was the very same organization that the Belfast linen manufacturers affiliated to in 1855.
Living behind the gothic facades of their newly built 'big houses', the
mill owners also were the architects of horrendous working condi-
tions for tens of thousands of Irish workers. For this purpose they
gathered the economic and legal forces of the land:

> From this you will gather that the enforcement of the law in
> Ireland provided some difficulties and many and amusing stories
> (if they were not tragic), which could be told of failure to
> enforce by reason of loop-holes, failure to get evidence because
> of prevarication, failure to get convictions because of technicali-
> ties presented by the defence to magistrates whose sympathy was
> with the employing class. (Smiley 1955: 107)

Hilda Martindale in her study of this system, *From One Generation to Another*, profiled the experiences of those who were subjected to mill life. Tellingly, the death rate of young people working in the mills of Belfast was twice that of the Manchester factories (Martindale 1944: 113). Children would be recruited into the mill system at the age of twelve. The work experience destroyed both health and life opportunities. By the start of the twentieth century one in six children in Ireland was illiterate. Schooling, which had been a national obsession in the post-famine years in many rural areas, in the cities had become a secondary concern to food security through mill work.

Life expectancy is a significant indicator of the real impact of the factory system on the communities that migrated to the mill towns in the years after the famine. While the mills' owners provided accommodation for most of their workers, wages could be clawed back into the profit cycle through rent. Working practices meant that whole families were ritually going through the mill system, generation after generation. The working conditions provide a snapshot of life in this machine. Women were released from work for as little as two days to give birth to children, sickness meant no wage, and the working conditions themselves of ten to twelve hours per day were suffocating, particularly for those in the machine rooms. C. D. Purdon, a doctor and campaigner against the mills, in his 1875 *Longevity of Flax Mill and Factory Operatives*, refers to lives of mill workers:

> The sanitary state of the Belfast factory district .... When about thirty years their appearance begins to alter, the face gets an anxious look, shoulders begin to get rounded – in fact they become prematurely aged, and the greatest number die before forty-five. (quoted in Smiley 1955: 108)

For those who worked in the carding rooms of the mills, the working life was estimated to be twelve years: starting at 14 years of age as operatives, they would be lucky to reach 30. In this part of the mill system the dust had a devastating effect. Diagnosed as chronic bronchitis with emphysema, byssinosis could be sourced to flax dust. The workers were conscious of the condition and the 'pouce' – a word thought to have been brought to the industry by the Huguenots and the French for dust – but were in no position to demand change. It killed tens of thousands. Action against the mills would mean the loss of jobs and eviction from the sought-after mill housing. Unbelievably, this form of bonded labour lasted until after the Second World War, when government housing authorities finally took over the upkeep and management of mill houses.

The economy of scale provided immense returns for the linen mill owners. With the cycle of linen production – flax production, bleaching where the linen was laid out in fields, weaving, dyeing, finishing, packing and selling – a range of skills were resuscitated across the industry. By 1890 Ireland had secured three-fifths of all employment in the linen industry in the British Isles. More specifically the development of the infrastructure for the industry was unprecedented: 'whereas in 1852 there was only a single power-loom in the Belfast linen industry, ten years later there were 6000' (Lyons 1963: 62). Subject to extraneous circumstances, volatile market conditions and an inability to adapt production techniques, by the close of the 1800s Irish manufacturing was still largely a hostage to market fluctuations. Furthermore, the divergence in the island's economy can be seen through the lens of the linen industry. Ó Gráda noted the growth and scale of this industry:

> Another important feature of the Irish linen industry was its marked localization within the island. By 1918 spindles were distributed among 50 owners, of whom 17 were in Belfast, 4 in Drogheda, 1 in Cork, 1 in Dublin, and the rest in Ulster. In weaving, it was the same story: by 1912 Belfast held 22,000 of Ireland's 37,000 power-looms, and the rest of Ulster another 13,000. (Ó Gráda 1994: 289)

While the north continued to industrialize at an unprecedented speed between 1850 and 1890, the southern half of the island struggled to consolidate its manufacturing base due to shifting macroeconomic demands and resistance to change by the landowning class.

The 'cotton villages' that were planned for a number of parts of the south found that the volatility of the cotton market could cause whole towns to rise and fall in fortune within months as this early form of globalization carried expansion and contraction in periodic sweeps. The 'cotton town' of Malahide, purposely built to support the finished product for shipping out, fell victim to the system even before the famine. Another, Balbriggan, had to diversify and eventually concentrate on the milling of flour. Westport, in County Mayo, with its French design and imported brick, gave all the impression that something particularly grand had come and gone. By the time of the famine, the cotton mills in the south were being adapted as workhouses. Nevertheless, for periods there was a flourishing of Irish cotton weaving, printing and finishing. At the beginning of the nineteenth century, Dublin's commercial centre was dominated by cotton producers and their thousands of looms, marking Cork Street, Bride Street, Francis Street, and Ardee Street with a once-prosperous industry. The Malcolmson Mill in Portlaw, Tipperary, by the 1850s was employing 1600 workers – almost half the population of the town – operating 900 looms, and importing cotton in a manner which highlighted its competitiveness with the producers of Manchester. Diversification in this location ensured that the core operation, cotton weaving, could survive periodic shocks. Ship production emerged as a by-product of the Portlaw economy, with some success. Ó Gráda was to point out that 'Malcolmsons' Neptune Iron Works produced the first steamship (the *European*) to carry live cattle from North America to Liverpool, and the *Una* was one of the first ships to pass through the Suez Canal' (1994: 280). Eventually, even the Portlaw Mill fell to the fluctuation in market trends and was to close in 1904 with the mill becoming a tannery and, as with other similar industries in the south, resorting to non-export agri-production.

The devastating blow to the cotton industry came during the American Civil War of 1861–5 with the blockade of Confederacy exports, halting the cotton shipments from the slave plantations of the southern states. Companies from Belfast to Cork had been benefiting from this trade and had been involved with cotton-producing plantations for decades. When the blockade enforced restrictions on the exporting of goods from the southern states, the Irish cotton trade went into depression. This was further undermined by the new US government's post-war tariff on cotton exports and a preference for English producers. In Ireland the linen industry was the main beneficiary. In 1861, 70 per cent of Irish linen was being exported to America and as the war intensified and the market was hit by a 'cotton famine', linen imports to the Americas increased substantially. In one year alone (1863–64) at the height of the conflict, linen exports from Ireland rose from £6 million to £10 million. Furthermore, employment in this industry went up from 57,000 in 1857 to almost 70,000 by the end of the 1890s (Goodman 2000: 12).

While the cotton industry was dependent on imports and global trends, the wool industry was in a somewhat different position. Australian imports supplied some of this market, but there was still the potential of sourcing and producing locally, without the need for heavy industry or the concentration of labour (for finishing) that cotton and linen were dependent on. Wool could rely on a customary economy across the island and a local market. The industry was linked organically to farming, and homespun and hand-woven clothing could still be produced by cottage looms. These industries also provided rural communities with the intensity of work and the wherewithal to avoid the move to the cities, which for rural townlands had a similar disintegrating effect as emigration.

With the end of the American Civil War there was a lull in the transatlantic trade, provoking an export downturn. As the country entered depression, political events again moved to equal importance with economic circumstances by creating a political vacuum that was filled by nationalistic fervour. The attempted Fenian rising of 1867 – a third salvo in the modern independence movement after the United Irishmen and the Young Ireland movement – and a failure in the potato yield over a number of years in the 1870s instilled a fortitude within much of Irish society that crystallized political momentum towards the ideal of Home Rule. The Fenians proclaimed a republic, citing grievances that contained a litany of economic references, revealing a definite socialist reference to their militancy:

> We have suffered centuries of outrage, enforced poverty and bitter misery. Our rights and liberties have been trampled on by an alien aristocracy, who, treating us as foes, usurped our lands and drew away from our unfortunate country all material riches …. The real owners of the soil were removed to make room for cattle, and driven across the ocean to seek the means of living and the political right denied to them at home. (*The Times*, 8 March 1867; Kee 1976c: 38, 34–44)

In contrast, the Unionist establishment in Dublin Castle and the north viewed industrial production as a stabilizing and conservatizing factor, and set about trying to encourage native industries through various endeavours. Wool and linen production were presented as exemplary trades. The industrial exhibitions of 1882 in Cork and Dublin in 1883 gave scope for debate on the potential for Irish indigenous manufacturing but predicated growth on the link to the British market. The key outcome of these exhibitions was the establishment of a select committee, appointed in 1885, which had the specific remit of monitoring local industrial development (Cullen 1964: 119). Its recommendations and initiatives were to influence the vision for and design of the economic base and its integration into the British economy until the south became independent in 1921.

Another more specialist debate that occurred in the 1880s revived ideas originally presented in John Hely Hutchinson's *The Commercial Restraints of Ireland* of 1779. He had argued that adaptation of traditional industries was the only possible way of releasing Irish commercial interests. The importance of this thesis was enhanced by the reprinting of his work in 1882 and again in 1888. The first significant review of Hely Hutchinson's work came through Edward Blackburne's *Causes of the Decadence of the Industries of Ireland* (1881) and subsequently J. G. Swift MacNeill's *English Interference with Irish Industries* (1886). Both lamented the loss of native industries, such as wool production, which they presented as being successful pre-famine, sourced rurally and exported extensively from across the island. This revival of interest in the historical and indigenous island economy coincided with and fed into the political tussles around the first Home Rule Bill of 1886. Advocates called for the revival of native industries and the relaxation of taxes imposed on Irish businesses, giving a spur in the debate on the possible benefits of an independent economy. However, the southern focus of this discourse also highlighted the evolving gap between the demands for advanced industrialization in Ulster's heartland and the intense arguments that were being ignited in the south around the land war and the role of land magnates in the impoverishment of the rural population.

In the 1870s across the south the land question remained the formative political dilemma, with the causes of the famine remaining 'live' issues. While actual land usurpation had been administered through the local agents' offices in the cities – driven by profiteering and not necessarily political intent – the common platform for opposition to the pattern of land ownership could be distilled into nationalistic reflection. Popular anger against landlordism could be easily manipulated into an argument for Home Rule, and while the interpretation was not defined in class terms, it nevertheless conveyed a political consciousness, localized and culturally inclined. Whereas ideological and class interpretations remained nascent until urbanization and unionization eventually brought forward concepts which were distinctly class-based, rural grievances consolidated anti-English sentiment in political discourse. Two key points emerge at this juncture in the history of the Irish economy. First, the proximity of small and cottage-based traditional industries made them vulnerable to the financial and industrial weight that was being formed in Ulster. Two Irelands had emerged. Second, the catastrophe of famine followed by land conflict and depression could be seen to be consequences of colonial expansion in the eighteenth century and by the establishment's anti-Irish racial fundamentalism in the early nineteenth. 'The orthodoxy that emerged at that time reflected the economic malaise of the period, and its acceptance was secured in the powerful upsurge of political feeling, which in time undermined both the land system and the Union' (Cullen 1964: 124).

The Irish radicalization process was expressed most forcefully by Michael Davitt (Micheál Mac Dáibhéid), a charismatic member of the 'Supreme Council' of the Irish Republican Brotherhood (IRB), who had served 15 years in Dartmoor Prison for attempting to organize a Fenian rising. After returning to the west of Ireland in 1879 he, along with parliamentarian Charles Stewart Parnell, formed the Irish National Land League on 21 October of that year, to campaign for 'fair rent, fixity of tenure and free sale'. It aimed to give tenants rights against eviction by landlords. His ultimate goal, taking a principle from the English socialists, was that of land nationalization. Within ten years the radicalization of his convictions had brought him to draw on the transitional programme of the International Workers Association for reform of Irish society (Kee 1976c: 74–9). The programme was articulated through his journal *Labour World* and promoted by the Irish Democratic Labour Federation which he founded in January 1891. The programme included universal suffrage, land rights, the building of worker's housing, maximum working hours, labour representation and free education. Davitt's work was to become the precursor to the trade union movement that was to develop in the 1890s.

Life in the cities, with congestion and rapid industrialization, had contributed to one of the harshest urban environments in Europe at that time. The life experiences and living standards of workers in Dublin can be seen from this 1862 City Hall survey of inner city life:

> We may safely venture upon the average of eight persons of each house, which gives us 64,000 people out of a population of 249,733, 50,000 at least of whom reside in a fetid and poisonous atmosphere .... The worst districts are the Liberties on the south, and the parish of St. Michan on the north side .... As a general rule, there is a green slimy steam oozing from a surcharged and choked-up cess-pool, through which the visitor is compelled to wade. (Robinson 1862: 517–18)

With the formation of a class of industrial and urban working poor and the ongoing and seemingly perennial deprivations for rural labour and small farms, Irish political and economic life was caught in the ideological mix of the late nineteenth century. The west of the island had come to identify with the Fenian movement (through the auspices of the IRB), the Gaelic League and the Celtic revival movement. Each was making its mark on the perceptions of Ireland internationally, drawing financial and political support from the diaspora. In the industrial east, socialism had started to evolve as a political force. In Dublin, the Irish Trade Union Congress (ITUC), the Independent Labour Party (ILP) and the Dublin Socialist Union were formed to campaign for workers' rights, developing links with the British Marxist Social Democratic Federation (SDF). By the mid-1890s they were organizing Dublin workers in a series of campaigns and marches, with branches being set up in Belfast and Waterford. The mobilization was successful enough for the fledgling trade union movement to organize a gathering of thousands in Phoenix Park in May 1895 to plan for action.

Emanating from the SDF, with increasingly acute ideological differences to the social democrats and the rurally inclined Gaelic League, James Connolly – together with Robert Dorman and T. J. Lyng – formed the Irish Socialist Republican Party (ISRP) on 29 May 1896 in a pub in Thomas Street, Dublin. In terms of industrial relations its intentions were clear cut and differentiated from the Home Rulers and social democrats. Its objectives were the:

> Establishment of an Irish Socialist Republic based upon the public ownership by the Irish people of the land and instruments of production, distribution and exchange. Agriculture to be administered as a public function, under boards of management elected by the agricultural population and responsible to them and to the nation at large. All other forms of Labour necessary to the well-being of the community to be conducted on the same principles. (Greaves 1961: 75)

Connolly adapted ten transitional actions from *The Communist Manifesto* (1848) and the Democratic Federation's *Socialism Made Plain* (1883) to argue the case for nationalization, the abolition of private banking, agricultural lending, a graduated income tax, a minimum wage, a maximum 48-hour working week, free education and universal suffrage. To maximize working class support he even resorted to Francesco Saverio Nitti's influential *Catholic Socialism* to appeal to the political awareness of religious workers.

In his first major political statement, published in *Labour Leader* in October 1886, entitled 'Ireland for the Irish', Connolly stepped outside the general internationalist mould of the socialist movement to introduce socialism and Irish nationalism as a single organic force dependent not on the neo-colonial idea of Home Rule, but on separation from the English colonial system. The influences on Connolly's work were unique enough: he had personal correspondence with and had met Eleanor Marx (Karl's daughter) and her husband Edward Aveling. He was also in communication with communist leaders across Europe (Greaves 1961: 84). In 'Nationalism and Socialism', published in the IRB's *Shan Van Vocht*, he reiterated the view that if an independent socialist democracy was not established, then English capitalism: 'would still rule you. She would rule you through her capitalists, through her landlords, through her financiers, through the whole array of commercial and industrialist institutions' (quoted in Greaves 1961: 85). Beyond Dublin, branches of the ISRP and the Socialist Society were established during a meeting in the Typographical Hall, College Street, Belfast, by Ernest Milligan, Robert Lynd, Samuel Porter and James Winder Good. In Cork, Con O'Lyhane used the commemoration of the 1798 rebellion as a platform to promote socialism there. The economic competence of this growing movement was not only ideologically formed, but also strategically focused. Parallel to these, ''98 Committees' were being set up across the island with notable cultural figures such as W. B. Yeats and Maud Gonne organizing demonstrations against what banners and flyers lambasted as the 'British Empire'. Conversely, while momentum was growing across the southern counties for separation, the Home Rule leadership under John Redmond were arguing that in economic terms separation would be unworkable. In a speech in Cambridge, he was adamant that 'separation from England was undesirable and impossible' (Greaves 1961: 94). Indeed, Redmond saw the link with England as indispensable for economic development on the island. These militant and constitutional juxtapositions were to set the scene within Irish political and industrial relations going into the next century. In a precursor of what was to come, events in South Africa turned its wars into a battlefield of the divisions fermenting across the island. Forty thousand Irishmen went to fight for the British against the Boers in the second Boer War (October 1899 to May 1902) under the pretext of fighting for the Empire. On the Boer side republicans sought another opportunity to engage with the British army. Michael Davitt, Arthur Griffith and Sean McBride – the latter two being rising stars of the republican movement – travelled to South Africa to participate in the Boers' resistance against Britain. At Robinson's Drift alone almost 500 Irishmen were killed fighting on both sides of that imperial conflict.

The increasing concentration of industrial labour in the major cities, with an evolving combination of work-related political activity, gave socialist politics an environment within which to flourish. Consequently, the nationalistic political blocs north and south, Unionist and Home Rule respectively, were joined by more militant trade union and socialist organizations. In the first years of the twentieth century the Gaelic League alone had 100,000 members, and with the political drive for independence being so strong Arthur Griffith was able to group various lobbies under the banner and organization of Sinn Féin (Ourselves Alone) in 1905. Griffith's newspaper, the *United Irishman*, with an estimated 250,000 readers was prominent in refining the economic nationalism that became so prominent in the post-independence years in the south (Ó Broin 2009: 175–9). Furthermore, the establishment of trade union branches presented the urban workforce with a leadership which was able to question the oppression of the factory system and capitalism.

Another major player in the development of a distinct and confident Irish trade union movement was Jim Larkin. His contribution to the labour movement on the island was unprecedented, founding the Irish Transport and General Workers' Union (ITGWU), the Irish Labour Party (with Connolly) and the Workers' Union of Ireland. Syndicalism had taken hold among many on the left during the Edwardian period, when the ideals of co-operative associations, workers councils, agricultural and urban cohesion, and labour as an engine for democracy provided a backdrop to the activities of the union movement. Disputes within the engineering industries in 1895–6 and 1897–8, and linen workers' strikes in 1897 and 1906, represented a coming of age for a distinctly Irish socialist movement. The National Union of Dock Labourers (NUDL), formed in 1889, which had significant membership in Britain, saw Larkin coordinating an unsuccessful strike in Liverpool in 1905. His arrival in Ireland signalled a more assertive leadership style with a focus on dockers' conditions and their right to be unionized (Morgan 1991: 94). Within months of Larkin arriving in Belfast he had organized between 4600 and 6000 dockers and carters, the vast majority employed by the Belfast Steamship Company. By 1907 Larkin had mobilized Belfast workers into a strike, with the core demand that companies address oppressive working conditions. It also enabled the dockers to view themselves as a concerted lobby. However, whereas post-famine fault lines remained a factor in the make-up of industrial relations across Ireland, they were distilled down to embedded sectarian divisions in Belfast. This legacy affected the trade union movement as well. A news-sheet from the women's section of the Irish Textile Workers' Union entitled 'To the Linen Slaves of Belfast' relayed solidarity from English workers, but dismay at the lack of militancy and the communitarian divisions within the Irish workforce. It noted that:

> they agree in condemning the conditions under which you work, your miserable wages, the abominable system ... which prevails, and the slaughtering speed at which you are driven. Many Belfast Mills are slaughter-houses for the women and penitentiaries for the children, but while all the world is deploring your conditions ... they unite in wondering of what material these Belfast women are made, who refuse to unite together and fight to better their conditions. (reprinted in Maguire 2006: 10)

As James Sexton later noted, workers were continually being frustrated by a seemingly intractable socio-religious divide:

> The prevalence of what I can only describe as the caste system throughout the dockers' fraternity, which [leads] to the creation of almost innumerably small clubs and societies all hostile to each other .... Quite frequently religious and political differences kept these bodies apart, and, indeed alive. (Sexton 1936: 109)

For a period Larkin was able to bring these disparate interests together in anticipation of better rights, wages and conditions. In response to the increase in syndicalist activity, strikes were followed by lockouts by shipping companies and other firms. In this first major confrontation, 160 dockers were expelled by firms in May 1907. They were supported in a strike involving 300 dockers and 200 carters. By July a further 1680 carters were on strike.

One incident stood out in the whole wave of industrial action that took place at this time, and that was the act of solidarity by 350 women from Gallagher's tobacco factory in north Belfast, who for a period suffered great hardship and resisted going back to work even after pleas from Larkin hiself. Nightly demonstrations were held at Corporation Square to protest against companies bringing in 'blacklegs' – strike breakers. At the height of the strike the army and police were used to disperse the strikers. On 27 June between 2000 and 3000 demonstrators attacked a convoy of blacklegs in High Street. 'The question of religion', the Royal Ulster Constabulary's Commissioner Hill reported to Dublin Castle on 1 July, 'does not enter into it at all – a fortunate circumstance, in view of the approaching Orange celebrations. I understand that there was never less party spirit in Belfast than at present. The strike is being conducted purely as a Labour dispute' (Dublin Castle file CSO – No.20333/08, SPO; quoted in Morgan 1991: 102). On Friday 26 July a red banner with the slogan 'Support the dockers and carters in their fight for trade unionism' was carried from Belfast's new City Hall up the Falls Road and down the Shankill Road by mill workers, dockers, carters, transport workers and various other unionized sections of labour in the city. For one moment in the city's history the communitarian divisions became a secondary concern. The northern establishment was, however, quick to reassert its influence and hegemony.

After introducing troops to the streets in ever greater numbers, an attempt by the local newspapers, the *Northern Whig,* the *Irish News* and particularly the *Belfast Evening Telegraph,* to introduce a sectarian pulse into the dispute eventually worked. Sectarian riots broke out on 10–12 August around the Falls Road, causing a number of fatalities. The immediate aftermath of the confrontation was a divided labour force and the sectarianization of the trade union movement between the northern-based NUDL and the southern-based ITGWU. The Home Rule crisis and the elevation of Edward Carson and James Craig to the leadership of the Ulster Unionist clubs to protest against Redmond's Home Rule bills brought Ulster's socio-economic and political life into the divided reality that would come to dominate Irish politics. On 23 September 1911 an estimated 50,000 Unionists converged on Craigavon to hear Carson denounce Home Rule. Another estimated 300,000 watched the demonstration make its way to the park. On 28 September 1912, Carson led 218,206 Ulstermen and 228,991 women in the signing of a covenant 'to refuse to recognize [the] authority … [of] a Home Rule Parliament in Ireland'. By 31 March 1913, 84,540 men had been enlisted into the Ulster Volunteer Force to physically resist Home Rule. At this stage the political and economic divergence between the north and south was complete, and the labour movement suppressed.

THE NEW REALITY

The most focused academic work on the development of the Irish economy in the Edwardian period came with the publication of

Alice Effie Murray's *A History of the Commercial and Financial Relations between England and Ireland from the Restoration* (1903). An academic from the London School of Economics and a friend of Sidney Webb, Murray was of the opinion that the 'difficulties' the Irish faced were primarily economic rather than religious or political. The influence of the English economy and the imbalance, 'estrangement', of economies meant that Irish economic development was largely bound to the reflex of English commerce. She noted that religious divisions were a facet of the system which distinguished economic development on the island, but that they were manipulated and to an extent manufactured to condition the economic and political environment. She made the observant point that: 'When Catholic emancipation at last came it came too late; the gift had lost its grace, and was powerless' (Murray 1903: 2). Subsequently, this divide would remain a feature of the island's development. The attitudes and actions of the respective hegemonic elites, the northern and southern factory and land owners, suggested that unlike other examples of this class, they had no loyalty to the people or the country they controlled. The picture she paints of the Irish economy is remarkably familiar:

> Irish manufacturing industry still concentrates itself in the north, hardly spreading beyond certain districts; emigration has been draining Ireland of her population for more than half a century; the class of absentees is far larger than it was before the Union. The great commercial expansion of the nineteenth century has conferred little benefit on Ireland; it has merely resulted in an increase of taxation to support trade in which she has little share. (Murray 1903: 3–4)

While progress was stunted, there was nevertheless an element of movement within the various economic sectors, where adaptation to new technologies and management systems could be seen. In particular, a number of initiatives had assisted in the improvement of economic conditions and co-operation between governmental and commercial activity. The first was the establishment of the Congested Districts Board in 1891. This set about encouraging and providing support for various aspects of agricultural and industrial production, such as enhancing methods of cultivation, co-ordinating the fishing industry to the point where it became self-supporting, developing industries such as lace-making and basket work, and supporting the wool hand weavers to generate a revival in that industry along the western coast of the island. The Board acted as an agency for economic development in areas that were deemed to be in poverty. The second major intervention came with the outworking of the 1896 Recess Committee's report on the Irish economy, which led to the creation of the Department of Agriculture and Technical Instruction for Ireland (1899). Its work included exhibiting Irish produce and assisting in the exporting of goods. The most prominent initiative of the period was a celebration of regional produce at the 1902 Cork Exhibition. A final example of active state engagement with the various native industries came from the Irish Agricultural Organization Society and its application of the 'Raiffeisen principles'. This was where moderate amounts of capital would be made available as loans to farmers or labourers by dedicated agricultural banks. The injection of this capital would enable produce which previously would have been for sustenance purposes to be released for market development. It was early micro-financing in its purist form and was celebrated by those such as Murray, Webb and Horace Plunkett as one of the main benefits of a co-operative movement.

Plunkett had brought the best of the European cooperative movement's ideas to Irish agriculture, working from the belief that productivity would be the measure of success. This was followed through by a distributive system that could assist agricultural communities to establish self-sustaining and profitable businesses. It was based on methods used in Denmark to group agricultural producers, collectively purchase equipment, secure joint loans and establish companies on the basis of producers having shares. By 1902 Plunkett's encouragement had led to the creation of 193 central cooperative creameries and 77 auxiliaries (Murray 1903: 427). Indeed, it was the incentive behind organizations such as the Co-operative Dairy Society, which was established in 1889 after a gathering of farmers in Limerick. In that same year 111 agricultural societies had been established, with the function of 'the cheapening of production by the purchase of good seed and of implements and general farming requisites' (Murray 1903: 429). The outcome of the reorganization of small rural businesses on the island was that it opened up a range of export opportunities for various societies and cooperatives. The Irish Industries Association, functioning in London but with offices in other major British cities, was able to co-ordinate a supply line which would bring woollen jumpers from Donegal, dairy produce from Limerick, embroidery from Dalkey and linen from Lisburn to the lucrative British and European markets.

Hand weaving and lace-making are the principal rural industries of Ireland; but there are many others, some of which are carried on in the workers' own homes and others in village workshops. The chief of these are hand knitting, hand embroidery, carpet-making, basket-making, iron-work, stained glass, wood-carving, stone and marble carving, bookbinding and leather-work, metal repoussé work, cabinet-making, porcelain, and silver and gold-smiths' work. Nothing approaching the excellence of Irish hand embroidery is to be found anywhere. (Murray 1903: 433–4)

The introduction of William Morris's utopian socialism to Ireland, which encouraged the development of cooperatives, guilds and the crafts industry, was an influence that proved popular across Irish society in the years up to the Great War. It played off the Home Rule image of what the island could be if given autonomy, and comple-mented the growing awareness of a distinct and independent Irish identity, gaelic in language and assertive in its difference.

Another noticeable facet of changes to the island's economy in Edwardian Ireland was the way in which the banking system adapted. As the financial stability of the various industries increased there was a corresponding expansion of the banking network. There had been a ten-fold increase in the holdings of the main Irish banks since the famine years, and this had come to manifest itself in the number of branches and the diversity of business activity that the banking sector was undertaking. In 1910 there were 809 branches across the island, up from only 165 in 1850.

The break-up of the monopoly of the Bank of Ireland permitted other financial opportunities. Relatively new alternative banks were increasingly linking the provision of services with the growing indus-trial enterprises. One notable feature of this diversification was the emergence of a northern banking sector. The Northern Bank, which had been established in Belfast (1824), the Belfast Bank (1827), the Ulster Bank (1836) and the Royal Bank (1836), all had their northern bases; the Hibernian Bank (1825), Provincial Bank (1825), National Bank (1835) and Munster Bank (1862) had southern provincial bases, while the Bank of Ireland (1783) remained Dublin based (Coyne 1901: 72–83: Hall 1949: 172–86). The banking system continued to expand in relation to commercial activities in the respective regions of the island, but what was formative was the systemic fault that had grown between Belfast and Dublin. Financial and fiscal operations in Dublin comprised a dedicated client base, which was a different market from the industrial clients of the northern banks. This was accentuated by restrictions placed on banking in Dublin, where banks other than the Bank of Ireland could not do business within a 50-mile radius of the capital. This exclusion created distinct regional financial bases, detached from the policy-making and governmental capital of Dublin. Taking the simple premise that politics follows economics, this demarcation assumes the inevitably of northern and southern financial differentiation and separate policy-making structures.

The Census of Industrial Production gives some insight into the Irish economy on the eve of the First World War. The 1907 census audited core industrial production, which was mostly concentrated in Ulster and shipped through Belfast, and consisted of linen, cordage, rope and twine. Securing the contract for building the *Olympia* and its more famous sister-ship, the fated *Titanic*, encapsulated the global influence that the industrial hub of Belfast had become. Six thousand dock workers were committed to these two commissions alone. With the largest mill network in the world, the most productive rope-works, the largest dry dock and the skills to design, build and fit 'unsinkable' liners, the industrial weight of the city brought it to a distinctly different economic position from other cities on the island. It also left it in a commercially advantaged position in the years leading up to the war.

In Dublin a number of firms stood out in terms of industrial activity peculiar to the capital's economy. From the 1907 census, W. & R. Jacob was employing almost 10,000 people in the production of biscuits. Brewing and distilling could also be seen as recognizable features of the Dublin economy, with Arthur Guinness & Co. Ltd producing two-thirds of the beer and porter on the island. Its productivity had always been unquestionable. Indeed, even during the darkest days of famine it had been producing 100,000 barrels per year (1846) and by the start of the war in 1914, 3.5 million barrels were being brewed. It was also known to be a benevolent employer at a time when the alternative, emigrating to England, could bring in up to a quarter more in wages. Guinness was an unusual employer, however; most were systematically exploitative:

> in Dublin as a whole the average earnings of the head of a family just before the First World War was just under sixteen shillings, though the average per entire family (based on a 1910 survey of 1254 families) was 22/6, with the majority earning less than a pound a week. (Lyons 1971: 68–69)

While industry had obviously adapted to the north–south reversal of fortunes, the treatment of labour by these celebrated globalized firms was exceptional. For most working in Irish industry, their experience was that of immiseration.

Within the context of a disparate industrialization process in the east of the island, industrial relations continued to ferment in a more conventional capitalistic augmentation. From 26 August 1913 until 18 January 1914, the trade union movement in Dublin led an estimated 20,000 workers in the largest industrial dispute the south was ever to witness – premised on the right of workers to union membership. The labour movement's conflict with over 400 employers, led by the Dublin United Tramway Company, focused attention not only on working conditions in the city through the Edwardian period, but on the conditions in which the Irish working class were forced to live.

With a death rate of 27.6 per 1000 of the population, Dublin was worse than Calcutta for the standard of living and depth of poverty in its slums. Tenements which had been constructed to sustain a post-famine workforce were desperately overcrowded, with almost 15,000 of them housing 30,000 families – in 1840 there had been only 353 tenements in Dublin. Eighty per cent of the 87,305 people who lived in the tenements lived in one room with their families. In November 1913 the Commissioners of the Local Government Board held an inquiry into conditions endured by the working class in Dublin. Their report from 20 February 1914 concluded that 'existing conditions of tenement life are both morally and physically bad' (http://multitext.ucc.ie/d/Housing_Report_Dublin_1913). A further 14,000 tenements would be required to give the city's citizens a basic standard of housing. The housing system designed for the 1840s had been merely added to by landlords in an attempt to capitalize on the influx of labour from rural Ireland, with impoverished living conditions being compounded by a lack of sanitation or health care. As well as contagious diseases such as tuberculosis, whooping cough and measles, circumstantial diseases such as cholera and polio, there was also a familiar pestilence for the Irish – as the Medical Inspector for Dublin, Charles Cameron, noted: 'It is certain that infants perish from want of sufficient food' (quoted in Doherty and O'Riordan 2011: 5).

Patterns of work in the city were erratic. Beyond the agri-food industry (including brewing) and transport there was no substantial industrial base. In Edwardian Dublin – the world of James Joyce's *Dubliners* – the unemployment rate was one in five, with many unskilled labourers vying for limited and often exploitative jobs.

William Martin Murphy, the spokesman for the Dublin Employers Federation and proprietor of the *Irish Independent*, represented the interests of businesses that dominated the city's economy. His power came from the extent of his personal influence over various ventures across the city, from the Dublin United Tramways Company to Clery's Department Store. His nemesis appeared in the guise of the now unemployed Jim Larkin. Larkin, having been removed from his role in the NUDL for encouraging industrial action, had formed the ITGWU on 4 January 1909. By the time of the Dublin lock-out in 1913 there were over 10,000 members of the ITGWU, and a confidence among its leadership that it could engage with the employers, and particularly Murphy, for better conditions. The union also attracted socialists who saw it as a means of challenging Irish capitalism, including James Connolly who had recently returned from the United States to take up a position as an organizer for the ITGWU. By 1911 the union was well established and managed, operating out of Liberty Hall, with its own newspaper – the *Irish Worker* – with an estimated circulation of almost 100,000.

Direct confrontation between Larkin and Murphy came on 27 July 1913 when Murphy instructed his employees not to engage in unionized activities, or to be members of the ITGWU. On 21 August he sacked 100 employees of the Tramways Company with the notice: 'As the Directors of the Tramways Company understand that you are a member of the ITGWU whose methods are disorganizing the trade and business of the city, they do not further require your service' (Doherty and O'Riordan 2011: 7).

In response Larkin organized a strike on 26 August by 700 of Murphy's 1700 tramways employees. Dock workers at Kingstown supported the action by refusing to handle products which were connected to Murphy's businesses. Sympathetic strikes spread across the city and when Larkin was arrested on 31 August for giving a speech from Murphy's own Imperial Hotel, riots broke out across the city. After one of the strikers, James Nolan, was killed by Dublin Metropolitan Police in a baton charge, his death became a rallying call for political opposition across the city. At his funeral, labour leader Keir Hardie provided the oratory in the absence of Larkin. Larkin at this point was in Mountjoy Jail. Out of these more violent confrontations with the authorities in Dublin, Connolly called together a defence wing for the union, the Irish Citizen Army. Increasingly this organization was to switch from advocating strike activity on rights and conditions to orchestrating direct military action.

The Dublin strike attracted attention from across the European trade union movement, with solidarity initiatives organized in Birmingham, Manchester and Liverpool. The real problem of hunger for the families of strikers in Dublin was relieved temporarily by the arrival on 28 September of the *Hare* carrying 60,000 boxes of food, 'family boxes', as an act of solidarity from the British trade union movement. At this point the intensity of the campaign and Larkin's challenge to the Dublin establishment met with more concerted opposition. The Irish Parliamentary Party, headed by Redmond and John Dillon, declared that Larkin was distracting from the primary political cause in Ireland – that of Home Rule; Arthur Griffith, the president of Sinn Féin, lambasted Larkin for getting Dublin workers involved in a vanity fight with Murphy; and William J. Walsh, the Catholic Archbishop of Dublin, condemned the provocative tactics employed by the ITGWU. As with the Citizen Army, however, the Sinn Féin leadership was also coming to the conclusion that rebellion was a plausible option.

On 29 September 1913 the government intervened with the establishment of a commission of inquiry, the Askwith Inquiry, which had the remit: 'to enquire into the facts and circumstances of the disputes now in progress in Dublin, and to take such steps as may seem desirable with a view to arriving at a settlement' (quoted in Doherty and O'Riordan 2011: 10). The inquiry criticized the strike leaders, while conceding in principle the right to strike. Christmas 1913 for the strikers was a particularly difficult period, with domestic deprivation underlining the fact that there was no resolution in sight. By the 18 January 1914 the ITGWU saw no point in continuing industrial action. The support from the British Labour leadership had waned and Murphy seized the opportunity by using his connections in the Irish media to claim victory over 'Larkinism'. At the annual congress of the ITGWU in June, Larkin reflected bitterly on the lock-out:

> The lockout in 1913 was a deliberate attempt to starve us into submission and met with well-deserved failure …. The employers claim a victory but the employers did not beat back organized labour in the city. I admit we had to retreat to base, but that was owing to the treachery of leaders in affiliated unions and betrayal in our own ranks. (quoted in Doherty and O'Riordan 2011: 12)

The monument to James Larkin in Sackville Street (O'Connell Street after 1924) in Dublin quotes a tribute from poet Patrick Kavanagh:

And Tyranny trampled them in Dublin's gutter
Until Jim Larkin came along and cried
The call of Freedom and the call of Pride
And Slavery crept to its hands and knees
And Nineteen Thirteen cheered from out the utter
Degradation of their miseries.

The result of the lock-out was significant in that it aggressively politi-cized the Dublin working class and radically realigned industrial relations on the island in general. It brought attention to the life expe-riences of the families in the tenements and highlighted the need for a mechanism of arbitration between union leaders and employers. Murphy went on being a successful proprietor; Larkin went to the United States and ended up being imprisoned for plotting revolution on 3 May 1920. Connolly – drawn increasingly to Pádraig Pearse and his desire for an Irish nationalistic uprising – co-led the rebellion of Easter 1916, a key marker in modern Irish history and a catalyst which, in one violent shock to the political system, was to encapsulate both the past and future of all the people on the island.

WAR AS STIMULUS

A number of significant moments in Irish history signalled an end to the traumatic birth of Irish industrialization with all its expansion, diversification, social disintegration, regional divergence, labour exploitation, poverty and strikes. Keith Jeffery awkwardly (and wrongly) presents this period just prior to the First World War as 'the last peaceful summer of Ascendancy Ireland' (Jeffery 2000: 72–73). The first significant moment was the crystallization of political forces north and south, the formation of respective hegemo-nies and paramilitary forms that would galvanize and concretize the poles of reaction in the two regions. The second was the dramatic sinking of the *Titanic* on 14 April 1912 with the loss of about 1500 lives, which came to symbolize the demise of often-romanticized Edwardian Ireland. The breaking point for the Irish economy and society came with the onset of war itself, which provided both the opportunity for adaptation to a war economy – yet again – and the trauma of a conflict with repercussions that would change the course of Irish history. The fact that serious academic attention to this key event in Irish history was only registered with a monograph 82 years after the end of the war – with Jeffery's *Ireland and the Great War* (2000) – gives an indication of the sensitivity of this conflict. Jeffery described the European war as 'the single most central experience of twentieth-century Ireland, not just, nor least, for what happened at the time, but its longer-term legacy' (Jeffery 2000: 2).

Over 200,000 men from the island of Ireland volunteered to fight for Britain. In reality the battle fields of Ypres and the Somme were to become the mire in which partition between north and south was moulded. The 'Irish' divisions of the British army, mostly south-erners and making up 60 per cent of the cohort, were recruited under Home Rule leader John Redmond's direction and a promise of Home Rule. They stood parallel in the trenches with the 'Ulster' division, formed largely from Edward Carson's Ulster Volunteer Force (UVF), and committed to the Unionist cause. It is arguably the paradox of Irish history that the long-feared conflict between the north and south was fought by proxy on the fields of Flanders. Roy Foster, in *Modern Ireland*, described Redmond's decision to support the war as a 'misjudgement' that changed the course of Irish history. For Carson, the blood-letting was to be seen as an act of loyalty to the crown.

The economy of the island was well placed both geographically and in terms of its economic infrastructure to service wartime needs. The production of flax had to increase to match the demand for linen uniforms. Likewise there were greater demands for munitions and agricultural produce to supply the English cities and the military complex. The war, in bland economic terms, was the catalyst for growth and for another boom (Lyons 1971: 63). The shirt industry, which was well established by the 1910s, found itself with unprecedented orders and struggled to supply demand. As Lyons notes, in *Ireland Since the Famine*, other features in the industrial organization of this period were notable:

> In the last quarter of the nineteenth century about twenty-five per cent of the work force consisted of juveniles under eighteen years of age and about seventy per cent of the whole total were women. But Belfast has the advantage that was denied to Londonderry of being able to redress the imbalance of the sexes by the employ-ment of male labour, not only on the heavier tasks in the linen industry, but also in shipbuilding, engineering, ropemaking and allied trades. (Lyons 1971: 64)

Going into the war, Derry contained 38 firms, employing 18,000 workers in the factories and an additional 80,000 in various supporting capacities. At the onset of war these firms were producing a staggering 20 million 'collars' (shirts) per year, primarily for export (Riordan 1920: 122–33). While hundreds of thousands of men were being shipped to France and Belgium, the industrial machinery needed the agility and cheap labour of women and children in the factories. The problem relating to labour supply came to head over the issue of conscription. The arguments for and against conscription into the British army were as economically charged as they were politically emotive – with one side arguing that Irish commercial links could only be enhanced by supporting the war effort, while on the other the increasingly militant independence movement decried the 'economic pressure' conscription and enlistment would create. The Limerick Young Ireland Society branch of *Cumann na nGaedheal* presented the absolutes of the latter position in the enlistment debate: 'Irishmen who enlist betray their country, degrade their manhood, and imperil their souls. They weaken agricultural commerce and industry by deserting civil life' (Rees 1998: 192–3).

Whereas Dublin suffered industrial decline and struggled to adapt to war production, the rural economy and the north-east were suitably adapted to benefit substantially from diversification by producing war supplies. The majority of recruits in the south came from the urban working class, particularly from the Dublin tenements. Political machinations were often left to those who had the opportunity or luxury to indulge in the discourse, while poverty in the Dublin city economy in the early years of the war left many with little choice but to find a military wage better than no wage at all. Many non-connected factories closed in Dublin, with some of the iconic names of Irish distilling disappearing at this stage. Guinness, the leader in the Irish brewing industry, cut its hours for its workers and reduced production. However, as Rees noted in *Ireland 1905–1925*: 'In rural Ireland, on the other hand, the war bought immediate and significant economic gains' (Rees 1998: 194). Farming practices changed to accommodate more intensive farming methods, agricultural prices were to go up and Irish produce was to supply the English market in a supporting capacity. Jobs were available in western counties, making it possible for younger farmers and labourers to secure a living in townlands where they would have struggled previously. It is interesting that in these areas popular resistance to the war and enforced enlistment into the army was most fervent.

In Ulster the situation was somewhat different. In securing war contracts Harland and Wolff (H&W) shipbuilders ensured ongoing work for upwards of 15,000 dockers. For its immediate competitor, Workman, Clark & Co. – which was within viewing distance of H&W – 10,000 other dockers laboured to build the merchant and navy ships necessary to prosecute the war at sea. In the first year of the war alone H&W was able to supply 256,547 tons of shipping, up from the 103,466 tons of 13 years previous. The scale of the contracts were such that the company had to outsource work to firms located the length of the east coast of Ireland, with component production and works ongoing in Dublin, Queenstown, Warrenpoint and Larne (Riordan 1920: 227–36). Belfast Harbour Commissioners (established in 1847) managed the flow of trade from the city *via* the lough, and with the proximity of the various mills, the sheer size of the quay and the volume of hull production, Belfast reasserted itself as a natural hub for shipbuilding.

War proved to be immensely profitable for the shipyards, coupled with a strategically safe position and an overwhelmingly Unionist workforce whose loyalty to king and country was not in question. By 1911 the population of Belfast had overtaken Dublin to make it the most populated city on the island. In that year's census the Belfast area registered 386,947 residents, while Dublin contained 304,802 (Mjøset 1992: 222). By 1915 it had one of the most productive war-dependent economies in Europe.

With the war restructuring the political and economic framework of the continent, the divisions in Ireland became so acute that eventually the diverse organizations advocating independence agreed to carry their cause to its logical conclusion. Bringing together starkly differing ideological and nationalistic positions, the Easter Rising of Monday 24 April 1916, became the consolidation of republican activity across the island. The rising, undertaken by insurgents from the Irish Citizen Army (ICA), the Irish Volunteers and *Cumann na mBan*, attempted to break the control of the British establishment in Dublin Castle by forcing the closure of state, industrial and strategic sites throughout the island. The aim was to provoke revolution in all areas where republicans were active, incite a popular confrontation with the British army and cripple British economic interests. The General Post Office in Sackville Street, the Four Courts, Jacob's biscuit factory, Boland's flour mill and St Stephen's Green – all important commercial centres – were to become the flashpoints of the rising. At the GPO, Pearse read out the rebels' agreed proclamation for a provisional republic. The imprint of the socialist ICA is very evident:

We declare the right of the people of Ireland to the ownership of Ireland, and to the unfettered control of Irish destinies, to be sovereign and indefeasible. The long usurpation of that right by a foreign people and government has not extinguished the right, nor can it ever be extinguished except by the destruction of the Irish people ... we hereby proclaim the Irish Republic as a Sovereign Independent State, and we pledge our lives and the lives of our comrades-in-arms to the cause of its freedom, of its welfare, and its exaltation among the nations .... The Republic guarantees religious and civil liberty, equal rights and equal opportunities to all its citizens, and declares its resolve to pursue the happiness and prosperity of the whole nation and of all its parts, cherishing all the children of the nation equally.

Outside Dublin the rising had temporary successes in Enniscorthy, which held out for three days, Athenry, where 1500 took part, and Ashbourne, where volunteers occupied four police barracks. With the reaction of the British Army and the police, and the turmoil of claim and counterclaim, the rising became the most significant violent shock in modern Irish history. By the 30 April the rising had been contained: '1351 people had been killed or severely wounded, 179 buildings with a valuation of £2.5 million had been ruined and some 100,000 Dublin citizens, almost one-third of the population, required public relief in the wake of the rebellion' (Rees 1998: 212). Some 1800 Irish Volunteers were transferred for internment in Frongoch Camp or Reading Jail, only later to be released under a negotiated amnesty in June 1917. In another theatre of conflict, and as if to re-emphasize the differences across the island, on the first day of the battle of the Somme (1 July 1916) the 36th Ulster Division suffered losses of 2000 dead and 3000 wounded. For the Unionist leadership this had reconfirmed the sacrifices made on behalf of the union and highlighted the perceived treachery of Irish nationalists. For Dublin Castle, the British Intelligence Service and the media, the most important political intervention in Ireland in the twentieth century was written off as a 'German Plot' (Costello 2003: 33).

The political ramifications of the rising and the war were to fix the economic and political formation of Ireland for the rest of the century. With the execution of the 16 leaders of the rising, including Connolly and Pearse, there emerged a new political counterweight to the Redmondites and Carsonites. In London by May 1916, Asquith had already decided that the island should be divided through a crude sectarian division between the six north-eastern counties and the southern 26. The economic implications were obvious to all. The republican Frank Healy noted during the election campaign of 1918 that partition would dissect 'six of the leading business counties', thus removing the economic viability of the 26 counties and the businesses 'that would ... help to finance the country' (Rees 1998: 223). Four years previously Connolly had foreseen the extreme repercussions of dislocating the north from the south, arguing that it would lead to a: 'carnival of reaction in both North and South, would set back the wheels of progress, would destroy the oncoming unity of the Irish labour movement and paralyse all advanced movements' (*Irish Worker*, 14 March 1914). Partition was to become an additional source of contention for Redmondites, separatists and Unionists alike. Carson railed against it with a belief that it would foster recrimination and cement religious divisions across the island. For republicans it was the worst possible solution, and created yet another point of conflict going into a guerrilla War of Independence.

While the war in Europe lasted, the economy outside the southern urban areas benefited from high prices for agricultural produce and industrial expansion in and around Belfast. The end of the First World War brought with it a contraction in the Irish economy, and with the War of Independence taking place concurrently the effect was the almost immediate collapse of certain sectors. This created a sense of displacement and rapid change in both north and south. While Sinn Féin's gains in the 15 December 1918 general election – where it collected 73 out of 105 parliamentary seats – represented an assertion of the national desire for independence, it also signalled a movement from one form of conflict to another, from rising to colonial liberation struggle.

Another aspect of post-war politics that benefited republicans was the Representation of the People Act. At a stroke it increased the Irish electorate from 701,474 to 1,936,673, thus giving political rights to a new constituency of men and women for the first time. In the aftermath of the Easter Rising and going into the independence struggle, this process of politicization would prove decisive. Irrespective of Ireland's position in the Empire, in January 1919 the Irish Republic was established with its parliament, the Dáil, sitting for the first time. This forced the issue of independence and military action. The journal of the Irish Volunteers, *An t-Oglach* (on 31 January), made it clear what was expected of its personnel: 'Every volunteer is entitled, morally and legally, when in execution of his military duties, to use all legitimate methods of warfare against the soldiers and policemen of the English usurper and to slay them if necessary' (quoted in Costello 2003: 29).

Two aspects of the War of Independence directly affected the economy and defined the type of engagement between the British authorities and the republicans. First, there was the deployment of 7000 men (mostly ex-soldiers) as a special military support for the Royal Irish Constabulary and 50,000 regular troops (Kee 1976c: 108). Known as the 'Black and Tans' due to their mix of military and policing uniforms, the newly employed ex-soldiers were to apply methods learned on the battlefields of the continent against the Irish population, with oppressive consequences. This introduction of British troops, recently returned from the traumas of war in Belgium and France, caused alienation across the south and in nationalist areas of the north. In economic terms, their activities under coercive legislation amounted to a scorched earth policy in parts of the island, and contributed significantly to the anti-English sentiment that had been galvanizing republican forces since the rising.

Beyond the summary executions and torture that visited whole counties in 1920 – the torching of towns such as Miltown Malbay, Balbriggan, Trim, Ennistymon and Lahinch, and the burning of Cork City on a number of occasions – the Black and Tans set out to attack the commercial infrastructure of the south and the morale of its people (Kee 1976c: 92–100). The methods that were used were the same as those employed in the towns across the continent, known by them as 'reprisal by burning'. It had the same destructive outcomes. Across County Clare it was the mills, bacon factories and creameries that were targeted. The harvests were burnt in a number of regions. The government itself even acknowledged the ferocity of the tactic and was later to pay £2,000,000 to the Irish government for the damage inflicted on Cork. Dublin fared no better, highlighted by the event that became known as Bloody Sunday, where on 21 November 1920 the RIC and regular army went into Croke Park, the Gaelic Athletic Association's headquarters, and fired into the crowd watching the Dublin and Tipperary Gaelic football match. Thirteen were killed and 70 injured. The *Freemans Journal* from the following day portrayed a scene 'unparalleled in the history of the country ... the bullets came in as thick as hail, dealing out death in their swift passage' (*Freemans Journal*, 22 November 1920; Mandle 1987: 193). 'It became the single most brutal act of the war.'

The second thing that influenced the form of military engagement that occurred in the 1918–21 period was something as simple as the mundane cycle of farm life. The rural population in the south was acutely aware of the food shortages that could hit the island if land was not tilled and managed properly. Military activities from republicans would have to come second to agricultural duties. With its extensive volunteer network throughout the island Sinn Féin assisted in this process by encouraging farmers to work out a division of labour between tilling, gazing, ploughing and fighting. 'Land grabbing', where land was taken from pro-British landlords and farmers, was also organized to acquire land for agricultural production for the designated Irish Republic. Counties Clare, Mayo and Sligo saw very active land grabbing and a corresponding growth in the support for the new Dublin administration. Although the Sinn Féin executive questioned the motivations behind this practice, it proved to be very popular at *cumann* (club) level (Rees 1998: 238–9). Demands for independence were consolidated in the south by the republican leadership forging one of the first anti-colonial struggles in the British Empire, and the message was straightforward: the Irish people were now at war with the British government.

Although there were coordinated attacks across the country, a series of guerrilla attacks and the occasional open battle between the respective sides, there was one commercial tactic that proved to be immensely effective. The Sinn Féin Standing Committee had already seen the worth of economic sanctions as an act of resistance, having announced a boycott of 'any and every direct and indirect tax' as early as 6 May 1918. They also instructed their supporters to refuse: 'to purchase any commodities, with the exception of necessary foods on which the British Government levies any tax' (see Lawlor 1983: 21). Furthermore, the involvement of the farming communities in the war signalled the arrival of a newly assertive and distinctly militant west of Ireland, confident enough to engage with 13,000 British troops in Cork County alone. Rural resentment was further heightened by the habitual commandeering of fuel, livestock and commodities by the police and army (Rees1998: 262). The economic war fluctuated as intensely as the military campaign.

With the onset of the War of Independence, the role of the Irish diaspora also came into play. Millions of Irish had taken the arduous journey across the Atlantic and through Ellis Island to establish lives in the cities of the United States. Their reasons for leaving were largely to escape, but their establishment and power in the American cities gave them a political freedom and economic weight that would never have been permitted in Ireland. This diaspora took centre stage in the logistical battle with Dublin Castle. Coordinating support for Sinn Féin and the establishment of the provisional government, together with the procurement of resources and intelligence to prosecute military engagement, meant a need for finance. Fundraising was subsequently to become a part of the Irish diaspora's experience, with the Irish in the United States effectively coming to bankroll the republican war through the Dáil Loan Scheme. Under the auspices of the minister for finance, Michael Collins, over £1,000,000 was raised for the support of the republican government. Most of the funding came through the Irish Self-Determination League, overseen in the United States by Eamon de Valera and James O'Mara. Dáil Éireann presented a prospectus in mid-1919 and by July 1920 the funds had been raised for financing the government's proposals. The *Prospectus* stated:

> The Loan, both internal and external, will be utilized solely in the interests of Ireland – an indivisible entity. It will be used to unshackle the Irish Trade Union Congress, and give them free access to the markets of the world; it will be used to provide Ireland with an efficient Consular Service; it will be used to end the plague of emigration, by providing land for the landless and work for the workless; it will be used to determine the industrial and commercial resources of our country and to arrange for their development; it will be used to encourage and develop the long-neglected Irish Sea Fisheries, and to promote the re-afforestation of our barren wastes; it will be available for, and will be applied to, all purposes which tend to make Ireland morally and materially strong and self-supporting. (*Dáil Éireann Loan Prospectus* 1919; also see Costello 2003: 75)

This appeal to the diaspora not only revealed the extent to which the Irish immigrant community had arrived in the corridors of power in cities such as Boston, New York and Philadelphia, but also provided an insight into the provisional government's vision for an independent Ireland.

While the de facto administration in Dublin was evolving slowly through the conflict, the war was an incompatible backdrop for the introduction of the Government of Ireland Act in 1920 by the British. The Act's most formative clause was confirmation of the partition of the island between the northern six counties and the rest of the island, designed in such a manner that the north could sustain an administration within the context of the British political and economic orbit. In December 1920, the Act came into force and while the south went into perhaps its most intense period of the conflict, the Unionist leadership in the north – at this point under the control of Northern Ireland's first prime minister, the landowner James Craig – celebrated the establishment of 'a Protestant Parliament for a Protestant people' (Farrell 1976: 91). Northern Ireland was formally established on 7 June 1921. As with similar colonial arrangements throughout the Empire, partition was orchestrated to mirror the political, cultural and economic divisions that marked the period, and was a convenient option for the London government.

In a report on the Anglo-Irish war in April 1921, the US Counsel in Dublin, Charles Dumont, presented data on the structural damage caused. The extent of the engagement between republican and British forces, verified by both government and republican sources, gives some insight into the intensity of the conflict. During the War of Independence 74 courthouses and 537 police barracks were destroyed, and 246 barracks damaged. Dumont also pointed to Sinn Féin's figure of 2000 homes destroyed (1921). Until the truce of July 1921, the War of Independence claimed the lives of 405 police personnel and 150 British soldiers, while 317 civilians were killed and 285 wounded – which included Irish Republican Army (IRA) personnel (Rees 1998: 263; Costello 2003: 126). Between June 1919 and June 1921, expenditure for security in Ireland rose ten-fold for the British government, while the income from fundraising in the United States for the Provisional government was steadily rising. Without a resolution, the war and the cost of the war were set to escalate.

While the situation had spiralled into lawlessness in many regions, international pressures were ongoing to achieve a settlement on the island. The most notable of these interventions came from a US initiative, the 'Committee of One Hundred on Conditions in Ireland', comprising 150 labour, church and political leaders. Their report of July 1921, the *American Commission on Conditions in Ireland 1920–1921*, gathered four days of hearings and testimony, and attracted substantial media coverage across the States. The conclusions criticized the methods and rule of the British govern-ment in Ireland, and brought forward what was effectively the opinion of the US government on the Irish situation, albeit heavily influenced by the Irish-American lobby. It stated that: 'In spite of this campaign of murder, arson, terror and destruction, the Imperial British Forces would appear to have failed to preserve British rule in Ireland' (*American Commission* 1921: 99–101; Costello 2003: 106). The British Labour Party's 'Commission on Ireland' report was published in January 1921. Written by a seven-member panel with a military advisor, its response was not as strong as the American Commission's – whose *Interim Report* had appeared at the same date – but the conclusions were also damning. The Labour report called for 'conciliation' and 'negotiation'. These two significant attempts to get the British coalition government to come to some resolution of the Irish issue can also be seen in a context where British trade unionists were calling for a general strike over the Irish question, and where significant sections of the British media – the *Manchester Guardian*, the *New Statesman*, the *Daily Herald* and the *Westminster Gazette* – had established desks dedicated to exposing abuses in Ireland. The international consensus that was building, particularly in the United States and among the European labour movement, demanded British government negotiations with the Irish Provisional government and almost universally promoted the option of the British government's withdrawal from the island (Costello 2003: 106–7).

3 PARTITION AND DEPRESSION (1921–1939)

With the signing of the Treaty between representatives of Dáil Éireann and the British government on 6 December 1921, the Irish Free State was established, a constitutional component of 'the Community of Nations known as the British Empire', with members of its Parliament swearing to be 'faithful to His Majesty King George V., his heirs and successors'. The south was now a member of the Commonwealth, with Northern Ireland awkwardly positioned within the union, yet administering its own state and economy.

While various clauses of the agreement on the constitutional arrangements with Britain plunged the 26 counties into civil war and defined the political poles in the south for almost a century, economically sensitive clauses were more subtly couched. For example, article five of the agreement stipulated that 'The Irish Free State shall assume liability for the service of the Public Debt of the United Kingdom ... and towards the payment of war pensions.' Article nine stated: 'The ports of Great Britain and the Irish Free State shall be freely open to the ships of the other country on payment of the customary port and other duties.' And article ten stated: 'The Government of the Irish Free State agrees to pay fair compensation ... to judges, officials, members of the Police Forces and other Public Servants who are discharged by it or who retire in consequence of the change of government.' The economic relationship with the new state of Northern Ireland further complicated the situation, with article fifteen making provision for 'Safeguards with regard to import and export duties affecting the trade or industry of Northern Ireland', and a 'settlement of financial relations' between both states. A boycott of the northern economy by the Dáil heightened the tensions as the relationship further deteriorated between the two fledgling states.

With the establishment of Saorstát Éireann, the Irish Free State, the demographic weight of the island shifted away from the cities and back to rural political bases. The movement for independence had been increasingly driven by the farming communities and with the creation of the 26-county state there emerged a policy bias towards a stratified agricultural sector. The new southern administration took on the burden of rebuilding an economy that had been emasculated from its industrial hub, wasted by the war and accorded the liability of transition. The Anglo-Irish war and partition had all but destroyed the manufacturing base in the south, and together with the large numbers of urban youth who were emigrating, the power base of the trade unions and the labour movement were substantially weakened. Sinn Féin, which had successfully navigated its way through the war, came out in a strengthened position, albeit divided over the question of partition. David Fitzpatrick, in *Politics and Irish Life 1913–1921*, commented that the party 'was heavily dependent upon the shopkeepers, employers and large farmers for income, and the Republican County Councils for their rates' (1977: 207). The problem of dislocation for the Irish Labour movement was further complicated by its lack of participation in policy making and lobbying in the first Dáil. It was given no role in the first government of the Free State and was to a large extent excluded from shaping the economic policies that were to bring the 26 counties into relative independence. Beyond the antagonisms surrounding pro and anti-treaty positions, the imbalance in labour representation would be an aspect of economic development that would mark the newly established hegemony and its economic policies. J. C. McCracken, in his *Representative Government in Ireland*, noted that both the first and second Dáils were made up of predominantly commercial and professional groups (65 per cent and 58 per cent respectively). This influence could be seen throughout the state's early economic architecture (McCracken 1958: 33–34).

Notwithstanding the composition of the government and the 'natural' inclination towards the larger farmers and commercial interests, the Democratic Programme that had been introduced as early as January 1919 did have some socially inclined elements. In planning for the restructuring of the post-war economy, the idea of social provision came into play – possibly in homage to Connolly by one of the Programme's authors, Sean T. O'Kelly. Resources would be secured to ensure that there would be some form of health provision for those perceived to be the most vulnerable within the new state, the old and disabled. Furthermore, there was a perception that the distinct geography of the island of Ireland could play a part in reconstruction, working towards: 'the development of the nation's resources, to increase the productivity of its soil, to exploit its mineral deposits, peat bogs and fisheries, its waterways and harbours' (quoted in Mitchell and O'Snodaigh 1985: 59–60). The document also affirmed the importance of the land issue by endorsing continued acquisition, thus consolidating support in rural areas. The growth in the size of farms during this period gives some indication of the extent of land acquired and the readjustment going into the Free State through a general policy of placating larger farmers across the south:

> Over a period of about 40 years, from the end of the First World War (1918), there was a general movement towards a consolidation in farm size. By the mid 1950s, 45 per cent of farms were in the range of 30 to 100 acres. The total area occupied by both tillage and pasture in the 26 counties, in 1930, amounted to about 11 million acres. (www.muckross-house.ie/library_files/Ireland_in_the_30s.htm)

While creating large farms was implicit in the strategic plan of the new administration, the assertion by the Dáil, and Collins in particular, that labour issues – class-divisive issues – should not be prioritized exposed the conservative ideological lineage of the new government.

> By the end of 1921, about one-third of Irish workers in the major insured industries were out of work, roughly the same proportion as in Britain .... Labour's position was progressively weakened until its best hope was toppled for mitigation of wage reductions rather than demand wage increases. (Fitzpatrick 1978: 32)

The Department of Labour had been established in 1919, and with a restructured bureaucracy, the voice coming through from the Department was effectively that of employers and farmers, under the auspices of Ernest Blythe and Darrell Figgis. Labour relations posed a different set of problems. Throughout the Anglo-Irish war the labour force in the cities had utilized strike action as a means of resistance and destabilization. Arbitration by the Department sought to bring residual industrial action to a conclusion in the interests of national unity. Particularly militant were the creamery trade unions in the west, which at one stage had tried to set up a Limerick Soviet, and the railway workers across the country who were involved in lockouts and a prolonged confrontation with employers that had been simmering since the 1913 strikes. As the economic implications of the Treaty took effect the system that had been in place under the British was merely adapted to the new dispensation, with labour relations being managed by the National Arbitration

Courts. Consequently, tensions were to remain high between the administration and the disaffected labour movement.

While the south fell into the reality of an immensely difficult reconstruction process, complicated by a vitriolic civil war, the north convulsed with the momentum of change. Ulster Unionists were reconciled to their new reality, while in the south two distinct entities emerged – one pro-Treaty, one anti-Treaty – with two differing views of what Ireland and its economy should be like. At the Anglo-Irish Treaty debate in the House of Lords on 14 December 1921, Edward Carson, leader of the Irish Unionists, lambasted the arrangements for breaking up the union as 'a revolver pointed at your head' (quoted in Rees 1998: 288). Supported by a group of Conservative Members of Parliament known as the Diehards, the Unionists threatened war with Dublin if the proposals were not changed. The Boundary Commission which was given the remit of deciding the border between the two states was a particularly sensitive issue for hardliners James Craig and his MP brother Charles, who saw the geography of partition as the key factor in the viability of the new state of Northern Ireland.

The north fell into an intense period of dissipation, a mixture of political confrontation over the arrangements, resistance by northern Irish nationalists and sectarianism. The nationalist community in the north came to refer to this period of Unionist state oppression as the 'pogrom'. Some 20,000 were forced to flee southward or move into the already congested ghettos where the nationalist and Catholic community had been concentrating since the 1880s. A Craig–Collins pact, orchestrated by Winston Churchill and signed on 21 January 1922, aimed to relieve pressure from the north–south stand-off. The ongoing economic boycott from the south was relaxed and the Craig administration agreed to take action to stem the spiralling levels of violence in the north. The pact lasted one week, and by February dozens were being killed in the north. One more attempt to broker a deal failed, and with the south increasingly destabilized by its own civil war, the northern issue was to become a secondary concern. In the spring of 1922 an attempted coup by republicans in the north failed, and after this partition became entrenched in both its political and economic form.

J. M. Curran was to point out in *The Birth of the Irish Free State 1921–1923* that the south almost stumbled into civil war without absolute and irresolvable reasons for conflict. Its damage was to be generational to Irish political and economic life. During the conflict three unstable governmental forms operated on the island: de Valera's

Cumann na Poblachta, League of the Republic, with its support in the west; Collins' Provisional Government and its Dublin base; and Craig's Northern Ireland. Each offered an alternative vision for the island and each acted in direct opposition to the others, with the political and cultural divisions being as complete as the economic dislocation. Collins's assassination at Beal na mBlath, County Cork, on 22 August 1922, shocked the country and left W. T. Cosgrave to assume control of the government in Dublin. His receipt of arms and support from the British army for the Free State forces adjusted the balance of power to bring their strength to over 50,000 by the start of 1923, vastly outnumbering the anti-treaty forces. The overwhelming force of the Free State's regular troops against the irregular republicans, a wave of executions by Cosgrave's government (77 in total), a lack of resources for the republicans, and mass imprisonment gave the pro-treaty forces an unassailable logistical advantage. With almost 3000 dead by 23 May 1923, chiefly among the defeated anti-treaty forces, de Valera proclaimed that the civil war was being 'suspended':

> Soldiers of Liberty! Legion of the rearguard! The Republic can no longer be defended successfully by your arms. Further sacrifices on your part would now be in vain, and continuance of the struggle in arms unwise in the national interest. Military victory must be allowed to rest for the moment with those who have destroyed the Republic. (quoted in Rees 1998: 312)

Encouraged by the defeat of the republican forces, the Free State set about consolidating its position. As an initial act, representing the southern administration, Ernest Blythe sought to formulate a conciliation policy with a satisfied Northern Ireland government.

The destruction to the infrastructure of the south was estimated to total £30 million, and together with the tens of thousands who were in need of hospital care, the extent of damage to private property and the demobilization of the Free State army, the beginnings of the new state were fraught. In Dublin alone the estimated damage caused during the fighting was £4 million. Economic depression and food shortages further undermined attempts to implement the optimistic project that had been lauded in 1918 to secure the sustainability of the Irish economy after achieving independence. The August 1923 election was marked by civil unrest between the opposing forces from the civil war, which Cosgrave's new political party (Cumann na nGaedheal) won. It then had to navigate the difficulties of a minority administration with only 63 seats out of 153 in the Dáil. De Valera's Sinn Féin gained 44 seats, Labour 15, the Farmers' Union 15 and independents 16. While initially absentionist, de Valera and his anti-treaty colleagues were by August 1927 to split with Sinn Féin and take up seats in the Dáil under the title Fianna Fáil. The poll was just sufficient to enable Cosgrave to take on the role of head of the Free State, with Ernest Blythe in the Finance Ministry and Joseph McGrath in Industry and Commerce. The tasks at hand were reconstruction and food security, with one of the first pieces of legislation for the new government being the Land Act of 1923. This transferred remaining landlord holdings to tenants, with the immediate effect being that it pacified areas which might otherwise have been opposed to the activities of the new administration vis-à-vis their position in the civil war. It also provided incentives to the farming community to stabilize production, leading to an increase that ensured food security throughout the decade. From a development perspective, while agriculture was able to support the indigenous market, its export market continued to be depressed.

From the outset of the Anglo-Irish Treaty, divergence between the northern and southern economies became structural. Comparisons between the states could be drawn from this period onward and the differences between the economies and the various sectors therein dominated policies and initiatives. In operational terms two alternative economic systems were being constructed, both standing in stark contrast to the British economy. K. A. Kennedy, in *Economic Development*, compared the average Irish income in the 1920s with the average British income. Whereas the average income in Northern Ireland stood at 61.8 per cent of the British level, the Free State income was 55.7 per cent. This was less than in the years before the First World War (Kennedy et al. 1988: 26, 21–4). The policies of Blythe and McGrath were in line with the power base that they had emerged from: bourgeois, intellectual and suspicious of organized labour. Their instinct – as with their civil service – was towards the status quo, and with economic policy this meant adapting a pre-war system to the new dispensation. Even with farming, demands to prioritize tillage as opposed to livestock were not accepted by the new government. This would have created more employment opportunities on the land for labourers and small farmers. Livestock farming meant larger farms with fewer opportunities for labour. The government was also resistant to industrial innovation, with the only significant evidence of industrial adjustment being the plan to bring electricity to the west of the island through the Shannon electrification scheme, which was completed in 1929 after four years of construction. While the austerity that informed the economic policies of the south in the 1920s reflected conventional economic theory, any popular expectations of a radical government dissipated.

Fiscal policy was relatively strict, taxation was to be low, the newly introduced Irish punt was pinned to sterling, and the agricultural sector was prioritized as the hub of economic regeneration:

> Exports were inflated by the effects of the civil war, but cattle exports (the best barometer of rural prosperity) rose by 27 per cent in volume and 12 per cent in value between 1925 and 1930. Butter, fresh pork, and sheep exports rose too. (Ó Gráda 1994: 390, 386)

In practice dairy and livestock farming became the measure of economic development for the Cumann na nGaedheal administration. Targeting the underdeveloped manufacturing sector, a fiscal inquiry recommended that tariffs should be limited to specific imported, mainly luxury, items. Patrick Hogan, the minister for agriculture, coined the slogan for the government's primary economic policy: 'one more cow, one more sow and one more acre under the plough'. Within the crucial British market this agricultural focus was evident, with Irish meat and dairy produce's share remaining stable or rising marginally (McKeever 1979: 76–9). The importance of livestock and pasture can be seen in comparison to the decline in grain production:

> Pasture was dominant, while the cultivation of grain continued to fall as it had since the Great Famine of the 1840s. Just over a million acres of grain crops were grown in 1921, this had fallen to just over 750,000 acres by 1931. In January 1930, the Honorary Secretary of the Irish Grain Growers Association appealed to Irish farmers to maintain at least the 1929 acreage of grain crops .... The number of cattle declined in the country from 4.4 million in 1921 to just over 4 million in 1931. Milch cows accounted for three quarters of these. The number of horses also declined slightly during this decade. However, at the same time, pigs and poultry experienced a sharp increase in numbers. The number of poultry rose by almost six million between 1921 and 1931. (www.muckross-house.ie/library_files/Ireland_in_the_30s.htm)

The Cumann na nGaedhael party ruled for over a decade after independence in the south. Its drive for reconstruction led it down a path of consolidation and restriction, of austerity in the interests of building the Free State. The focus on limiting tariffs and searching for compatible markets brought the economy to a situation where control of selective markets assisted the growth of the privileged sectors. This was met with policies that attempted to be compatible with other European and American growth-oriented markets. In the drive to reduce tax, the standard rate went down from 25 per cent in 1924 to 15 per cent in 1927; the income of farmers was exempted from taxation and this left a fiscal system that was largely driven by customs and excise duties and rates on property. Consequently, the imbalance created a mechanism which was heavily dependent on the rate returns from urban tax payers, leaving little revenue for the government to invest in public services. From this period on, the role of the Catholic Church in the provision of social services was fixed in southern Irish society. Its involvement as a quasi-state provider was to have a profound and lasting impact onto the development of the society, with aspects of religious order practices proving controversial, undermining both the long-term social policy of the state and the Church's role in Irish society.

The depreciation of agricultural prices worldwide after the boom of the First World War had been further complicated by a series of bad harvests in Ireland in 1923–4. Livestock and dairy produce were increasing in terms of market share, yet tillage was being reduced year in year out. By 1929–30 it accounted for only 16 per cent of the value of gross output, though it had been 22.5 per cent at the beginning of the First World War (O'Connor and Guiomard 1985: 89–97). This adjustment can also be seen in the amount of government expenditure that was being directed towards tillage in the early years of the Free State, averaging out at 2 per cent per year. Other interventions by the government seemed to be out of kilter, such as the 1927 Intoxicating Liquor Act which prohibited the sale of alcohol on Good Friday, Christmas Day and Saint Patrick's Day. There was also the creation of a loans scheme for farmers, administered through the Agricultural Credit Corporation. This was one of a number of state agencies that the government established to stimulate economic growth, the most prominent of which were the Dairy Disposal Company and the Electricity Supply Corporation, both from 1927. The benefits of the credit injection would eventually pay dividends and was intended to be a functional investment into agriculture.

The most formative elements of agricultural policy were the re-establishment of the trade supply to the British market and the standardization of produce – such as Irish butter, beef and eggs – to distinguish the quality of Irish products in the wider market. From this sector one product excelled in export markets and helped to sustain the Irish economy in the years after the Free State was established. This was based around the continual demand for beer, and stout in particular, supplied by Guinness in Dublin. Three-quarters of the produce was exported, mostly to Britain, and in 1926 this single product accounted for 30 per cent of: 'total manufacturing value added in Ireland' (Kennedy et al. 1988: 47). The freedom of access to the British market for this produce ensured its role in the Irish economy and to an extent it underwrote the economic viability of the first years of the state.

The Censuses of Population from the 1920s were to catalogue a freeze in employment patterns, so much so that the global depression of 1929 was to have only a marginal impact on an already deflated labour market. Indeed, in the five years from 1926 to 1931 employment rose by 4850, an increase of 970 jobs per year. Some sectors lost out. The construction industry was deflated by the lack of public expenditure and restrictions on the development of manufacturing industries. As Jon Press pointed out in *The Footwear Industry in Ireland 1922–1973*, a lot of the new jobs created during this period were livestock-derived and demanded larger numbers of women for the peculiar types of work that emerged – such as shoemaking (Press 1989: 33, 46; Daly 1987: 71–75). What was endemic to this economic realignment was the role of emigration. This historical problem exacerbated the overall economic situation in the 1920s, as civil war, partition and poverty drove people from the island. As Kieran Kennedy calculated in *The Economic Development of Ireland in the Twentieth Century*:

> In fact emigration in the decade 1921–1931 averaged 33,000 per annum, higher than the figures for either of the two previous decades 1911–21 (19,000 per annum) or 1901–11 (26,000) per annum .... The estimated decline in population from 1922 to 1931 was 89,000, or nearly 10,000 per annum. (Kennedy et al. 1988: 38–39)

In the first decade of the state, emigration was factored into the strategy for economic recovery, as was the north–south divide. The crude sectarian carve-up of the island had contributed to demographic shifts, including the decline in the non-Catholic population in the south, which went down by 132,500 – from 327,000 to 194,500 – between 1911 and 1936 (Girvin 2006: 47). In a Dáil Éireann debate on 19 November 1930, future taoiseach Seán Lemass highlighted the effects of the loss of so many – mainly young – people for the economy, giving an indication of the establishment's understanding of the severity of the situation: 'If it were possible to estimate in terms of money the loss which the state has endured in consequence of emigration, it would be shown that the capital loss ... would amount to five or six times our national debt' (Dáil Éireann debate, xxxvi, 91, 19 November 1930).

THE NORTHERN 'DOMINION'

The parliament in Northern Ireland, which was under the jurisdiction of Westminster, inherited an economic infrastructure that differed immensely from the system that was in place in the south. The political control of that economy meant that it was organically tied to the ebbs and flows of the British economy. Financial, fiscal and monetary policies were shaped through the Treasury in London, yet the north was cut from a natural economic hinterland in the Free State. It was to remain the only region of the United Kingdom to have a border economy to deal with, and all the dislocation that this came to represent.

This point was further complicated by the fact that both the southern government and a significant minority of the population in the north considered the six counties to be a constitutional component of a united Ireland. Republican aspirations were to reconstitute it as such. Partition was disliked on all sides – Unionists felt that it was a manifestation of the break-up of the United Kingdom, while nationalists believed that it stifled the political and economic destiny of the island in general. The British government took the view that it was a interim measure until the Boundary Commission and the Council of Ireland could decide on a more effective arrangement. Partition was to be temporary. The long-term sustainability of the economy of the six counties was not a factor that was considered (Harkness 1983: 43; Dixon 2008: 56–7). The sectarian divide was incorporated into the architecture of the new northern state – as permitted through the agreement – and settled immediately into an apartheid-like arrangement. In 1921, Catholics in Northern Ireland amounted to 33.5 per cent of the population, thus encapsulating a permanent and sizable minority within the six counties (Darby

1983: 102). For the population in the north, the sectarianization of the region was perhaps the most pressing implication of partition. It soon became a feature throughout many aspects of the society and was to evolve as the state moved from crisis to crisis. Indeed, the administration seemed to be only able to sustain its hegemony through maintaining a suspicion of external and internal subversion. As Paul Bew and Henry Patterson commented in *The British State and the Ulster Crisis*:

> The role of sectarianism was less in founding the state than in influencing the form that it took …. By openly demonstrating its distrust of Catholics, by excluding them, with rare exceptions, from all but the most menial types of government employment, and by maintaining a form of exceptional legislation (the Special Powers Act) and an often openly partisan judicial system, it demonstrated to the Protestant population just how seriously it took the threat of Catholic subversion. (Bew and Patterson 1985: 4–5)

Prime minister Craig voiced the reality of the new arrangement: 'In the South they boasted of a Catholic State …. All I boast of is that we are a Protestant Parliament and a Protestant State' (quoted in Dixon 2008: 58).

Generally, the living standards of people in the north had been better than those in the south due to industrial employment patterns and better wages. Throughout the 1920s there were opportunities not available to those in the south, and consequently by 1926 there were almost as many in employment in the northern six counties (505,000) as in the rest of the island (762,000). Furthermore, in that year more than three times the number were employed in industry in the north (34,000) than in the rest of Ireland (10,000) (Kennedy et al. 1988: 99). Unemployment was averaging out at 20 per cent during the 1920s and, unlike the south, when the Great Depression hit the United Kingdom, Northern Ireland saw job losses and unemployment rising to almost 30 per cent. The figure was influenced by both the region's links to the economic base in the United Kingdom, with its exports being affected, and the numbers involved in manufacturing. Exporting had become crucial for the survival of the industries of the north and the link with the UK economy had become its lifeline.

The aspirations of the south to decouple from the British economy paradoxically led to a differentiation from the activities of business and government in the north. The immediate impact of this could be seen in the border areas where, on both sides, businesses and economic activity were forced to look away from their natural hinterland and towards the largest northern or southern (in the north and south respectively) economic hubs. It was a differentiation that was to depress commercial activity in the border regions for decades.

The first government of Northern Ireland was a microcosm of the state's hegemony, a gathering of Unionist politicians and senior members of the Orange Order whose focus remained the idea of empire that had driven Edward Carson and a pre-Great War socio-economic mentality. John Andrews, the minister for labour, and the ministers for finance, Hugh Pollock and John Milne Barbour, managed economic policy under the leadership of James Craig. Their aim was to ensure that the links between London and Belfast were absolute in opposition to Dublin. This resistance to Dublin's perceived pressures on the northern administration was reinforced by sectarianism. Dawson Bates, the minister for home affairs in the mid-1920s, refused Catholic appointments to his ministry. 'In 1927 Edward Archdale, the Minister of Agriculture, boasted that there were only four Catholics in his ministry' (Bew et al. 1996: 57). The Orange Order, within this culture of anti-Catholicism, took on the unofficial role of monitoring Catholics and surveillance for the ministries. Andrews brought this to a further extreme by ordering a register of Catholics who worked with or for the Northern Ireland government. No minor personality in the administration, Andrews – from a mill-owning family and the highest figure in the Orange Order in government – was successively minister for labour (1921–37), minister of finance (1937–40) and prime minister (1940–3). Bates had a particular influence over the economy and had the favour of Craig, yet his sectarian make-up was central to his political and personal demeanour. Sir Basil Brooke, a rising star in the administration, stated in 1933 that:

> [he would not have] a Roman Catholic about his own place ....
> He would point out that the Roman Catholics were endeavouring to get in everywhere and were out with all their force and might to destroy the power and constitution of Ulster. There was a definite plot to overpower the vote of Unionists in the north. He would appeal to loyalists therefore, wherever possible, to employ good Protestant lads and lassies. (quoted in Dixon 2008: 59)

Such blatant sectarianism resulted in the skewing of public funding towards political and religious lobbies that were keen to support the new regime. It rapidly sectarianized the fabric of the state and society itself. In the bigger picture, Westminster was increasingly leaving Stormont to sort itself out.

The *Ulster Year Book* from 1929 maps the composition of the workforce in 1926, with 38.8 per cent of the 'gainfully occupied' in manufacturing, textiles, shipping, engineering or building – 221,505 in manufacturing and building alone. Agriculture employed 25.9 per cent of workers. This represented a substantial industrial workforce concentrated in Belfast at this stage. State revenue for 1927–8 amounted to £10,524,735, coming from both local taxes and transfers from London. Expenditure amounted to £10,303,315 of which 49 per cent went on social services, 12 per cent on law and order, 15 per cent on administrative departments, while 14 per cent was returned as an 'imperial contribution' to the UK Treasury. Notwithstanding the fluctuating fortunes of the linen and ship-building industries, the depression affected the population of the north in a familiar manner to the south, with a total of 57,500 emigrating between 1926 and 1937 (Harkness 1983: 46–47). While agricultural production remained relatively stable and adaptable to innovation, the contraction within industry caused more uncertainty within the main cities and towns. Half the population of the north lived in rural areas, and after the NI (Miscellaneous Provisions) Act of 1928 and the easing of export opportunities, productivity expanded, increasing the north's British market, particularly for potatoes, meat, eggs, orchard and dairy produce. The Milk and Milk Products Act (NI) of 1934 ensured that the production and marketing of agricultural produce from the region was as competitive as possible, covering areas as diverse as animal welfare and hygiene.

As in other places, unemployment in the industrial sectors became problematic as the north moved further into the Great Depression. The linen industry was noticeably exposed, making it vulnerable outside the fortunes of war production. Also negotiations between the various ministers and shipping lines became increasingly tense, compounded by the demands of a revived labour movement. The shipyard in Belfast had one major casualty of the depression – that of Workman, Clark & Co., on the Antrim side of the lough. Its contracts dried up to the point of closure in 1934, its workforce a mere 10 per cent of what it had been in 1924. In an unusual act of state intervention, the Loans Guarantee Acts (1922–38), the government moved to guarantee loans from private enterprise for shipping orders. Another major attempt by the government to manage industrial decline was with the introduction of the New Industries (Development) Acts of

1932 and 1937. The Acts took a broader view of the geo-economic location and attempted to draw on international investment. It worked to a degree in that Short & Harland arrived in Belfast to produce aircraft in 1937, creating more employment – eventually rising to 6000 – than the shipbuilding industry. The 1930s were, however, a period of industrial decline across the north in comparison with the early years of the century. Its location, its history and its increasingly antiquated production techniques, left the region floundering – until the war. Harkness was to comment:

> Increasing government caution and red tape, indecision and division of responsibility between ministries, and the inability to offer substantial taxation, wage or insurance concessions compounded Northern Ireland's natural disadvantages of distance, lack of raw materials and absence of cheap power, so that it remained amongst the most depressed areas of the kingdom. (Harkness 1983: 50)

The situation was complicated by the conservatism of the representatives of the old industries sitting in Stormont. Their disregard of the social needs of the public reflected a lack of understanding of any economic development theory. Furthermore, there was an innate distrust and suspicion of the Keynesianism that was to rescue the general British economy from depression, and a steadfast refusal to implement reform to the education system or to ensure unemployment benefits. In stigmatizing those out of work, it gave the administration a harshness that was, in British and Irish terms, Victorian. Sending in troops to quell food riots during the depression embittered the society to the role of government. The Northern Ireland government had a tendency to direct policies in its own peculiar way, in a fashion that was to affect long-term economic growth. This continually frustrated the Treasury in London. Sir Richard Hopkins, the controller from the Treasury, was to comment of this period:

> When the Northern Irish government was set up it was expected that their revenues would be sufficient both to meet their expenses and to provide a substantial contribution to Imperial services (defence, debt, &c). This expectation was realized at first fully and later in a diminishing degree. Since 1931 Northern Ireland has been in effect a depressed area. So far from receiving any large Imperial Contribution we have invented a series of dodges and devices to give them gifts and subventions within the ambit

of the Government of Ireland Act so as to save Northern Ireland from coming openly on the dole. (Hopkins, 8.2.39, PRO T. 160/1138/15586; cited in Bew et al. 1996: 62)

Relief schemes, a raw nerve to the historical memory of Irish north and south, were to become a feature of life in the north. Just over a decade on from being led into the slaughter of the Great War, thousands were being forced to labour on road works for food rations. In 1932 these schemes were being managed by the Ministry for Labour, with opposition from the Ministry of Finance due to the cost and, apparently, the embarrassment of having to appeal to the Treasury to support this kind of programme. With unemployment relief handouts, food riots and a stagnating economy, the early 1930s represented a period of intense crisis for the administration. Hugh Pollock spoke of 'the disgrace attendant on the insolvency of the province' (PRONI CAB 9A.40.1 'Imperial Contribution', Pollock to Andrews. 1.9.30; cited in Harkness 1983: 53). In the middle of the crisis, the new grandiose neoclassical Stormont Buildings were opened by the Prince of Wales on 16 November 1932, with Craig displaying characteristic bullishness. Bankrupt as it was, the Ulster government was introduced to the world as a high point of imperial power. To enable the north to pay for itself the Finance Act (NI) 1934, the Valuation Acts Amendment Act (NI) 1932 and the Employment (Agreement) Act (NI) 1936, all attempted to restructure its economy so as to make it more functional within the net of the Treasury. This effectively meant the revaluation of the state for the purposes of survival and impacted onto the imperial contribution from Northern Ireland. In 1930–1, this contribution was £545,000, yet by 1934–5 it had declined to a mere £10,000.

Where the situation was most acute was in the urban communities that were subject to immense deprivation during this period. In 1932 unemployment stood at 27.3 per cent, with both Irish nationalist and Unionist working-class communities struggling for food and basic healthcare. Craig resisted the introduction of a health stamp which would have provided sickness benefit, only to concede and introduce it after pressure from London. The Victorian principles of 'improvement' and 'utility' remained intact in the dominant ideology of Northern Ireland in the 1930s, and could be seen by the provision of outdoor relief, the workhouses and work schemes. The number of people registering their families for relief gives some indication of the levels of poverty: 'relief cases mounted steadily during 1932, the Belfast board of guardians recording 884 in early January, involving

4008 persons, 1985 in mid-June, involving 9144, and 2612 by 10 September, involving 11,983' (Harkness 1983: 69).

For those subjected to relief, it meant hunger and the humiliation of seeking food support from the congested relief centres. The hunger was eventually addressed after riots by the unemployed on the Shankill and Falls roads in Belfast, and the scare of the emergence of a communist movement which, against the cultural norms, threatened to cross the traditional and officially sustained sectarian divide. The result was that a third of all government revenue was redirected towards poor relief in 1933–4. It amounted to some £331,494 and led to the creation of an unemployment board through the Unemployment Act (NI) 1934 and the Poor Relief (Amendment) Act (NI) 1937, which enabled poor relief to be distributed at discretion. Problems that remained included poor sanitation caused by a lack of investment in the infrastructure, energy shortages due to the high costs of importation, almost one in three unemployed, a lack of health services, and housing which for a significant minority was unfit for habitation. Together with widespread hunger, public policy negligence came to blight the lives of the population of the north through the 1930s (Ministry of Home Affairs, quoted in Lawrence 1965: 151). Governmental intervention, however, appeared unorthodox to an Ulster administration that remained suspicious of the gathering consensus on socialist economics in Britain.

With the state of Northern Ireland formed by the early 1930s, the identity of the region was marked by a series of expensive iconic projects: the Silent Valley reservoir opened in 1933, the Ulster Museum opened in 1929, and Stormont's own Parliament Buildings with their greco-imperial garnish, which were positioned so they could be seen across large parts of Down and Antrim. Edward Carson's death on 22 October 1935 marked the point of consolidation for the northern state, with his requiem service being held at St Anne's Cathedral in Belfast. It signified the coming of age of ideological forces that had been fermented in the dislocation of pre-partition and pre-war Ireland. The hegemony had been embellished by heightened fear of the Dublin government and anti-Catholicism, shaping policies and initiatives which would come back to haunt Stormont a generation later. Sectarian conflict spread throughout the north in the 1930s, culminating in organized attacks on Catholic pilgrims as they tried to return from the 1932 Eucharistic Congress in the south; in July 1935 nine were killed in Belfast in sectarian riots; in March 1936, 514 Catholic families were forced from their homes in Belfast alone; and 13 people, coming from both communities, died in the run-up to the most intense fighting of that year.

A report by the National Council for Civil Liberties in May 1936, addressing the special powers of the Northern Ireland state, concluded that sectarian and repressive discrimination were implicit in the operations of the regime. The Stormont government's official report on the conflict, *The Disturbances in Belfast in 1935*, on the other hand blamed 'anti-loyal' elements – including republicans – for orchestrating the violence (PRONI CAB 9B/236). In 1938, as preparation for war was concentrating the energies of most other countries across Europe, a Home Office audit of governance in Northern Ireland concluded that it was 'a Protestant "state" otherwise it would not have come into being and would certainly not continue to exist' (cited in Harkness 1983: 80). The *Ultach* initiative, comprising critics of the state largely from Belfast's radical intellectual circles, branded the state 'totalitarian' and demanded that the British government intervene. In a Europe succumbing to authoritarian regimes, the north – as with the south of Ireland – was rapidly becoming less of a concern for others.

ECONOMIC WAR

In the Irish Free State by the late 1920s there was some quantifiable economic growth, but it was marked by the Cumann na nGaedheal government's lack of innovation and vision in regard to manufacturing. Import substitution, gambling on experimental monetary systems, relying on specialization and comparative advantage within the agricultural sector had imposed immense pressures on the economy. The new Irish punt had been pegged to sterling, and while monetary policy seemed to at least stabilize the financial system, it reflected the fact that sterling represented more than the English economy, but was a global currency (Kennedy et al. 1988: 26; Ó Gráda 1994: 382). This was driven home by the need for the administration to develop a greater knowledge of sterling as a currency, and for prudence on the part of the Treasury in Dublin. Correspondingly, the administration managed a frugal fiscal policy which was notable for its 1927–8 reduction in the standard income tax from five shillings in each pound to three shillings: that is, from 25 per cent to 15 per cent. The consequence was the reliance on alternative revenue raising and the hugely unpopular reduction in pensions for the elderly. The party had long abandoned its role as revolutionary manager of a new state. Going into the Great Depression and entering its last year in power, it had come to represent a beleaguered establishment intent on maintaining its political base in the middle class and large farms around the country. Furthermore, for the first time since before partition the class issue re-emerged as a feature of Irish politics.

Until the depression the Cumann na nGaedheal government held rhetorically at least to the principles of free trade with deference to its powerbase. The increasingly popular policy of protectionism had been spreading across Europe, yet the instinct of the administration had been suspicious of government participation in the economy. Hogan had acknowledged the practice of tariff imposition to be problematic in restraining the infectious impact of the international markets at a time of contraction. In the *Economist* in November 1927 he commented that 'We have tariffed, on the admission of anybody who has examined the matter, almost fifty per cent of our tariffable imports. And that is called Free Trade? I accept that definition of Free Trade' (26 November 1927; Ó Gráda 1993: 387; O'Brien 1936: 360–1).

The Fianna Fáil party only decided to take seats in the Dail in June 1927, but with a groundswell of support across the Free State it had built up the momentum that was to take the anti-treaty leadership – led by de Valera and Seán Lemass – into government on 9 March 1932. Immediately, the new administration set about engaging the old enemies at home and abroad through an 'economic war', based on self-reliance and protectionism. Lemass quipped:

> The late Government was able to solve, partially, its unemployment problem by the annual emigration of 25,000 or 30,000 young people. That is ended. Those 25,000 or 30,000 people who, in other years, found an outlet through the emigrant ship are remaining at home or have to be provided for at home. (quoted in Ó Gráda 1994: 379)

In an interview for *Time* on 11 April 1932, de Valera made his intentions clear and again asserted his republican principles. 'Britain', he proclaimed, 'cannot frighten us'. Although the south had been struggling throughout the late 1920s to engage with the broader open market system in a manner that many European countries had been rejecting, the onset of depression carried its dominant economic interests to similar conclusions to those of Fianna Fáil. As other states began to prioritize and protect indigenous markets by closing their economies, so did the south.

The Cosgrave administration had sought to curb spending and reduce debt, appeal to foreign investment where possible and enhance aspects of the agricultural economy to stimulate economic growth. The de Valera administration after 1932 brought a different type of vigour to the country, changing both the Irish government's political style and its economic policies. One commentator on Irish affairs, the future US president J. F. Kennedy, saw de Valera and his party as holding on to principles that predated the foundation of the state itself, while continuing to be fixated with the British connection:

> De Valera is fighting politically, the same relentless battle they fought in the field during the uprising of 1916, in the war of independence and later in the civil war .... He feels that everything Ireland has gained has been given grudgingly and at the end of a long and bitter struggle. Always it has been too little and too late .... They have not forgotten, nor have they forgiven. The only settlement they will accept is a free and independent Ireland, free to go where it will be the master of its own destiny. Only on these terms will they accept the ending of the partition. (J. F. Kennedy 1946; quoted in *Sunday Times*, 14 March 2010: 13).

With an equally zealous minister for industry and commerce, Lemass, the focus of policy was to draw from the economic nationalism that was the predominant theory of the day. Protectionism was promoted as a means of disengaging from the dominant neo-colonial economy of Britain. The nationalistic motivations of the party at this point cannot be overstated and the assertiveness of this position can be seen clearly in the 1928 economic policy document *Fianna Fáil and its Economic Policy*. De Valera drafted the policy himself:

> If the servant was displeased with the kicks of the master and wanted to have his freedom, he had to make up his mind whether or not he was going to have that freedom, and give up the luxuries of a certain kind which were available to him by being in that mansion. (de Valera 1928: 3)

Beyond the rhetoric, a series of plans sought to realign the south with the economic thinking of the day; the motivations appeared to be deliberately marginalizing. The *Statistical Year-Book of the League of Nations* of 1940, the index on international economic performance, noted that between 1929 and 1938, of the smaller European economies, the Irish Free State was the most aggressively protectionist, with its imports and exports combined dropping by 64 per cent (League of Nations 1940: 189).

The Finance Act which was introduced in May 1932 was a first major act of this realignment process in that it imposed *ad valorem* duties of between 15 and 75 per cent on 38 different types of produce and imposed bespoke duties on five other types. It meant the closure of certain markets with Britain and severe restrictions on others. For the Irish population it resulted in a reduction in the variety and quality of goods that were in supply. The rationale behind the strategy for economic disengagement from the British market contained three elements. First, the new administration needed to distance itself from the Cosgrave era by reigniting civil war sentiments that were familiar to the Fianna Fáil political base. Second, the protectionism that was being advocated around the world in the wake of the Great Depression seemed to be logical enough as a means of job creation – the conventional response to systemic economic inactivity. Finally, there was the desire to slow down or halt emigration, which was perceived to be a legacy of colonialism (De Valera 1928: 7–8). The political hook for the implementation of the policies that were to dominate much of the 1930s was the discourse on independence, the perennial question of Ireland's relationship with Britain.

The anti-colonial engagement accelerated after 1 July 1932 with the government withholding the land annuities that were being paid to London. Simply ignoring the agreement that had been made by Ernest Blythe (the former Irish minister of finance) and Winston Churchill (the British chancellor of the Exchequer) in March 1926, de Valera held on to the annuities for the Irish Exchequer. The savings amounted to the equivalent of 20 per cent of tax revenue for the State. While the impact on the British economy was minimal, the effects were harder on the population of the Free State. The British response was immediate. On 12 July 1932 (a symbolism not considered in London) an *ad valorem* 20 per cent duty was placed on most of Ireland's agricultural imports into Britain. The retaliation by de Valera came as soon as the 13 July with the Emergency Imposition of Duties Bill – which meant that the Irish government could impose any and further duties as and when it wished. The first casualties were key imports such as coal, steel and iron, and as the tussle intensified this list increased. In a sequence of exchanges, quotas, regulations, import licences and tariffs were introduced to firm up the protectionism. In return the British duty on agricultural goods was raised to 30 per cent by November. Export exemptions which had been in place were rescinded by the UK's Import Duties Act (1932). By 1933 the restrictions on cattle importation came into force, with up to 66 per cent of profits going in duties to the Irish Exchequer. After 1 January 1934 there was a complete restriction on the importation of beef and veal from Ireland to Britain. Although the intensity of the dispute was beginning to wane by mid 1935, the damage to the Irish Sea market would take decades to repair. As Kieran Kennedy pointed out in *The Economic Development of Ireland in the Twentieth Century*:

> An indication of the range of goods involved may be seen from the fact that in January 1936 the official import list containing nearly 2000 categories showed over half of them subject to tariffs, many in the range 50 to 75 per cent. The average tariff level rose from 9 per cent in 1931 to 45 per cent in 1936. (Kennedy et al. 1988: 43; Ryan 1949; Neary and Ó Gráda, 1986/1991: 254)

James Meenan re-emphasised the point: 'at the end of 1931, the list of tariffs covered 68 articles including nine revenue tariffs. At the end of 1936 it covered 281 articles including seven revenue tariffs. These figures do not include a profusion of quotas and other restrictions. At the end of 1937 it was calculated that 1947 articles were subject to restriction or control' (Meenan 1970: 142).

The Irish Control of Manufacturing Acts (1932 and 1934) attempted to wrestle industrial ownership from the control of foreign nationals, restricting shares and voting rights for business owners who were not Irish nationals. The move attempted to recoup influence for the government over manufacturing that could be proved to be benefiting non-Irish interests. The initiative was also linked to the shift in production priorities across the various sectors of the economy to enhance those sectors that were perceived to be core to the principle of national self-sufficiency. Government support was also allocated to tillage and, in a reversal of the previous government's priorities, smaller farmers were actively encouraged to move away from cattle and sheep production towards tillage. The changes in agriculture could be seen in the employment patterns and earnings from the period:

> Between 1926 and 1936 the total number of men and women employed in agriculture fell from just over 644,000 to just over 605,000. This trend later accelerated, partly due to increased emigration during the Second World War (the Emergency). Wages were low for a farm labourer; earnings could amount to less than 15 shillings a week. (www.muckross-house.ie/library_files/ Ireland_in_the_30s.htm)

Other programmes aimed at shaping the Irish economy into a form that was less dependent on imports included the development of quasi-state bodies that were tasked to diversify and create options for indigenous supply. Many were to become components in the evolution of the Irish economy. The Turf Development Board (1934) provided an alternative source of energy to the importation of British coal, Aer Lingus (1936) from the outset became the dominant Irish air transport service, and Ceimici Teoranta (1934) worked to encourage the indigenous production of chemical goods for the Irish market. In the early years of the Fianna Fáil administration, seeking the ideal of self-sufficiency was the government's primary reaction to the lack of control that accompanied the freer market that had been evident in the depression years, and all that that had entailed. Interestingly, John Maynard Keynes referred to the various exchanges of the Anglo-Irish economic war as merely 'a trend' which would not service the economic interests of either side, but which would adversely affect the Irish economy. He advised against ideologically driven economic policies, advocating job-creation as the essential dynamic for economic growth. In reference to his *General Theory* – as guest speaker at the first Finlay Lecture at University College, Dublin, on 19 April 1933 – Keynes argued that the Irish government should use deficit spending to create jobs, and spend its way out of depression. Furthermore, he cautioned against rejecting the international economic system:

> Ideas, knowledge, science, hospitality, travel – these are things which should be homespun whenever it is reasonably and conveniently possible, and, above all, let finance be primarily national. Yet, at the same time, those who seek to disembarrass a country of its entanglements should be very slow and wary. It should not be a matter of tearing up roots but of slowly training a plant to grow in a different direction. (Keynes 1933: 181)

He also presented the warning that was to apply to other European states in this period:

> Italy, Ireland, Germany, have cast their eyes or are casting them towards new modes of political economy. Many more countries after them, I predict, will seek, one by one, after new economic gods .... We do not know what will be the outcome. We are – all of us, I expect – about to make many mistakes .... We do not wish, therefore, to be at the mercy of world forces working out, or trying to work out, some uniform equilibrium according to

the ideal principles, if they can be called such, of laissez-faire capitalism. (Keynes 1933: 184)

De Valera and his senior economic advisors listened to this classical Keynesian argument for kick-starting economic recovery, but decided that a crude tariff system driven by internal market forces would be more effective (Keynes 1933: 187–90). The model introduced at this period – based on closing the external market, shifting agricultural produce to tillage and encouraging medium-sized indigenous enterprise – may have stood against cautionary wisdom and stunted natural economic growth in the south, but it had its logic in that it consolidated a political constituency with bias towards small farmers and labour. This was the rationale behind the policies (Ryan 1949; Neary and Ó Gráda, 1986/1991: 253).

With de Valera and Lemass introducing an aggressively protectionist economic system for the south, the attempts to sustain jobs by concentrating on the indigenous market inadvertently affected agriculture. Exchange quotas brought some relief to the sector, but the value of some products (such as livestock) fell by up to 50 per cent between 1932 and 1935. There appeared to be a fixation on food security as a base-line economic policy at the expense of growth or speculation in other sectors. Cereal production came to dominate agriculture, leading to skewed economic growth, an imbalance in the allocation of resources and finances and, significantly, the stunting of industry in a more general sense. Criticism of the policies came from across the board, not only those who heard what Keynes had to say, but also those advising the government of the day. Economists berated the policies in *Studies*, the *Economist*, and the influential *Round Table*, which pointed to:

> a heterogeneous shambles of tariffs … while the government have been seeking to build up little industries which can never hope to do an export trade, the Danes, with the aid of their better standards and methods, have captured the huge British market. (*Round Table*, xxix: 594; Quoted in Neary and Ó Gráda, 1986/ 1991: 251)

The policies did however register some changes, in that there was a rise in the number of people who were securing indigenous industrial employment. The emergence or adaptation of companies in this period gave some indication of a shift within industry itself. Working to the legislation and extraneous circumstances, businesses sought to adapt. This is reflected in the number of largely Dublin-based companies that were established during this period:

> Between 1922 and 1930 there had been only one public issue of shares, and that for only £15,000. By 1933 there were twenty-four quoted Irish industrial companies with an aggregate capital of £5 million. By 1939 there were seventy-eight companies, with a combined capital of almost £10 million. The *Times Issuing House Year Book* recorded three new Irish companies in 1933, nine in 1934, twelve in both 1935 and 1936, and ten in 1937. (Ó Gráda 1994: 398)

For these new businesses, imports were needed to bring raw materials for assembly or manufacture in Ireland. Businesses attempted to circumvent the protectionist legislation by producing goods that did not need to look to the British market. While the structural adaptation affected profitability for businesses implicated in the economic war, it also brought strains to industrial relations. Those in work were witnessing industrial changes which were marked by irregular working patterns, periods of poverty and unemployment, and options that meant engaging in new industries where they were unsure of production methods or where employment was unstable. Among the Fianna Fáil faithful, continuing to confront the British was a popular position to take, but the Dublin Chamber of Commerce took a different view altogether of the policies:

> The Council regards with increasing anxiety the effect of the present unequal struggle with Great Britain, which, if continued, must lead, by rapid process of financial exhaustion, to the annihilation of our external trade and the permanent and substantial diminution of our internal trade. (Dublin Chamber of Commerce, 12 November 1932, National Archives, 1064/3; quoted in Ó Gráda 1994: 411)

The trade union movement had been engaged in an ongoing struggle against a depressed manufacturing base, mass unemployment and governmental restrictions that had suppressed industrial action. In the midst of this environment one initiative stood out in an attempt to reassert the role of democratic socialism within Irish society. A new movement emerged in 1934 and rallied under the banner of a 'Republican Congress'. It was able to gather a myriad of leftist groups together to represent socialist interests on the island and, crucially, to participate in the anti-fascist cause that was emerging across the continent of Europe. The joint secretary of the organization, Patrick Byrne, in his 'Memories of the Republican Congress', reflected on the forces behind this realignment, suggesting that something different was occurring across Irish politics through the radical dialogue between leftist groups north and south:

> There was a quarter of a million unemployed in the island out of a population of about four millions. Conditions in the north were, if anything, worse than in the Free State. The shipyards were almost at a standstill. 20,000 workers in the linen industry were idle. In the slums of Belfast 8000 children were declared by the Belfast Executive Committee to be suffering from malnutrition …. There was mass unemployment, poverty and starvation in the crowded slums of Dublin, Waterford, Cork and elsewhere; stagnation in the countryside. Evictions from smallholdings, and mass emigration was on a scale unequalled since the 1880s. (Byrne 1984)

The unrest that developed in the 1930s was in part driven by desperation, but also could be seen to have leadership in the tradition of Larkin and Connolly. Two distinct groups emerged within the Republican Congress – one advocating the organic movement of a 'United Front', the other wanting the establishment of a socialist party that could bring together the diverse strains of labour, radical republican, trade union and communist thinking that stretched the length and breadth of the island. The constituency was in a way ahead of the contemporary political forces, as the *Irish Press* at the time noted: '10,000 unemployed marched in protest against the scale of relief paid in certain distress schemes. Eight shillings a week for a man to support his wife and family' (4 October 1932). Furthermore, in rural areas the ongoing payment to landlords in Britain through the Land Commission set up by the Free State government as a term of the 1921 Treaty was causing widespread distress over a decade after independence. A campaign of refusing to pay was initiated by Peadar O'Donnell, chair of the Congress, who came to articulate the case for the rural community. The issue eventually brought the Fianna Fáil administration into confrontation with the Westminster government and directly led to its withholding annuities from the south to Britain.

Parallel to the labour and small farming communities agitating for more favourable conditions, in Athlone on 7–8 April 1934 the leaders of various socialist and republican organizations met to agree a new agenda for the Left in Ireland: 'We believe that a Republic of a United Ireland will never be achieved except through a struggle which uproots capitalism on its way. We cannot conceive a Free Ireland and a subject working class.' The terminology drew on two contemporary alliances, the popular front movement that was bringing together the various anti-fascist groups on the continent, and the republican and trade unionist traditions. The trade union movement in Belfast responded to this incentive with the assertion that:

> We are convinced that the horrors of the capitalist economic system, the menace of Fascism ... the question of Irish National unity are inter-related problems, the solution of which can only be found in the solidarity of the workers, small farmers and peasants North and South.

Importantly, this was signed by the president of the ITGWU in Belfast, Murtagh Morgan, and the chair of the Belfast Trades Council, William McMullan, among others. The Republican Congress also set up a weekly paper, *The Republican Congress* and later *The Irish Democrat*, and set about organizing demonstrations against fascism and poverty, forming residents' groups, documenting levels of poverty and picketing exploitative employers. Curiously, the Congress also ceremoniously gave back weapons that its members would have retained to the Fianna Fáil administration, mostly republican guns dating from the civil war. One activity of the Congress in particular was highlighted by Byrne – that of campaigning for housing rights:

> The Tenants Leagues, run by Republican Congress personnel, organized rent strikes for better conditions. On one occasion the Third Dublin District Committee carried on a rent strike for two months affecting five streets in the vicinity of Westland Row, and finally won a 25 per cent reduction in rent. At the same time the Fourth District Committee won rehousing by the Dublin Corporation for the tenants of Magee Court, a collection of filthy cottages fit only for the vermin abounding therein. (Byrne 1984)

Against this community development work and against the popular front's organization with all its limitations, emerged the surreal gathering of the Irish Blueshirts, a reactionary grouping emanating from Cumann na nGaedheal. Containing elements of the southern police it was led by the eccentric former police commissioner Eoin O'Duffy. The Blueshirts conspired to attack progressive groups across the south as a means of provoking publicity for fascism, culminating in a vicious confrontation with those attending a Republican Congress Easter ceremony at Glasnevin Cemetery in April 1936. De Valera attempted on a number of occasions to intervene in this political battle that was working itself into Irish politics, fearing that if it was left unchecked one group or the other would be in a position to stage a coup in the south. In 1934 he set up a new Volunteer Force with the intention of disciplining former IRA combatants, followed by the introduction of the Military Pensions Act which provided pensions for war veterans (Lyons 1963: 532). With the onset of the Spanish Civil War, the crystallization of the right and left across Europe, the Congress's project realigned its priorities, and as with the Blueshirts, the leadership decamped to the battlefields of Spain. With activists from the Congress fighting for democratic republican Spain against Franco's fascism, their colleagues in Ireland set up 'Spain committees' to help send supplies to Almeria in Spain. Frank Ryan led Irish activists to fight in the International Brigades for the Spanish republicans under the title the 'Connolly Column'. A number of the Congress's key personnel were killed: Charlie Donnelly, Kit Conway, Jack Nalty, Dinny Coady. In all, 320 Irish volunteers fought on the republican side of the Spanish Civil War, 730 Blueshirts signed up for Franco and fascism. Ironically, de Valera's threat had emigrated.

The economic tussle with Britain and the ideological flux of the mid-1930s rocked both the politics and economics of the island. The statistics from this period are telling. Even though tariffs and quotas suppressed trade, the economy of the Irish Free State remained dependant on exporting to the United Kingdom. Going into the economic war, around 90 per cent of exports were in this direction, and conversely in 1931 up to 7.8 per cent of British exports were going to the Free State. The introduction of the quotas and restrictions on exports, however, had led to the stagnation of the Irish economy for almost a decade. By the mid-1930s, exports from Ireland were worth approximately half of what they were in the late 1920s. Livestock exports in particular, which were profitable through most of the 1920s, by the mid 1930s were worth only one-third of their previous market value. 'From 1931 to 1934 the value of United Kingdom imports from the Irish Free State dropped from £36,500,000 to £17,200,000; the value of United Kingdom exports to the Free State dropped from £30,500,000 to £19,500,000'

(Bromage 1938: 518). Goods other than those produced locally were either scarce or were commodities, mainly luxury items, that were unaffordable to the vast majority of the population.

Partition continued as an enduring contradiction in de Valera's strategy. Driven by ideological zeal and political pragmatism, he had helped to seal the border in a manner that could not easily be remedied (Neary and Ó Gráda 1986/1991: 6–8). Border inspections were increased to restrict imports to the south, and high tariffs were introduced to undermine competition from the north. The agricultural sector's output went down dramatically, and with prices decreasing by 40 per cent between 1929 and 1935 farming incomes were reduced accordingly. As a consequence smuggling across the border became a national pastime and became 'wholesale'. The *Economist* on 26 October 1935 joked that up to 100,000 cattle from the Free State had become part of 'conducted tours across the border'. The illegal trade carried with it significant repercussions: first, it compounded the economic differences between the north and the south, and second, it created a structure which ensured that partition was effective for the informal economy. The practice became hard to dislodge from the day-to-day commerce of border communities.

Another major casualty of the economic war was the export stalwart of the 1920s and the company that had resuscitated the Irish economy in the years immediately after the Treaty: Guinness. As the most profitable manufacturing company in the south it opted to relocate in 1936 to the Park Royal site outside London. The result was a reduction in the brewing of stout in Ireland: 'the decline in Irish exports from 1.3 million barrels in 1935 to 0.8 in 1938 closely matched the increase in output at the Park Royal brewery' (Kennedy et al. 1988: 47). The disappointment was not lost on Guinness itself, which released figures in 1939 almost as if to prove its level of commitment to the Irish economy: 'Total amount of government duties and taxes paid by the Company, from its formation in October, 1886, till June 30 1938 ... £221,778,000. Maximum amount of government duties and taxes in one year ... £16,141,559' (Guinness 1939: 32).

Industrial productivity did improve in certain sectors in the 1930s, but comparative measurement places growth into the context of the depressed state of manufacturing in the last years of the Cosgrave government. Growth often looked better than it actually was. House building through reconstructive investment accounted in part for the extent of growth in the construction industry in the mid-1930s, and consequently there was a quantifiable increase in those who were indexed in industrial employment. Indeed, the numbers employed in construction rose between 1931 and 1938 from 110,600 to 166,100 (Kennedy et al. 1988: 47). This noted, the unemployment figures continued to be a legacy of a constrained industrial sector and reached 145,000 during this period.

The pragmatic nature of the government's policies, matched with the topical nature of protectionism as economic theory during the period, brought the economy of the south to a relative level of growth in comparison with other regions of the British isles. For the general population, income levels were largely unchanged, the variety of goods for sale had been restricted, and as the 1930s went on emigration to Britain again became an obvious feature of family and community life. The industries that had been created in the south were primarily established to supply the indigenous market, including 'boot factories, canning plants, clothing manufactories and sugar-beet refineries' (Bromage 1938: 519). Drawing on the instinct of many economists of the time, eventually there was a realization that the Fianna Fáil policy of protectionism and economic struggle had been stunting Irish economic growth. This was even acknowledged by insiders, such as Seán MacEntee, the minister for finance, and purveyor of the policies:

> In an effort to cope with unemployment we have increased tariffs, we have fostered tillage, we have subsidized dairying and pigs and livestock production, we have developed the sugar-making industry; we have raised the prices of agricultural commodities, we have shortened the working hours of the employed and given them holidays with pay, we have introduced quota restrictions and established virtual monopolies. We have more regimentation, more regulation, more control everywhere. And more unemployment. (Seán MacEntee, UCDA, P67/125; quoted in Ó Gráda 1994: 420)

The economic policies that had brought the Fianna Fáil administration to power had been exhausted by the late 1930s. On 29 December 1937 a new constitution was framed, *Bunreacht na hEireann*, superseding the statutes of the Free State and providing for the institution of an Irish presidency. Crucially in economic terms the new constitution for the State of Eire provided clauses which could facilitate negotiation and accommodation with the British government and any of the British Commonwealth of Nations. The

British response was nonchalant: 'to treat the new Constitution as not effecting a fundamental alteration in the position of the Irish Free State, in future to be described under the new Constitution as "Eire" or "Ireland"' (quoted in Bromage 1938: 521). Within the south, the rise of European fascism and the real possibility of a European war brought an air of caution to the practicalities of managing an economy under such geo-political uncertainties. The outcome was a strategic recalibration of the relationship with the British government, and in economic terms the 'phoney war' of the mid-1930s came to a close with the Anglo-Irish Trade Agreement of 25 April 1938. The unusual premise to the agreement was that the republican party in Ireland, Fianna Fáil, had entered into a mutual agreement with the British government based on 'relations of friend-ship and good understanding' (Irish Government 1938, preamble). De Valera even visited London to work on the strategy, with the relationship becoming so involved that Craig, the prime minister of the Stormont administration, called an election in mid-1938 to justify the existence of the northern state to London.

While economically de Valera was hailed at this point by (the now renamed Cumann na nGaelheal) Fine Gael as a convert to the 'open' economy for relaxing the relationship with London, political unification of the island remained very much on the table. 'Partition', de Valera told the *New York Times*, 'was one of the first things discussed at the London conference and one of the last. To the extent that there is no reference to partition in the agreement' (6 May 1938). On the ending of the economic war Lemass was bullish: 'The economic war is over. It is, I suggest, a complete waste of time to discuss who began it. The important fact is that we won it' (*Dáil Éireann*, lxxi, 183, 28 April 1938).

The 1938 negotiations concluded with three aspects to the agreement – the first related to the use of ports in Eire (Cobh, Berehaven and Lough Swilly) and defence in time of war, the second to financial claims, and the third was in regard to trade relations. A particularly sensitive element of the agreement was with respect to the withholding of the land annuities. During the negotiations it was estimated that the amount owed through the outstanding annuity and other financial obligations from Eire to Britain was in the region of £80–100 million. This was considered an impossibly high figure for the Irish side to raise. Eventually, and together with other claims by the British government, de Valera agreed to pay the British Government a lump sum of £10 million on or before 30 November 1938. This transfer was completed before the half-yearly returns for the Irish Exchequer on 1 October. In return the British government removed the duties against Irish imports that had been put in place by the Irish Free State (Special Duties) Act of 1932. Emergency customs duties that had been introduced by the Irish government on imports into the country were abolished on a *quid pro quo* basis. Some quotas were retained, for example on beer and sugar, but this was to ensure an equalization of market development between the countries' produce. The agreement covered an extensive array of goods, specifically naming silk, coal, coca, agricultural and fishery products, lamps, motor cars and yarns; it also addressed UK and Canadian imports, minimum duties and packaging duties, licensing provisions, and in the spirit of the occasion 'care and management of duties' (Irish Government 1938, Arrangement of Sections).

As well as reciprocal arrangements for the free entry of named goods and the preference for certain products, the agreement created a Prices Commission which would have the role of reviewing protective tariffs. This Commission could suggest changes that would be beneficial for the evolving relationship, and while it was an Irish agency the British would have 'full rights of audience'. Its role would be to review the developing system:

> in accordance with the principle that such duties and restrictions upon goods produced and manufactured in the United Kingdom shall be replaced by duties which shall not exceed such a level as will give to United Kingdom producers and manufacturers full opportunity of reasonable competition while affording to Irish industries adequate protection having regard to the relative cost of economical and efficient production, providing that in the application of this principle special consideration may be given to the case of industries not fully established. (quoted in Bromage 1938: 529)

What the agreement represented was not only the mechanism of trade, but the reproach of a former colonial power and the colonized. Of immense significance for this period was the acceptance of the *Bunreacht*, the new constitution, by the British government and the invitation to de Valera to enter into partnership on trade. It was also an acknowledgement on both sides of the Irish Sea that there was an economic interdependence that was both historical and organic, and if worked appropriately could benefit both parties. De Valera carried the Anglo-Irish Agreement and the *Bunreacht* into the elections of 17 June 1938, and subsequently secured an overall majority in the Dáil for Fianna Fáil.

The post-colonial engagement that marked the economic inter-action between Eire and Britain in the 1930s followed a familiar pattern of positioning, personality conflicts, retraction and hardship. The judgements made by de Valera's administration proved to have a high level of support within the republican areas of the south, and framed the type of Ireland that de Valera had wanted to establish. This post-colonial fight also highlighted the awkward relationship that Eire was forging with Britain and the disregard that the British establishment had developed for its smaller neighbour. Patrick McGilligan in the Dáil Éireann debate on the economic war on 13 November 1935 stated the problem bluntly:

It was to a great extent a bluff .... We had these catch cries of the minister that we could get markets elsewhere; that Great Britain must buy; that we could cut off British supplies and would have Great Britain on her knees in no time .... The Fianna Fáil govern-ment has made a demonstration to the world of what exactly our strength is. (*Dáil Éireann*, lix, 850, 13 November 1935)

4 THE IMPACT OF WAR (1939–1957)

The relaxation of economic restrictions between Ireland and Britain was timely in the context of international developments and post-depression readjustment, but the rapprochement was caught within the uncertainty of the pre-war period. It meant that commodity importation could give the population more options in terms of day-to-day necessities, and the ongoing commitment to encourage manufacturing saw improvements in supply and demand. With the outbreak of the Second World War the situation shifted significantly, this time placing the island in the desperate position of having the north fully engaged in the conflict, and suffering immensely as a result, and the south controversially opting for neutrality. Economic policies were immediately subjected to extreme external political circumstances.

De Valera's response to the German invasion of Belgium and the Netherlands was characteristically sanguine:

> Today these two small nations are fighting for their lives, and I think I would be unworthy of this small nation if, on an occasion like this, I did not utter our protest against the cruel wrong which had been done them. (quoted in Girvin 2006: 98)

The strategic intervention at this point was notable because he did not voice concerns about the invasions of Denmark or Norway, and was muted in his opinions on the invasion of Poland. However, his comments were measured to the extent that he saw an opportunity to pressurize the British government on the issue of the six northern counties and partition. De Valera was to get all-party support in the south for neutrality, with many not wanting to complicate the recent history of the war of independence, civil war, depression and economic 'war' with a world war. For the south the official stance on the crisis was to call a state of emergency. De Valera stated that:

> We should have war all around us. We may not be participating ourselves in the war, but we shall have conditions here almost the same, so far as the question of supplying the material needs of our people is concerned, as the condition we would have if we were actually a belligerent. (quoted in Girvin 2006: 63)

Successive British prime ministers, Neville Chamberlain and Winston Churchill, proposed an end to partition in return for active support against Germany, but were rebuffed by de Valera because of the possibility of a Germany victory. The best that de Valera could do was to provide tactical support and to 'favour' the Allies over the fascists. From the lens of the summer of 1940, the Nazis might win the conflict and the Irish government did not have the wherewithal to gamble against this. Furthermore, the Irish administration was keeping one eye on how the United States was dealing with the crisis, with its non-committed approach being a signal for de Valera to wait and watch.

The economy suffered in a number of ways during the Emergency, and while neutrality frustrated the relationship with neighbours both northward and eastward, the effects were impacting on both the quality of life of people across the south and their loyalty to the state. Indeed, more southern citizens – a contemporary estimate of 50,000 – went to fight for the Allies during the war than joined up from the north of the island, with an estimated 40,000 (Lyons 1963: 557). The figure was revised by the time – in April 1995 – taoiseach John Bruton acknowledged their contribution in the fight against European fascism, when at the Irish National Memorial Park he referred to an estimated 150,000 Irish men and women who had 'volunteered to fight against Nazi tyranny in Europe, at least 10,000 of whom were killed' (quoted in Girvin 2006: 257).

To stem the haemorrhaging of the population the government introduced a recruiting drive for the Irish defence forces. Over 30,000 extra regular troops were taken on by 1942 to provide protection against any impending invasion from Germany – or Britain. Twice as many (c. 26,000) were emigrating per year by the early 1940s as had emigrated during the depression years of the 1930s, with 198,000 passports and travel permits being registered by the Emigration Commission between the years 1940 and 1945. While many went to join the British army, many more went for the more traditional reason of finding work in British factories. The emigration levels were all the more striking given the restrictions that the Irish government placed on movement during the war. Farm labourers and the sons of farmers had restrictions placed on their movement and were prohibited from emigrating, while doctors and the clergy were the only two named professions eligible to use private transport. In 1939, 7480 new cars were licensed, yet by 1941 this had dropped to as little as 240. Key characters in the government provided role models, with Seán Lemass resorting to a bicycle to get around Dublin, showing in a very visible way the austerity demanded in times of adversity. In *A Rocky Road,* Cormac

Ó Gráda painted the picture of a transport network that had all but ground to a halt:

> The virtual absence of motor fuel meant that some freight switched back to the railways in 1939–45, while passenger services were drastically curtailed. Train speeds also dropped, as trains tried both to conserve and substitute fuel; the journey from Dublin to Cork (160 miles) might take ten hours. On the Grand Canal there was a return to horse-drawn barges. (Ó Gráda 1997: 13)

For the southern Irish population, scarcity was the most notable feature of life during the Emergency. The shortage of petrol meant that travel for the general population almost ceased, imported goods virtually disappeared from the shops, rationing was introduced, and fuels such as coal were largely unobtainable. The weekly allowance that was introduced for certain foods meant that at one point an individual's weekly allocation would be half an ounce of tea, six ounces of butter and half a pound of sugar. In response the government set up the Department of Supplies which would monitor produce availability, coordinate supplies and manage the use of raw materials. Its job was basically to feed the population during the Emergency. Living standards went down significantly, and although there were supplies of Irish staples such as potatoes, meat and dairy produce, beyond this – with imports such as tea, coffee and fruit – there was great scarcity. In the cities pigeons were substituted for chickens, nettle tea for imported real tea, carrots could be smoked, and curtains could be recycled as clothes. Horses were reintroduced to agriculture and industry, returning the economy in part to the production methods of the nineteenth century. While the various schemes may have kept hunger at bay and the quality of food that was being provided was still better than many of those regions of Europe that were fully engaged in the conflict, it was still deprivation and, as in the rest of Europe, food supplies were significantly lower during the war. With agricultural produce being restricted due to the shortages of fuel, fertilizer and animal feed, the best that could be achieved under immensely difficult circumstances was the maintenance of pre-war levels of key foodstuffs. Interestingly though, Eire's gross national product (GNP) was the same per capita at the end of the war as it was at the beginning. Beyond the routine of the rationing and parochialism that dominated people's lives, news from the war on the continent filtered through on licensed radios, censored newspapers, letters from emigrants in Britain and word of mouth from those who had been transversing the border.

The Scientific Research Bureau was set up in 1941 to explore possible alternatives to the products that were being exhausted due to the shortages. Experimentation, while often eccentric, on occasion produced definite results – such as the development of flour from potatoes, gas that could be produced from peat, and pesticides from tobacco. The Turf Development Board, another agency, refined the production techniques and mechanism for the extraction of turf for fuel as a replacement for coal. Backing this up was the Special Powers Order introduced in 1944, which prohibited the use of gas for domestic heating and created an instant market for turf.

Generally, industry suffered, struggling to overcome shortages against centralized supply systems. Companies could not get the fuel to keep machinery working, components for equipment were in short supply and becoming scarcer, supply and delivery lines were restricted. Coal imports dropped by 33 per cent during the war and oil ceased to be available for large sections of the economy. Consequently, production levels went down dramatically during the Emergency and stayed at a static level for the duration of the war. Statistics from the mid-1940s showed that: 'manufacturing output fell to a low point in 1942, nearly 25 per cent below the 1939 level, and only in 1946 was the 1939 overall level surpassed again' (Kennedy et al. 1988: 50). The export of basic food supplies became a mainstay of the profitable economy, with the British market accounting for virtually all exports. Given the ongoing supply of meat products in particular to the stressed British market, the Irish imports were repeatedly referred to as evidence of support given to Britain during the war.

To enhance this, in 1941 the Irish government created the state-sponsored agency Irish Shipping to coordinate the supply of goods to Britain. The agency purchased eight ships and leased five others which were to be used for transporting supplies. Of these the *Irish Oak*, the *Irish Pine* and the *Vassilios Destounis* (*Irish Poplar*) were attacked by German submarines or aircraft, the former two being destroyed. The response from the Irish government to the attack was to assert that the actions were against international law and it pursued claims for compensation. The issue of shipping continued to be a controversial one throughout the war with the refusal of the Dublin administration to let the British use Irish ports out of fear of reprisal from Germany. It was an issue that Churchill found particularly vexing:

The fact that we cannot use the South and West coasts of Ireland to refuel our flotillas and aircraft and thus protect the trade by which Ireland as well as Great Britain lives, is a most heavy and grievous burden and one which should never have been placed on our shoulders. (Winston Churchill, speech, *Hansard*, House of Commons, 5 November 1940)

With production going down and imports at a standstill, wage levels were also affected by the Emergency. While the war economy in the north showed a quantifiable growth in manufacturing opportunities and increases in wages, southern workers, positioned outside the variable growth rates of the war economy, saw their incomes decrease by 30 per cent. This resulted in industrial unrest and, in reaction, the outlawing of strikes. In Britain, Keynes had been brought in to design a wartime economy which would seek out growth while maintaining a reasonable standard of living in adverse circumstances. Ireland was factored into this equation as an area that could complement this strategy while enhancing the clauses of the Anglo-Irish Agreement. Agriculture and fisheries' representatives from both sides of the Irish Sea met to discuss the possibilities as early as 20 March 1940. The British consensus on Anglo-Irish economic cooperation was that:

> In general it must be borne in mind that Eire's economy is complementary to and not competitive with that of the United Kingdom and consequently that, so far as possible, undertakings should be avoided which would further force Eire in the direction of economic self-sufficiency. (UK Public Records Office, Ministry of Agriculture and Fisheries 83/87, 'Meeting with Irish Butter Representatives' 19 March 1940; quoted in Girvin 2006: 162)

As the war went on the population of the south became recipients of an unexpected feature of the Emergency. The growth of the economy in the north due to wartime production and employment meant that wages there had increased substantially. Workers were also returning from England with disposable income and little to spend it on. By the summer of 1942 the south was becoming a destination to get away from the conflict, and in turn a fledgling tourist economy developed, adapting to host trainloads of workers and troops from the north on vacation. By all accounts Dublin became a city that was known as an escape, 'a pleasure city', where the war discipline of the north did not apply. Rationing was used as a means of profiteering, and exchanging goods that were brought in by these visitors became a pastime. With the perennial problem of the malfunctioning border economy, black-marketeering became a way of life for those living in the border counties. Indeed, throughout the war up to 1000 people per year were convicted for operating outside the constraints of the formal economy. This black market was almost impossible to control given that, from various accounts, up to a quarter of a million Irish from the south had been working in the war industries, were members of the Allied forces – mostly the British Army – or were smuggling across the border. Visits home, or visitors from the north, brought an economy in its own right. They also gave the people of the south some indication of life and hardship for a northern population that was taking its measure of the Nazi *blitzkrieg*.

WAR ECONOMY IN THE NORTH

With the outbreak of the war, the political and economic differences that had been developing between the north and the south of Ireland over the two decades of partition were reinforced. Officially, 3 September 1939 marked the point when the systemic reaction to partition went into overdrive, when the north entered into the Allied engagement with the Axis, and when against concerted international pressure the south opted out of the conflict. In this the experiences of the respective populations and economies were substantially different. Indeed, the military station at Grey's Point, North Down, holds the claim of firing the first Allied shots at the Germans when, minutes after war was declared, the local commander decided to fire on an unidentified (Scottish) fishing trawler in Belfast Lough.

This type of confusion also resonated throughout a dislocated northern government which, by and large, had left the region unprepared. In November 1938 an Air Raid Precautions Act was introduced which drew from Whitehall intelligence information about the possible nature of the conflict to come, taken largely from the experiences of the Spanish people during the Nazi bombing raids of their civil war. The 1939 UK Civil Defence Act brought into force measures that would attempt to prepare the population, if not practically then psychologically, for war. The Blackout Order of September (1939) was an immediate and visible indication of what was to come. The June 1940 Ministries (NI) Act put another structure into place which was to have longstanding implications for the north of Ireland in that it realigned effective authority from

Stormont to Whitehall, thus making the administrative control of Northern Ireland more deferential to the centre of power in London (Harkness 1983: 82). For the duration of the war Northern Ireland was functionally operating at the behest of Whitehall:

> Many matters which in peace would have come automatically under the jurisdiction of that parliament [Stormont], were now 'for the duration' *ultra vires*; food rationing would be controlled from London; prices of flax and farm produce normally fixed on recommendations from London; and the allocation of raw materials to Northern Ireland determined by a supply ministry in London. Moreover, policy on these and many other issues would be formulated in the war cabinet and its committees at Westminster in light of broad strategic and national considerations often having little or no bearing on the special requirements of Northern Ireland; and the Northern Ireland parliament was not able to express its opinion very emphatically, because all these matters arose from a state of war or were connected with the defence of the realm. (Blake 1956: 26)

On 24 November 1940 Craig died while prime minister of Northern Ireland. John Andrews, the minister of finance between 1937 and 1940, took over as prime minister and remained in that position until 1943. He was deputized by one of the most senior freemasons in Ireland, John Milne Barbour, who had been parliamentary secretary to the minister of finance since the founding of the state, and then during Andrews' rule served as minister for finance. Caught with depleted powers Andrews and Barbour went into a role of reacting, where possible, to external and extraneous circumstances. The management of the economy in the war years came largely through the offices of Whitehall while continuing to be funded from the central purse.

In Stormont the war was initially treated as an opportunity to refresh local industry for new business, supporting the imperial cause and enhancing the position of the regional administration against the perceived threat from Dublin and the republican community in the north. As the conflict became ever more real, and with the threatened invasion of England in April and May 1940, the Stormont administration finally acted to build air-raid shelters, provide gas masks, extend rationing, restrict petrol and coal supplies and organize a civil campaign to counter Nazi actions against the north. The popular opinion of the day considered this to be too little too late – tinkering with a 'very rudimentary civil defence system' (Davison 1979: 83). For the purposes of rationing and in view of the possibility of conscription, a register was taken of the whole population in the north. Between June and August 1940, 26,000 people were admitted into a Special Constabulary. Later redesignated the Ulster Home Guard, it was funded by the Treasury to protect the north against German attacks, possible invasion and the 'internal' threat – tackling the increasingly active militant republican forces of the north. In practice maintenance of the status quo was to take precedence over the defence of the realm.

Industrially, the north stumbled into the production of military equipment. Throughout 1940 no new investment came into industry, unemployment was rising and at that stage the existing munitions factories in Northern Ireland 'had the worst record of production in the United Kingdom during the early months of the war' (Paseta 2010: 1). The early phase of the war, the 'phoney war', was met with relaxed disbelief in Stormont. As the conflict began to roll out westward into the Irish and North seas, circumstances forced structural readjustments not seen on the island since the famine years. A number of events and altercations swiftly fixed the economy of the north into the general war economy of the Allies. Crucially, the Belfast 'Blitz' in April and May 1941 brought the continental experience of devastation directly to the population of that city. The last-minute nature of preparations for war meant that the north was wholly unprepared for any sustained attack. With no searchlights to locate planes, little anti-aircraft cover, no fighter aircraft cover and inappropriate barrage balloons, the city and other areas around the north were left vulnerable to bombing raids. The perceived wisdom in Stormont had been that the north would not be a target for the German bombers. This changed in April 1941.

A Ministry for Public Security had been established in mid-1940 to look at regional defences in the face of attack, and as late as March 1941 its minister, J. C. MacDermott, concluded that defences were 'not satisfactory' (Harkness 1983: 85). A decade after the war ended, J. W. Blake, in *Northern Ireland in the Second World War*, recorded MacDermott's sentiments at the time – and the sense of ignorance: 'The period of the next moon from, say 7th to the 16th of April, may well bring our turn' (Blake 1956: 167). Only 15 per cent of the households in Belfast had been allocated air-raid shelters. On 7 April six German bombers attacked the city in order to destroy the fuselage factory at Harland and Wolff, killing 13 people and wounding 81. On the night of 15–16 April 180 bombers delivered a sustained attack on the city, causing the highest casualties for one night of any city in Britain and Ireland (Farrell 1976: 158; Paseta 2010: 1). That night 745 people were killed in Belfast, with 1420 injured. The bombers also had the freedom to attack Derry, killing 15 and Bangor, with the loss of five more. Belfast city centre was laid waste, with whole streets disappearing. On 4–5 May 200 bombers returned with greater tonnage and firepower. Eyewitnesses spoke of hundreds of Luftwaffe planes raking gunfire across the city and dropping high explosives and incendiaries onto residential areas and industrial sites alike. In Belfast 150 were killed that night, 14 the night after.

Many parts of Belfast were left in rubble. The aircraft factory at Shorts and Harland's in the docks were seriously damaged; High Street was destroyed; York Street and the Markets areas were devastated, and across the city upwards of 50 per cent of housing and the city's infrastructure were extensively damaged. The human cost went beyond the fatalities – people with horrendous injuries wandered the streets in the days after the attacks looking for medical assistance and shelter. On the night of 4 May hundreds of terrified young people were locked into the Ulster Hall during the raid to prevent them getting in the way of fire-fighting around the city hall; St George's Market, a Victorian centrepiece of Belfast, became a morgue, while the Falls Baths were drained to make way for the hundreds of bodies that needed to be stored before mass burials could take place. 56,000 houses were damaged during the raids, 3200 totally destroyed, leaving upwards of 100,000 people homeless across the city. Feeding centres had to be established and 26 emergency camps were set up to provide shelter for the displaced families. Thousands fled to the Belfast hills for safety, sleeping out from Cave Hill to Hannahstown. The House of Commons parliamentary debate on the events of April and May contained a statement by Tommy Henderson, the Member of Parliament for the Shankill area, noting that:

> The Catholics and Protestants are going up there mixed and they are talking to one another. They are sleeping in the same sheugh, below the same tree or in the same barn. They all say the same thing, that the government is no good. (House of Commons, *Hansard* 1941, Volume 24: 828–29)

There was a general consensus on the lack of action taken by the Stormont administration before and after the attacks. Controversially, it was not until a shared coalition was in power six decades later that the Northern Ireland government could find the resources to build a monument to those killed in the Blitz (in 2009). Blake noted that: 'the degree of shelter protection available to the citizens of Belfast was probably lower than that in any other British city of comparable size and vulnerability' (quoted in Lyons 1963: 729–30). The helplessness was palpable:

> More than all else it was this tragic aspect of the raid which left indelible memories: of the queue at the mortuary in St George's market where men and women tried to identify their missing; and of the public funeral ... when Protestants and Roman Catholics joined in prayer, and, as the cortege of five covered wagons moved slowly through the scarred city streets paid their last respects to over 150 of the victims. (Blake 1956: 233–34; also see Lyons 1963: 730)

The sea war had placed the island in a unique position between the United States and Britain. However, with de Valera refusing access to ports in the south, Derry and Belfast took on a strategic importance that would lead these cities directly into a frontline role in the conflict at sea. Belfast became a hub for ship production and a base for minesweepers, and on 5 February 1942 Derry formally became a part of the US Atlantic Fleet Command. The latter action led to a formal protest by de Valera regarding the unauthorized use of Irish ports. It was not received well by the US authorities. The adaptation of the economic infrastructure of the north began in earnest after the blitz, when Belfast was deemed to be ideally placed for significant wartime production. This shift in manufacturing was largely driven through the auspices of the industries themselves at the behest of the Ministry of Defence, and saw unemployment going down in the region from 83,655 in January 1940 to 39,606 in July 1941. Productivity in the north accelerated to unprecedented levels after the blitz. The records of Harland and Wolff, and Shorts – situated on the reconstructed docks site in east Belfast – reveal a concentration on war production. Harland's tripled its workforce and diversified its production into making landing craft and tanks, as well as substantially increasing its shipping production:

> By December 1944 there were almost 31,000 employees at Harland and Wolff; altogether Queen's Island launched 170 Admiralty and merchant ships between 1939 and 1945, including 40 corvettes, 27 minesweepers, 11 frigates and three aircraft carriers. The firm also repaired 30,000 vessels and manufactured 13 million aircraft

parts, over 500 tanks, thousands of field guns and hundreds of searchlights. Shorts of Rochester set up at Sydenham in Belfast in 1938 and its workforce rose to 23,000. By the end of the war it had built 1200 Stirling bombers and 125 Sunderland flying boats. Mackies made 75 million shells and 65 million parts for bombs. (BBC NI, *Belfast Blitz* 2010, online)

The ability to adapt industry to such dedicated production techniques is striking. Shorts diversified its production to build bombers and flying boats, and tragic revenge became a simple motivating factor for increasing productivity among the workforce. Munitions factories were established across Belfast, with numerous smaller firms contributing to levels of productivity that accounted for millions of shells and supporting equipment. The size of the contracts meant that outlying towns across the north could be tied in to an invigorated industrial complex.

The rope-works, linen and textile industries were likewise adapted at the behest of investment contracts from the War Office and the Admiralty. Producing 200 million yards of cloth for 15 million finished shirts per year, the Ulster uniform became the mainstay of the Allied armies' kit until the end of the conflict. The production of battledress was to revive the Derry mills and facilitated the influx of Derry women into the factories, a process that was to become a feature of the city. With the production of rope, Belfast alone supplied a third of the War Office's requirements for military use; flax production went up from 21,000 acres of cultivated flax in 1939 to 124,000 by 1944; compulsory tillage orders meant farms operating at an increased productivity for war time supplies; two million parachutes were produced for the D-Day invasion; munitions, uniforms, tents, fabric for airplanes and even specialist fabrics such as rayon were being manufactured on a unprecedented scale. The war economy reshaped the base of Ulster's industry and, with a combination of rebuilding, war contracts, an ideally distant location and a skilled workforce, it brought a boom which the north had not seen since the post-famine years. Employment patterns give some indication of the extent of this structural adjustment:

In shipbuilding, for example, the numbers employed went up from 7.3 thousand in 1938 to 20.6 thousand in 1945. In engineering the increase during the same years was from 14.0 thousand to 26.1 thousand. Most remarkable of all, the aircraft industry, which before the war had been struggling to establish itself, rose from a mere 5.8 thousand in 1938 to 23.5 thousand in 1945. (Blake 1956: 395; also see Lyons 1963: 731)

Even though there was a persistent level of unemployment across the north, moderated to a large extent by emigration and military service, skilled labour was in demand because of the north's competitive wages and the rate of productivity (Blake 1956: 383–94, 413–26).

Paradoxically, the Stormont administration continued the policy of being suspicious of the labour movement throughout the war and even went as far as introducing anti-trade union legislation and outlawing strikes. As expected, this resulted in growing support for the trade union and labour movement in the north, and industrial action – which amounted to three times more days lost per worker than in Britain. Between 1941 and 1945 there were 523 strike days for every 1000 workers, in comparison to 153 in Britain (Paseta 2010: 1). Investment in broad terms rose dramatically in the war years and should have given the north an injection of wealth that could have matched the returns that came through to the region during the American Civil War, Crimean, Indian and African wars of the late 1800s. The investment was tempered, however, by the financial liability the Second World War imposed on the British Treasury. The imperial contribution which the north continued to pay, which had stood at £1.3 million per year at the beginning of the war, rose to £36 million by the end of the war, bringing total transfers into the Treasury from Northern Ireland during the war to £131 million. The profit from the productivity of the 1939–45 period was repatriated (Harkness 1983: 95).

Another factor which contributed to reshaping the form of the northern economy during the war was the influx of troops from across the Allied countries. Within a month of the United States entering the war in December 1941, 4000 troops had arrived in Belfast. By May 1942 38,000 US personnel were stationed in the north, and by the time the 15th US Army Corps had arrived in February 1944 there were 120,000 – amounting to one US soldier for every twelve locals. The impact was pervasive on the society. Mill owners' stately homes were commandeered for the officer corps and tented towns were erected to prepare the US troops for the impending invasion of Europe. This presence was reinforced by the building of airstrips across the north which could accommodate the movement of tens of thousands of troops at short notice. By March 1944 Northern Ireland was one of the most heavily militarized areas under the control of the Allied Command. With this concentration of troops came an influx of disposable income that spawned the building (or conversion) of dance halls and bars across the north to provide leisure outlets for the tens of thousands of troops temporarily resident there. Football pitches were adapted as baseball pitches, traditional dance halls were converted to jazz and swing clubs, and a black market emerged to process US luxury goods into the regional economy.

The inability of the Unionist Party leadership to cope with the management of such a sophisticated economy rankled within the ranks for the modernizers and caused a dislocation between the establishment of the Party and the communities it purported to represent. Increasingly the Unionist working class was turning to the left and to the Northern Ireland Labour Party, which was encouraging a social democratic alternative to the regime as it had evolved since partition. This move away from the establishment figured significantly when the Unionist Members of Parliament acted on 30 April 1943 to replace Andrews with Basil Brooke, known within the party as a reformer. Brooke, while possessing all the credentials expected of a prime minister of Northern Ireland, also had an eye towards modernization in the post-war period. In one of his first presentations to his new administration, he outlined the priorities:

> to continue to maintain the existing constitutional position of Northern Ireland, to bring the utmost vigour to the task of assisting the war effort of the United Kingdom, the empire and the allied nations, and to make further preparation for dealing with the problems of the post-war period. (Brooke, Northern Ireland House of Commons debate, *Hansard* 26, col. 466, 11 May 1943; quoted in Harkness 1983: 97)

While maintaining a one-party state, Brooke heralded an approach more conciliatory than any of the previous Unionist prime ministers, and sought to release the economy for a more flexible means of development than the previous trenchant leaders. This was complicated by a review of the budgeting arrangements by the Treasury and the insistence that, as of 1946, the Northern Ireland budget would have to be subject to agreement by the Treasury each year before going to a Joint Exchequer Board.

It was the first determined attempt to discipline the Stormont regime by the new socialist government of the United Kingdom. Estimates for subsequent financial arrangements would have to be submitted to the Treasury for scrutiny and substantial items of expenditure would have to be agreed through consultation between the Stormont Ministry of Finance and the Treasury in London. This, in theory, provided a stronger method of accountancy and gave the Labour administration in Westminster an influence over Unionist Party control of the north. A further implication of the new socialist administration to the state of Northern Ireland was the formation of the welfare state, a policy which Stormont had opposed. The Social Services Agreement of 1949 introduced London-funded services that were to change the living standards of the population of the north, and included family allowance, free healthcare at the point of need, national assistance and state pensions. Based on a National Insurance Fund, national insurance was introduced in 1948 to ensure state support for all during unemployment and maternity, for orphans and widows, for the elderly and to cover the costs of burial. The costs were to be borne by the Treasury, a subvention that cost the United Kingdom £36 million in 1946. This was to rise dramatically each year to reach £60 million by 1960 (Lyons 1963: 740).

POST-WAR RECONSTRUCTION

The north and the south suffered in different ways during the Second World War. The neutral position of de Valera, while popular with his Fianna Fáil colleagues, had left Eire internationally isolated and economically vulnerable to the changes that were occurring in the post-war world. The north had engaged fully in the war economy and, with its regime in Stormont holding close to the demands of the War Office in Whitehall throughout, it was to come out the other side in a favourable position vis-à-vis the Allies' plans. The most noticeable feature of post-war Ireland though was the extent of the schism that divided it politically and economically. Going into the new dispensation of a peaceful Europe, partition had become a distinct and seemingly intractable legacy of the old order. The economic differentiation which had prevailed between north and south had created a substantial difference in living standards for ordinary people. With almost full employment in the north, substantially higher wages and the availability of luxury goods from imports, the quality of life for the average person was discernibly different from that of their counterparts in the south. However, wages continued to be well below those on the British mainland, as the *International Labour Review* of November 1948 was to show. Between 1938 and 1946, across industry the gap between the wages for Irish and British men grew from 16 per cent to 32 per cent, and for women from 8 per cent to

31 per cent (*International Labour Review* 1948: 699–700). In the
north there may have been a closer parity with the south, but the
east–west divide was extensive.

With the end of the conflict in Europe there was a political
silence across the island as both regional administrations withdrew
to take stock. From the establishments' point of view there was
a need to get back to the securities of the pre-war hegemonies.
In the south this meant returning to the austerity that encapsulated the refuge that was de Valera's island, and by implication
to the worst economic growth in post-war Europe. His vision of
Ireland is often cited as one 'bright with cosy homesteads … and
the laughter of happy maidens' (de Valera, St Patrick's Day address
1943, Radio Éireann, RTÉ archives). Economically it was frozen in
time. Eire had survived untouched by the devastation wrought on
just about every other country in Europe, but it had an economy
which was dated and reclusive, caught outside the dynamic enterprise that was occurring across the continent based on industrial
adaptation and the internationalization of indigenous economies.
Eire had not been ravaged in the way that other areas had been,
including the north, and ironically it had financial reserves, not
having entered into the debt cycle other countries had to resort
to in order to service war provision. It was also caught on the
periphery of the new economy in Europe and remained isolated
for a considerable time, whereas other regions were developing on
a platform of creating new markets and industrial regeneration.
Post-war Eire could not find a role in this new region-to-region
network that stretched across Europe and was driving development
forward. For some, Eire's neutrality and the economic war with
Britain still rankled, leading to other regions avoiding Irish produce
and opting for the more openly competitive continental market.
The geopolitical position taken by many countries connected to
the Irish economy in the post-war years, such as fascist Portugal
and Spain, further complicated the situation. This complex of relationships was often accompanied by inappropriate policy-making
initiatives by the southern government.

The make-up of the evolving European market, with its technological (electronics) industries, the production of luxury goods and
the ability to activate new market opportunities, remained frustrating
for Irish producers. Their industries were under-resourced, agricul-
turally focused and lacked capacity. Again Ireland's main export was
to be human capital, the young, through a process of emigration that
was to reach unprecedented levels by the 1950s. The British market

was the most immediate outlet for goods and people, but remained problematic due to post-war reconstruction policies which included restrictions on agricultural imports in support of its own farming communities. There was also the attraction of the innovative welfare state in Britain, which had put into practice the most progressive proposals from Keynes through the Beveridge Plan and the creation of a mixed economy driven forward by major investments in the public sector. The National Health Service, social housing schemes and education reforms were to change British society.

Furthermore, the Marshall Plan was introduced across Europe. This feature of European reconstruction brought substantial funding from the United States to create a new infrastructure to mirror the commodity-driven open-market economy of the United States itself. While question marks were placed over the Irish need for post-war reconstruction, Marshall Aid was forthcoming in the form of £6 million, with a further £40 million in loans from the fund – the 'counterpart funds'. The influx of dollars meant that the government could readjust aspects of the import market to secure essential supplies from the United States, and while the restrictive Control of Manufactures Acts of the 1930s still kept tariffs at an exploitative level, some US imports did flow through:

> In 1947 imports from the United States accounted for well over one-fifth of all Irish merchandise imports (£29 million out of £131 million) ... the value of Irish imports from the United States rose to £18.5 million in 1949 and £20.8 million in 1950. (Ó Gráda 1997: 23)

In the high street what was noticeable was that luxury goods were getting through, including chocolate, tobacco, fashion clothing and fruit. There were also urgent imports such as wheat and petrol that were able to stimulate other aspects of economic development. Going into the 1950s, the funds from the United States represented almost 50 per cent of Irish governmental investment.

Notwithstanding the stunted nature of the southern economy, there was evidence that tentative changes to industry were bringing dividends to the society in general. There was a realignment of sorts within industry to take on board the potential of the new technologically driven environment and changes to consumer demand. The number of cars that were registered went up to 17,524 in 1950, a substantial departure from the 1946 figure of 2848 (Ó Gráda 1997: 22). Eire's GNP rose by 3 per cent on average by the end of the 1940s, and there was a quantifiable measure of restructuring and industrial growth which aspired to the new markets on the continent. Indeed, production went up by 10.7 per cent on average between 1946 and 1951, which reflected not only an increased level of investment but also the contrast with industrial activities in the pre-war era. Interestingly, even with the growth in productivity and importation, exports remained at a similar level to the pre-war years. The changes to industrial production and investment could be seen to be taking effect in the labour market as well. It was the first time since the Great Famine that the population of the island rose. The move from agricultural labour to industry and construction signalled a shift in the employment patterns within the economy and, while emigration went up from rural areas, unemployment actually went down from 9.3 per cent in 1947 to 7.3 per cent in 1951 (Kennedy et al. 1988: 58). Migration to urban environments within the south gave some indication of the increased opportunities that were opening up across the country.

The contrast between the suppression of the 1930s and the evident potential of the more open economy of the late 1940s gave rise to calls for modernization. The conflict between economic aspirations and a governmental reliance on the old system had provoked tensions which eventually encouraged a new political understanding for the new context. Viewing what was happening elsewhere in Europe, Irish people were wanting more commodities and luxury goods than the government was permitting to come through. Furthermore, necessities continued to be rationed throughout this period while tariff duties continued to be imposed on many luxury imported items. The leisure economy that was becoming so prevalent in other western European countries in the process of recovery was restricted in the south, putting the region again out of tune with cultural changes that were taking place in other societies. Church censorship had become a feature of the control of Irish society and a rallying point for those demanding social change. Demand was growing for commodities that were in scarce supply and, with the outmoded industrial infrastructure, low wages, restrictions on imports and an authoritarian suspicion of external influences on Irish society, there remained a deficit between the demand and supply of goods, cultural freedoms and traditional *mores*. Even though unemployment fell over the same period by over 3 per cent to 7.3 per cent, strikes were to become a feature of the period, with many protesting about the intensity of the depression and governance of the economy. A Labour Court was inaugurated in August 1946 to provide an outlet for industrial action, but strikes were ongoing, particularly throughout 1946 and 1947.

With the Irish punt still linked to sterling, fluctuations in the British market invariably impacted on the Irish economy. When sterling was devalued in 1948 the Irish monetary system had to reciprocate and depreciate accordingly. This put further stress on exports. The result of this was a significant balance of payments deficit, which meant the government could no longer sustain economic growth at the levels it was operating at. The result was financial instability. As Kieran Kennedy commented:

> This position deteriorated sharply in 1951 when a large current payments deficit of £62 million, equal to nearly 15 per cent of GNP, coincided with reduced capital inflows due to exhaustion of the Marshall Aid funds. This led to a decline of nearly one-sixth in external reserves. Underlying the deficit was a large increase in imports from mid 1949 to mid 1950, due to sharply rising import prices. (Kennedy et al. 1988: 59)

In the event the government returned to the comfort zones of harnessing public expenditure – and 'bunkered' down. Technically, it had been in a position to innovate and invest through the use of reserves that were accrued throughout the war, or by using Marshall Aid funding in a manner that could have assisted indigenous business development and public sector investment. This was resisted and the result was virtual stagnation for almost a decade after, and an entrenchment that (again) relegated the Irish economy to the peripheries. There was the possibly of spending the reserves to activate a manufacturing base that was faltering in reaction to British government economic policies and restrictions, and indeed to look at the integrating continental market at this point. The government held back, retreating to the confines of austerity measures at a point of potential expansion. This inactivity had a devastating impact on the confidence of those seeking to adjust the Irish economy. The result was a depressionary cycle that would blight the 1950s, against the backdrop of spontaneous growth in numerous other regions throughout western Europe. The contrasts were not lost on the increasing lobby of modernizers. In a way the Irish population was becoming defiantly more European while the establishment of party, state and church were attempting to hold on to the traditional safeguards.

The demand for change was eventually registered with the shock election of an inter-party administration in 1948, which had the result of stabilizing the policy framework and refreshing Irish politics, now released from the dominance of Fianna Fáil. The new Clann na Poblachta government, under taoiseach John A. Costello, injected a sense of realism into the policy arena to carry the national discourse beyond the civil war politics that had dominated Irish society since the 1920s. It gave the country its first taste of the modernization process that was occurring in other countries and an understanding of the concerns that were driving this change. The new government quickly revisited the historic economic conundrum by renewing its working relationship with the British government. There had been a realization of the isolated nature of the economy and an appreciation of the influence of investment and external markets on economic growth for enhancing the standard of living. In this there was an acceptance that sector-specific trade arrangements could be the way forward. The trade agreement with Britain in 1948 encouraged a more interactive relationship than the previous strained system, providing a much needed outlet for Irish produce. The British agricultural sector had been operating a similar protective mechanism to that of the Irish sector in the years immediately after the war in order to secure adequate food production and to ensure that the internal market in Britain was sustainable. The agreement meant that there were restrictions on certain agricultural imports from Eire, but that other products – manufactured goods – could have a freer flow into the British market. It profiled manufacturing and relaxed regulations on the exchange of produce. Furthermore, the 1949 Land Rehabilitation Project repositioned the agri-economy by bringing land back into use that had been set aside due to lack of investment. This proved very popular across rural areas.

The most noticeable public policy aspect of this period was the governmental response to the post-war need for social housing, emphasized by T. J. Murphy, the minister for local government. In all 110,000 houses were needed and from 1950 there was an expansive building programme which achieved a rate of 12,000 new builds per year, a rate not seen on the island since the growth of mill housing in Belfast at the close of the nineteenth century. Equally striking were the new health policies and the campaign by Dr Noel Browne to eradicate tuberculosis in the south. In terms of policy interventions this single act was to become one of the most enduring legacies of independence. As B. Hensey noted in *The Health Services of Ireland*, upwards of 4000 people were dying of the disease per year (Hensey 1959: 105, 134). Browne not only knew how to treat the condition, significantly he had the professional background and the influence to radically reform sanatoria across the country. New staffing and medical advances were introduced with dramatic effects. The death rate went down by 90 per cent by 1952.

Both the south and the north of Ireland participated in the Council of Europe after 1948, and this was considered to be a particularly important forum for the southern politicians to voice desires about engaging with other European regions and moving away from Britain's political and economic orbit. Represented initially by Costello and the minister for external affairs, Seán MacBride, a new vision of Ireland could be launched on the international stage – with relative distance from de Valera who was still viewed with suspicion on the continent due to perceived fascist and nationalistic sympathies. Indeed, during de Valera's participation at the second session of the Council of Europe, the president of the Council, Paul-Henri Spaak, had to intervene with the appeal: 'We must not allow every Debate to become the object of a dispute between the Representatives of Ireland and Great Britain .... I beg you to keep the matter in hand' (quoted in Hederman 1983: 35). Beyond this rhetorical bickering and posturing there was, however, a serious level of engagement with the proposal for European integration and the Irish role within this type of configuration. De Valera was later to comment on the deliberations taken at that time and the important conclusion that was reached:

> The idea of a complete Federation of Europe was most attractive, but when one got down to the details it was not easy to find a workable scheme ... Close co-operation for specific purposes, such as the Schuman plan – the 'European Coal and Steel Community' – was quite a different matter, and he believed, in present circumstances, that that was the most fruitful line to pursue. (quoted in Hederman 1983: 34–35)

This discourse would reshape the attitudes of the Irish political establishment so as to encourage links with other economies and would give the government impetus to realign policies in a manner that could complement the ongoing process of European integration. The idea of participation in the broader European market generated interest and support from the earliest days of the process. For example, the *Farmers' Journal* of 3 June 1950 commented:

> The countries of Europe need Irish food and Ireland needs free

access to their markets. If the proposed new arrangement could be achieved then it might well mean the end of partition and the entry of Ireland fully into a Europe secure in its strength and rid of most of the barriers which today prevent free movement and trade among nations.

In practical terms the debate about membership of the European Community had begun. On 13 June 1951 de Valera regained power.

The 1950s were years of recurring depression for the south of Ireland. Expectations and aspirations were high among the population, but disengagement from broader trends in the global economy left a caustic frustration and a sense of helplessness that resonated throughout the provinces. A seemingly timeless rural society which had changed little in generations, with rundown cities that struggled to keep the young from emigrating, summed up life in Ireland at this point. In policy terms the methods of dealing with the crises were seen by many as a national 'death-wish' for Irish society (Chubb and Lynch 1969: 1–2). There seemed to be no solution to the bouts of depression. Employment patterns give some indication of the volatile nature of the economy of the period:

> In 1951 the total number of persons at work was only 12,000 more than in 1926. The net increase of 159,000 in industrial employment over that period had been almost wiped out by a decrease of 147,000 in agricultural employment. Even taking the wastage from emigration into account, the Irish economy was able to create new jobs for no more than 800 people each year. (Lyons 1963: 573)

Trade flows went down year on year; agricultural prices were deflated on an ongoing basis, exports decreased correspondingly, while import costs were grossly inflated. Consumer demands were at a high due to the knowledge of and availability of leisure-based consumer products and white-goods in Britain, Europe and the north. The response of the government to this increase in demand was to introduce extraordinary import levies in March and July 1956. With economic policy being managed after the collapse of the Clann na Poblachta coalition by Seán McEntee for Fianna Fáil and later Gerard Sweetman for Fine Gael, successive governments through the 1950s sought to impose additional levies before reaching a point where levies peaked at 60 per cent on imports in March 1956. One major concession was made, however, with preferential rates for the UK and Commonwealth imports – they were levied at 40 per cent.

In both 1952 and 1956 the Dublin government reacted to the international contraction of markets in the usual manner with further cuts to public spending. The impact of resorting to 'corrective' measures can be seen after the 1955 crisis when government spending itself was reduced by 15 per cent and the public sector's percentage of national income dropped from 35 per cent to 30 per cent. Correspondingly, the employment levels in public-sector-related jobs is telling, as spending on capital projects was drastically reduced. Between 1955 and 1958, employment in construction declined from 74,000 to 56,000, causing an exodus of young and skilled labour, mostly to England:

> In the worst year 1957, the net loss of population due to emigration reached 54,000, while between 1951 and 1961 it totalled over 400,000. The slight gain of population between 1946 and 1951 was erased, and by 1961 the population had declined to 2.8 million, more than 5 per cent below the level at the foundation of the state. (Walsh 1979: 28)

Emigration was higher than at any time since the 1890s (Kennedy et al. 1988: 62). From a longitudinal analysis, from the famine (1841 census) to 1951 there had been a decline of 55 per cent of the population in the 26 counties that were to become the Irish Republic. The decline in the northern six counties was less, but still significant at 17 per cent (Mjøset 1992: 222). The problems continued. The shock of the decline in external reserves and a collapse in the credit status of the Republic left the Department of Finance deflated and forced it to act in a manner which would control the balance of payments and retrieve the credit rating, but cause further hardship across the country. It was not until 1958 and active engagement with the international markets that signs of growth would be registered in the GNP. The 1957 budget that was introduced to confront the depression was deflationary, aimed at cutting public expenditure as a means of stimulating growth. A third of the Public Capital Programme was cut, with a particular target being the building of social housing across the south. This led to further unemployment in the building and construction sectors and throughout this period the loss of almost 20 per cent of that labour force.

The course of the economy of the Irish Republic throughout the 1950s was against the international trend, where integrated

markets were rising and export-driven growth was facilitating industrial diversification and unprecedented growth patterns in many
European regions. The success of the Treaty of Paris of May 1951
(where six countries established a common market for key industrial commodities) revealed the opportunities that were possible
with a more cohesive interaction between sectors and regions, and
presented a model of co-ordination that was to dominate post-war
reconstruction on the continent. Trade in Ireland declined by 14 per
cent in the decade up to 1957 (Kennedy et al. 1988: 61). The
reaction by the Irish government to the stagnation of the economy
was to resort to deflationary measures that would further stress
the economy and go against the grain of economic wisdom across
the board. These stifled growth and frustrated companies in their
attempts to stimulate production and market conditions in ways
that were evidently working elsewhere. The economy stagnated
throughout the bulk of the decade as companies were forced to rely
on a domestic market that was not in a position to purchase. The
Irish Banking Review of July 1958 reflected on a situation where:
'Ireland [had] been suffering from a mood of pessimism in recent
years. Expressions of despair about the future of the country are
heard on all sides' (quoted in Ó Gráda 1997: 27). The economy had
become static, being held to the pre-war rates of growth against an
obviously changing macroeconomic tide. The sense of desperation
at the historical management of the economy of the Irish Republic
can be seen in one particularly telling paragraph of the Department
of Finance's groundbreaking 1958 report *Economic Development*,
or the 'Grey Book' as it became known:

> After 35 years of native government people are asking whether
> we can achieve an acceptable degree of economic progress. The
> common talk among parents in the towns, as well as in rural
> Ireland, is of their children having to emigrate as soon as their
> education is completed in order to secure a reasonable standard
> of living. (Department of Finance, 1958a: 5)

5 MODERNIZATION AND THE CONFLICT ECONOMY (1958–1987)

The early 1950s marked a low point in post-colonial economic development for the south of Ireland. The conservative policies with which the government sought to reverse the fortunes of the island only accelerated the pace of decline and impact of depression. In July 1956, the *New York Times,* alarmed at the state of the Irish economy, put it bluntly: 'the balance of payments has reached so dangerous a state of disequilibrium that we are within sight of national bankruptcy' (*New York Times*, 29 July 1956). This dislocation occurred within the context of a European economy that was undergoing a period of unprecedented growth and restructuring, leading to an integration process which was to successfully bring six disparate economies from Western Europe into a common market. In contrast, the years up to 1958 in the south were marked by a lack of growth, unprecedented levels of emigration and a self-doubt that was to stimulate a debate that was to alter the way in which Irish economists and civil servants were to view the patterns of economic interaction on the island as a whole. Before this date the relevant departments did attempt to introduce policies that would encourage investment and growth; however, political constraints prevented them from looking at methods that could have taken the south in the direction of other European regions. Evidence of a change of direction, though, could be seen after the government formally joined the World Bank and the International Monetary Fund (IMF) on 8 August 1957.

The quasi-governmental agency that was established in 1949 to monitor and stimulate industrial growth, the Industrial Development Authority (IDA), had been given the dubious task of trying to attract inward investment. The strategy had been enhanced with the setting up in 1951 of An Foras Tionscail, the Underdeveloped Areas Board, which had the remit of delivering financial support to new industries in rural areas in an effort to stimulate business. By 1956 this had been extended to the remaining parts of the Republic, with a focus on capital investment and technical assistance. Out of an initial mapping exercise of the economy, these agencies built up knowledge of the needs of industry across the state and were able to highlight aspects of investment that could possibly bring returns. This included support such as staff training, skills enhancement, the covering of plant costs and development investment. Further to this, the Córas Tráchtála, the Irish Export Board, was set up to locate foreign markets for indigenous producers. The new markets would provide an opportunity to circumvent the protectionism that had dominated economic policy in that new products would not frustrate the production of already existing tariff-protected goods.

The fruits of this internationally focused strategy were to emerge eventually. With the Department of Finance taking a leading role in the reform of economic policy, an international interpretation of the potential of the Irish economy started to take shape, shifting the department from its historical conservative role in managing economic affairs. The constraints that had been placed on business regarding exports, imports and investment were redefined, resulting in innovation being considered as a means of market stimulation. From this point forward new products were given priority. In May 1958, after co-ordinating research on the potential for growth, the Department's new Secretary, T. K. Whitaker, presented the policy document that was to change the direction of economic policy in the Republic. Based on the work undertaken by the Capital Investment Advisory Committee, he was tasked with looking at the design of public investment in the Republic. His approach was to take the Irish economy, dissect it and target deficiencies that had been undermining growth. The recommendations that were put forward in the policy document could subsequently be adopted as policy. The no-nonsense approach of the report stated the problems clearly and exposed a sequence of serious weaknesses across the economy: with its low real income, savings, investment, productivity and national product. It advocated 'A great and sustained effort to increase production, employment and living standards is necessary to avert economic decadence' (Department of Finance, 1958a: 2).

Interventions that hastened development included the two Finance Acts of 1957 and 1958, the Industrial Credit (Amendment) Act of 1958 and the government's own White Paper on *Economic Development,* which was released for public consumption in November 1958. The paper stated: 'public and private development of a productive character must be stimulated and organized so as to overshadow the non-productive development which now bulks so largely in public investment' (quoted in Walsh 1979: 31). The Finance Acts opened a decade of tax relief to new products for export, and the Credit Act enlarged the budget of the Industrial Credit Company to direct state funding into capital projects which could assist new industries. The Central Bank was the first to step up to berate the government's policies and support the strategy of realignment.

What Whitaker was able to do was to set out in stark economic terms the reasons for underperformance in the Irish economy at a time when external market growth and the diversification of production should have been a catalyst for change. The countries grouped under the Treaty of Paris (1951) were forging forward with a strategy that gave their collective gross national product (GNP) a rate of growth of 42 per cent between 1949 and 1956. Britain's GNP rate of growth was 21 per cent, while the economy of the south of Ireland remained at 8 per cent – a figure unchanged since the start of the war. It left a noticeable difference between economic development in the Republic of Ireland and its immediate neighbours in Britain and Europe (Department of Finance 1958a: 11). The Census figures were to highlight the most immediate effect of this disparity – emigration:

> Not only was there a steady decline in the number of people working (in agriculture it dropped from 597.2 thousand in 1946 to 378.7 thousand in 1961, and in manufacturing industry from 187.6 thousand to 179.4 thousand between the same two dates) but the number leaving the country continued to be formidable. Net emigration for 1951–6 was 196,763, for 1956–61 it was 212,003. These rates were nearly three times the pre-war rates and for the decade 1951–61 in particular were higher than for any other comparable period in the twentieth century .... Between 1931 and 1960, while the total number of males engaged in all forms of agriculture had dropped by 24 per cent, those working on farms of one to thirty acres fell by 50 per cent as compared with a 12 per cent drop on farms of a hundred acres or over. (*Census of Population 1961*, Volume 1, Table 1; adapted by Lyons 1963: 625, 627; also see Crotty 1966: 167–78)

By focusing on the weakness of the economy and drawing from the long-term faults in policy design the *Economic Development* report brought to the fore the structural causes that had been debilitating Irish markets and industries. Public sector investment had usually been targeted at the behest of political interests, and thus economically sensitive areas which could have created jobs and private capital had often been subjugated to export and import restrictions. Furthermore, agriculture remained as if it was providing for a different century, never mind a European market, emigration seemed to be endemic, and there was a lack of productivity across the economy. All these features came through in the report and set the context for change.

The influence of the *Grey Book*, as it became known, can be measured not only in the way it was able to justify the adaptation of the vagaries of the Irish economy to ideas that were common currency across other European countries, but in the fact that the government accepted its recommendations. This core document was to be the framework for the first Programme for Economic Expansion, brought before the Oireachtas (the houses of parliament) in November 1958. The programme included a timeline for the restructuring of the Irish economy, and particularly its agricultural and industrial sectors. Productivity and exporting were to be the central outputs, with government investment being targeted towards high-growth markets. For industry this meant a release from the constraints of the past and an opportunity to access new markets, with a confidence that the Irish government would act in a supporting capacity. It also meant a more considered application of protectionist measures, working to the strengths of Irish producers. As the programme stated:

> Hence, it must now be recognized that protection can no longer be relied upon as an automatic weapon of defence and it will be the policy in the future in the case of new industries to confine the grant of tariff protection to cases in which it is clear that the industry will, after a short initial period, be able to survive without protection. (Government of the Irish Republic 1958b: 38)

This opening up of the system was further enhanced by the introduction of the Industrial Development (Encouragement of External Investment) Act of 1958 which provided incentives and tax concessions for companies considering investment in the south. Drawing from the continental model, new industries were to be encouraged and the government's investment strategy would go as far as to pay for the machinery, locate the companies and promote the goods in external markets. A five-year plan was budgeted at £220.4 million.

In the debates around the implementation of the programme, and indeed the *Grey Book* itself, ideas about the possible future of the economy of the south were anticipating wide-ranging adjustments. Its

Keynesian import is important. Carrying forward the proposals set out in the Provisional United Trade Union Organization's 'Planning Full Employment' policy document (1956), industrial investment and state planning had been considered a means of stimulating growth towards the ideal of full employment. It called for a comprehensive state-based investment facility which would stabilize employment and stem the tide of emigration. The programme moved towards this aspiration of the unions. Academics who were involved in discussions around the new direction for the Irish economy saw the strategy as a way of actively catching up with other regions in Europe. For the first time the evolving Scandinavian model for advanced growth (a progressive mixed economy with a prominent public policy) was acknowledged as a possible alternative for the Irish economy. Various cornerstones of the Irish economy were confronted, such as the creation of jobs that would encourage young people to stay and social bargaining. Donal Nevin, in the Symposium on Economic Development, held on Friday 1 May 1959, brought the sensitivities of a number of the lobbies together:

> The aim of economic development is not, of course, the provision of employment for the sake of employment. But the employment aspect must, in the context of the Irish situation, be regarded as of primary importance if our people are to be imbued with the will and the enthusiasm necessary to carry through a comprehensive development programme. While economists look to the trend in real national income and keep a weather eye on the balance of payments, trade unionists, for example, will tend to ask: how many more jobs will be provided? The psychological implications of this approach should not be overlooked by the economists. (Symposium 1959: 129–30)

The programme was fortunate in that it was introduced at a period of change throughout the global economy, as industry and technology were adapting to a new consumer-based market system. The Irish initiative coincided with this movement within the European context and was quickly able to link into a number of sectors that had been shifting from the constraints of post-war austerity to export-driven commodity production, employing multi-location production techniques. Furthermore, the idea of loan-driven industrial expansion would be able to provide the much-needed capital for companies seeking to attract the new markets. Taking a leaf from the *Grey Book*: 'If sufficient capital is not available from home resources, every effort should be made to obtain it abroad on reasonable terms' (Government of the Irish Republic 1958a: 44). The modernization process could be recognized as the point at which the Irish economy opened to external influences. Its impact could be measured by a decline in the numbers emigrating:

> The Census of 1966 showed an actual increase in the population of 62,411 persons, while emigration reached a new low. The total for the five years 1961–6 was 83,855, little more than a third of the previous intercensal period, and the annual net rate per 1000 had fallen from the disastrous 14.8 of 1956–61 to 5.7 between 1961 and 1966. (Lyons 1963: 630)

Changes in the Irish government's approach to economic integration were boosted by the election of Seán Lemass as taoiseach in June 1959. From this point on, trade, with the emphasis on exports and attracting multinational corporations, became central to the regeneration of the Irish economy, and indeed internationalization in that regard. What was noticeable about the expansion of the economy in the period of the first economic programme was the injection of the Keynesian method of enhancing market activity together with public sector investment. Under the Public Capital Programme, fiscal policy was expanded, and with investment coming through from alternative sources the anticipated cuts to social spending were circumvented. As Kennedy and Dowling pointed out in *Economic Growth in Ireland*, public capital expenditure continued to grow even during the deflationary policies of the mid 1960s, with the leverage of foreign borrowing (1975: 233–6). The changes in policy and ideological form reflected a new generation, post-civil war, with a more vibrant attitude to multi-layering economic policies that included foreign direct investment, strategic borrowing, the diversification of various sectors, employment and an acknowledgement of the importance of the general standard of living. The first programme was also robust enough to adapt to soundings from international fluctuations in industrial development and, significantly, to integrate Irish industry in accordance with macroeconomic circumstances. One further factor highlighted the point that the Irish economy needed to work within the context of the emerging Common Market, and that was the geographical location of the island.

Economic Development was categorical in its preferred option for the future of the Irish economy, and this was for the Europeanization of industrial and agricultural sectors. Entering into an integrated market system was presented as the only way out of Ireland's historical isolation: 'There is really no other choice for a country wishing to keep pace materially with the rest of Europe' (Government of the Irish Republic 1958a: 2). This assertion from a new generation of policy makers was an open riposte to the often-cited comment of de Valera at the Council of Europe on 17 August 1949 when he warned his continental neighbours: 'If the nations here on the mainland of the continent consider that they cannot wait for us, perhaps they should consider going on without us by an agreement among themselves for a closer union' (quoted in Kennedy and O'Halpin 2000: 49). As a vulnerable peripheral region of the economic bloc that was to become the European Economic Community, an alternative vision of the island's future started to take shape. While it had remained outside the Treaty of Rome and was not permitted to join the European Free Trade Association (EFTA), the Republic had successfully negotiated for Marshall Aid and entered the Organization for European Economic Cooperation (OEEC), albeit with trepidation. The experience of working with continental civil servants provided a favourable environment to the sequence of three applications to join the EEC. The rate of economic growth for the countries participating in the Community and the fact that they offered an alternative to the historical dependence on the British economy, gave the Department of Finance advisers a strategy in the making. In the mid-1950s there still remained a high level of confusion within political circles in the south as to the rationale behind integrating economies. In January 1958 *The Statist* surveyed British attitudes to the Irish debates over trade liberalization and protectionism:

> Ireland's attitude seems to be one of refusing to accept that she will not get exceptional treatment .... The fact is that no expert appraisal has yet been made of the likely implications on individual Irish industries of a free trade area in which all participating countries would be treated equally. (quoted in Hederman 1983: 56)

Ireland's position outside the framework of the European integration process would leave it peripheral, searching for compatible markets to work with in order to secure trade with prospective partners. Before deciding on the EC path one other option had to be considered and this was in partnership with the United Kingdom. Dublin began negotiations with London about joining the 17-strong EFTA. From the extent of exchange between the Irish and British markets, this would have been a natural route to follow. In the years up to the establishment of EFTA, the Republic had been exporting 89.2 per cent of its produce to the United Kingdom and only 5.5 per cent to the six states that comprised the signatories of the Treaty of Rome. Furthermore, in terms of imports, the Republic was bringing in 51.5 per cent of its produce from the United Kingdom while only sourcing 8.3 per cent from the European 'Six' (Fitzgerald 2000: 5). Returning to the economic fold of the United Kingdom would, however, have meant a political realignment that could cause internal disagreements and reopen the sensitivities of the older generation of republicans. Whitaker reframed the issue with the belief that partition would be entrenched further if the Republic was to continue to resist the pull of the UK markets. Remaining outside EFTA 'would mean the erection of another barrier between Northern Ireland and ourselves' (quoted in Hederman 1983: 54). Nevertheless, to effectively readjust the Irish economy, external partnerships were crucial and foreign investment would be necessary, irrespective of its source.

The debate about Irish participation in EFTA reached breaking point on 10 February 1958 with a symposium in Belfast organized by the Irish Association for Cultural, Social and Economic Relations. Gaining significant coverage in the media, the debate about EFTA was brought centre stage, emphasized by Lemass's rapprochement to the northern establishment with his statement that all-island integration within this network would benefit north and south alike.

The possibility of integration within EFTA was however knocked back as early as May 1959 when the British and Swedish governments objected to the Republic's membership (Fitzgerald 2000: 6). While this was perceived to be a setback it convinced the Irish government to approach the European Community in a more determined manner, and also laid the ground rules for a more bespoke arrangement with the United Kingdom. That was to become the Anglo-Irish Free Trade Area Agreement (AIFTAA) – signed in December 1965 and taking effect in the summer of 1966. In this mechanism agricultural produce from Ireland gained favourable access to the British market, while industrial exports had restrictions removed. From the British perspective industrial tariffs would be phased out over a ten-year period to secure ease of access for British goods into the south of Ireland.

The drive to promote industrial exports was significantly enhanced by the Committee on Industrial Organization (CIO) which created, from June 1961, a partnership forum between industrial representatives, the civil service and trade unions. Its job was to locate and encourage those industries that would be ideally suited for export markets. Its loans scheme was later to be complemented with a grants support scheme.

The EEC route provided something new for the Irish government that would eventually locate it in a dynamic developmental process which would, significantly, be outside the orbit of and dependency on the British economy. The correspondence and exchanges between the Irish and British premiers of the day, Lemass and Harold Macmillan, showed that from the Irish point of view any strategic repositioning would have to have definite economic advantages. The tactical decision to apply for EEC membership was undertaken as a means of tracking the British decision to do likewise. With the various criteria in place and a general consensus on the future position of the Republic in the European market, the government set about publicizing the benefits of Irish membership to the population. The industrial sectors envisaged a rapidly expanding market with exports at the hub, whereas with agriculture the Common Agricultural Policy (CAP) was acknowledged as a support mechanism for a range of produce and the rural community in general. The Irish Congress of Trade Unions (ICTU) also saw the appeal of participation in a labour market of seven or more countries, the opportunities offered by the freedom of movement and strengthened links with the union movement across the continent. Membership would enhance the profile of the ICTU. For the government the attraction of the CAP was the deciding factor on which direction they should turn. Lemass put the dilemma of membership very succinctly in a Dáil debate on 11 December 1959:

> There are now two trading blocs in Europe into neither of which this country can enter, accepting the full obligations of membership, without taking what most of us would regard as an undue risk. This country is predominantly agricultural. That fact must determine our thinking and our policy in this respect as in all others. (Lemass, Dáil debates, 11 December 1959, Volume 178; quoted in Laffan and O'Mahony 2008: 16)

Foremost in the mind of Lemass was access to the larger European market, particularly for agricultural produce and to extract Ireland from its dependency on Britain. This issue was to dominate Lemass's remaining time in office. Focusing on this goal and conditioning the civil service to this pathway meant that the population was steadily prepared for a different economic reality within the context of the

European Community. In a keynote address to the Dublin Chamber of Commerce on 8 January 1959, which was reported in all Irish papers at the time, Lemass was explicit about his intentions to enter a free trade association:

> It seems clear that if an agreement for a European Economic Association came into operation we could not afford to remain outside it but generally we conceive it to be in our interests in the present state of our economic development (*Irish Times*, 9 January 1959).

The commitment of the government to this particular policy can be seen in its publication of the *European Economic Community* White Paper of 30 June 1961. Again Whitaker's hand could be seen throughout the document, arguing for realignment and the effective liberalization of trade within the context of an emerging and dynamic continental trading bloc.

The timing was notable, with Ireland submitting its application on 31 July 1961 and the United Kingdom submitting its on 10 August. They were two of four applications to be submitted around the same time to the Community, the others coming from Denmark and Norway. On 18 January 1962, Lemass delivered a justification for membership to the EEC Council of Ministers highlighting the economic history of the island and the series of problems that had frustrated its development. The Council returned with 15 questions requesting information that would justify Ireland's membership (Maher 1986: 375–80). After protracted discussions with representatives from the Council of Europe, accession negotiations began in October 1962. This was backed up with a tour of the capitals of Europe by Lemass to give the Irish case momentum within the various member states. The result was the confirmation by Emilio Colombo, the president of the Council of the EEC, that the six states of the EEC had unanimously agreed to open accession negotiations with Ireland. The prospect, as understood by the Irish government's representatives, was that the country would enter the Community on 1 January 1964.

While the Irish delegation to the EEC was anticipating membership, the relationship with the United Kingdom was to impact adversely on the plans. Due to ongoing tensions between London and Paris regarding UK membership of the Community and an uncompromisingly Gallic approach to the British by French president Charles de Gaulle, UK membership was vetoed. By proxy, and due almost exclusively to the dependence of the Irish economy on the

UK market, Ireland was also subjected to this veto. Membership of the Community would have to be delayed until such time as France was willing to accept UK membership. Lemass, almost in a nationalistic reaction to being caught helpless inside the British economic orbit, set about committing the republic to EEC membership as a policy mission: 'to prepare and plan for our entry to an enlarged Community, taking every step which will further this objective and avoiding any that might make it more difficult to attain' (Lemass, Dáil debates, 30 January 1963, Volume 199). Membership of the Community was to become a national obsession through the 1960s and was to have a dramatic effect on the nature of Irish society as well as the economy. As Brigid Laffan and Jane O'Mahony noted of Lemass's vision in *Ireland and the European Union*:

> The Ireland he was trying to change was an Ireland in which agriculture was still the most important economic activity and source of employment and a society in which the influence of the Catholic Church was pervasive. Irish society was deeply conservative in terms of its values and mores. The imperative of generating economic activity and jobs would have a transformative impact on Irish society. Membership for Ireland was not about ending centuries of conflict, it was about embedding Ireland in an external environment that would enable it [to] address the challenge of economic modernization. (Laffan and O'Mahony 2008: 23)

The drive to get the Republic into the EEC coincided with the implementing of the *First Programme for Economic Expansion* which ran from 1959 to 1963. Its successes ensured a qualitative improvement in the standard of living and employment opportunities, and presented a new framework within which the Irish economy could develop. The statistics spoke for themselves about the transformation of the economy: 'Thus, whereas net agricultural output was only 1 per cent higher in 1963 than in 1957, industrial output in 1963 was 47 per cent above its 1957 level' (Lyons 1963: 630). The extent of the influence of this alternative model can be gauged from the second programme, which was intended to run from 1964–70. This strategy assumed – wrongly – that Ireland would be a member of the EEC and could develop its economic base on this premise. Knitted throughout the *Second Programme for Economic Expansion* were clauses to permit compliance with the various articles of the Treaty of Rome. The programme had to be curtailed after only two years because of the level of integration that the administration was anticipating. While there was a return to this strategic approach in 1969, the south was forced to play a waiting game. Furthermore, the second programme got caught up in something completely different: the uncertainty of macroeconomic instability, an international oil crisis, global recession and the tumultuous outbreak of civil conflict in the north. The programme had to be withdrawn.

OPENING THE NORTH

Northern Ireland, as the industrial anchor on the island, emerged from the Second World War in a relatively advantaged position. Its commercial infrastructure had been able to weather the storm of the post-war decline and, with its organic links to the British market, it was in a natural position to maximize the opportunities that were opening up in the new commodity-based international market. Shadowing its potential there was however the underbelly of economic history in the region – a depressed labour market, a divided union movement, sectarian polarization across the society and a stubborn conservative administration in Stormont under Basil Brooke. The make-up of this post-war economy was framed by the Ireland Act of 1949:

> It is hereby declared that Northern Ireland remains part of His Majesty's dominions and of the United Kingdom and it is hereby affirmed that in no event will Northern Ireland or any part thereof cease to be a part of His Majesty's dominions and of the United Kingdom, without the consent of the parliament of Northern Ireland.

Within this constitutional pretext, the disparities and disadvantages were patently obvious: 'Income per capita in Northern Ireland was less than two-thirds of the United Kingdom average in 1959–60, whereas the unemployment rate since 1950 ranged persistently from three to five times the national average' (Steed and Thomas 1971: 346).

Unlike the south where agriculture remained a dominant feature of the economy, in the north two industrial centres had emerged around Belfast and Derry, the locations for four out of every five jobs. In November 1950 the Re-equipment of Industry Bill was tabled with the Northern Ireland Government. Its key task was to encourage industrial adaptation and 'the payment of grants towards expenditure incurred in the re-equipment or modernization of industrial undertakings' (NIHC Debates, *Hansard*, Vol. 34, 1928). With upwards of 33 per cent of capital investment being allocated through this bill, it displayed some understanding within the administration of the urgency of managing decline in the traditional industries. This dilemma was to provide the backdrop for economic development in the north for the next decade. On the cusp of the region's unemployment level entering double digits, Basil Brooke made the situation plain to Stormont: 'we are now faced with the stern necessity of making our books balance' (NIHC, *Hansard*, December 1951, Vol. 35, 2572).

The 1950s highlighted some of the nuances within the economy of the north, with its lack of diversification, resistance to island-wide economic cohesion and regional isolation leaving it vulnerable to the processes of modernization. The patterns of employment in this decade give some indication of the role of traditional industry in maintaining the hegemony under pressure. Almost 20 per cent of the workforce were employed in agriculture, 30 per cent in textiles and linen, and 30 per cent in the shipyards (Isles and Cuthbert 1955: 97, 101). The problem of demand in the post-war era meant that by the beginning of the decade employment in the textiles and linen industries was dropping by 5 per cent per year, with the outlook being one of systemic decline. Coupled with the introduction of synthetic fibre as an increasingly competitive textile, managing for a sustained period of contraction seemed to be the only future for northern industry. 'Between 1954 and 1964 the number of jobs in plants employing 25 or more (the great majority) fell from 56,414 to 33,957. The number of plants fell from 298 to 200' (Bew et al. 1996: 115–16). The role of the shipyard is also important to note at this period, given that Harland and Wolff was the biggest single employer on the island. While the textiles industry could be seen to be susceptible as early as the late 1940s, shipbuilding retained its market until the start of the 1960s when, within the first three years of that decade, it lost 40 per cent of its labour force. As Thomas Wilson pointed out in *Economic Development in Northern Ireland*, the unemployment rate in Northern Ireland averaged out at 7.4 per cent, which was four times the UK average (Wilson 1965: 23–4). Constraints in the labour market meant that unskilled labour in the north was the lowest paid of the various UK regions.

The Isles and Cuthbert Report of 1957 gives perhaps the most insightful analysis of the economy of the state since partition and, while assertively partitionist, it offered an economic complement to the work of Whitaker in the south. It began with masonic panache and spoke to only one section of the northern community: 'To the Right Hon. Lord Glentoran ... We have the honour to be, My Lord, Your obedient servants' (Isles and Cuthbert 1957: v-vi). Glentoran, the Stormont minister for commerce, also happened to be from the Dixon family, the shipping and timber magnates. What was innovative about the report, officially titled *An Economic Survey of Northern Ireland*, was that it anticipated the collapse of the traditional industries, shipbuilding and linen mills. The report argued that new industries producing, for example, synthetic fibres, chemical and electrical engineering, regionally dispersed, were necessary for the rejuvenation of the faltering industries that were clustered largely in the urban centres. The report looked closely at the types of investment and finance in the region and found a number of anomalies that would frustrate the kind of economic development that would be necessary for market-focused, export-driven growth. Importantly 60 per cent of industry in Northern Ireland was privately owned and tied to conventional means of capital generation and credit. Therefore the risk-taking necessary for restructuring and investment had been disabled.

Isles and Cuthbert focused on the potential failings in the regional economy – as did Whitaker in the south – and stated clearly that dependence on British government subsidies, which was being used to prop up failing companies, stifled adjustment towards a more productive, growth-based economy. It also meant that foreign investment, when it was coming into the northern economy, was avoiding an increasingly antiquated industrial base with falling productivity. In a word, traditional industry in Northern Ireland could not *compete* with other similar companies and was caught in a position where it was being artificially sustained, dependent on the government's direct financial support and unprofitable. This inability to innovate and invest meant that productivity and employment were destined to decline.

> Thus the general problems of economic development in the province (as distinct from the country as a whole) have to do with the causes and effects of the relatively low level of income and the causes and effects of the relatively large volume of unemployment and narrow industrial structure with which the relative lowness of income is associated. (Isles and Cuthbert 1957: 5)

Isles and Cuthbert also complained about the state of the regional accounts – or more precisely the lack of accountability on the part of the Stormont administration – which left the two Queen's University academics struggling to get an estimate of the overall balance of payments for Northern Ireland. Stripped back, the issues of investment and employment were presented as the keys to growth in the region:

> So far as the immediate effects on employment are concerned, it would not matter whether the government, or other public authorities, invested in the construction of works serving the needs of industry – such as harbours, docks, roads, bridges, dams, drainage works, and the like – or whether it concentrated on the provision of public amenities and social needs, such as schools and educational buildings, hospitals and other public building, recreational facilities, and houses. The investment of funds in such works at a time of heavy unemployment would directly provide work …. Moreover, if carefully selected and planned, the programme of works might, as a by-product, have the lasting effect of either improving and cheapening various services for industry commensurately with the cost of the investment, or of providing the public with an important addition to general amenities. (Isles and Cuthbert 1957: 368–9)

This inability to change could be seen from one very telling statistic from the early 1960s – the subvention from the Exchequer in London had increased by a startling 600 per cent between 1946 and 1963 (Goodman 2000: 16). As calculated in a second major analysis of the Northern Ireland economy at the time, the Hall Report (*Report of the Joint Working Party on the Economy of Northern Ireland*) of 1962, employment in manufacturing had declined by 28 per cent between 1950 and 1961 (Hall 1962: 70). For both reports what was crucial for the economy to adapt was capital investment coupled with the diversification of industries.

The reaction of the Stormont administration to the declining industries, against the recommendations of the economists, was to attempt to prop up the big employers and to privilege those firms that had political or historical links to the Unionist Party. The reason for this blatant nepotism can be seen in the composition of the leadership of the Unionist Party. Of the 14 Belfast Members of Parliament for the regional government, twelve were the managing directors of large local firms – predominantly linen and shipbuilding. Between 1955 and 1961, £123 million was used to keep traditional industries solvent (Hall 1962: 58). These industries were further assisted through the introduction of a number of Acts that had the intention of protecting the firms: the Re-equipment of Industries Act, the Capital Grants to Industry Act and the Industrial Development Act. Working from this legislation Stormont could pump state investment into the failing industries. By 1964, 40 per cent of labourers in the shipyards had been made redundant. James Goodman noted that 'In the same period, employment in textiles fell by 16,000 to 56,000, and in 1961, 8000 workers were laid off from the shipyards, reducing the workforce to 16,000' (Goodman 2000: 17; Bew and Patterson 1979: 134). Between 1950 and 1960 agricultural employment also went down by 28,000, or one third of the total (Bew et al. 1996: 117). Parallel to this adjustment process and in a period of exceptional growth elsewhere, investment in new industries was starting to find its way through to benefit a younger generation of qualified and skilled workers who were looking to gain employment outside the traditional firms. Multinationals Viyella, ICI and Courtaulds were to become a very visible presence in the north in the late 1950s and early 1960s, circumventing the constrictions put in place by the politicians by directly investing in a new generation of white-collar employees. With evidence mounting regarding the contraction and stress on the regional economy, the ruling Unionist Party chose to ignore the various warnings. That was nothing new. In November 1950, the Stormont minister for finance, Brian Maginness, had outlined the 'dangers' of modernization:

> While I am sure the [Ways and Means] committee are in full sympathy with the government's policy of attracting new industries, thereby diversifying our industrial set-up and mitigating, as far as possible, the effects of any setback in world trading conditions upon our principal export trade, there is undoubtedly a feeling that these new industries may have had an adverse effect on existing industries, notably in the attraction of labour to modern, well laid-out factories. (NIHC, *Hansard*, Vol. 34, 1000; cited in Bew et al. 1996: 120)

The ignorance of Stormont was reflected in another area of life in the province, that of working class politics. This manifested itself for a time with the Northern Ireland Labour Party, which came to make ground across the erstwhile divided working class communities and increased its support by upwards of 15 per cent (Bew et al. 1996: 128). The extent of the mismanagement of the economy, at a time when other parts of Europe were experiencing an unprecedented boom, was marked at the beginning of 1961 with the announcement that 16,000 workers would be made redundant in the aircraft and shipbuilding industries. Ten thousand went in the shipyards alone, spurring the Confederation of Shipbuilding and Engineering Unions to organize 20,000 employees to walk out and demonstrate against the government's inactivity.

The response of the Brooke administration proved that it was wedded to the policies that were proving so destructive to the regional economic base. What came back from the Unionist MPs was a demand for tax reductions for business, a mantra which was not received well by an increasingly assertive trade union movement. The only major 'concession' that Brooke was able to extract from the Westminster government was a commitment to consider the Hall recommendations and to look at where employment opportunities could be enhanced in the region's industrial and agricultural sectors. This second major analysis of the northern economy in four years set out a strategy for change within an economy where employment in manufacturing alone had declined by 28 per cent between 1950 and 1961 (Hall 1962: 70). For Hall, Isles and Cuthbert what was crucial for the economy to adapt was capital investment coupled with the diversification of industries. Change continued to be resisted.

The Brooke administration's Ministry of Finance, headed by the enigmatic Terence O'Neill, reacted to the circumstances by attempting to negotiate a series of concessions from the Treasury by highlighting the deteriorating circumstances in the north. Central to the request was a 50 per cent increase in state aid to Ulster's industry. This was carried to the Treasury on the back of a promise of wage cuts, increased productivity and the rationalization of traditional industries – processes that could not be halted anyway. The principal motivation behind the plan from the administration was to maintain the economic base as effectively as possible in a time of destabilization. The recommendations from the Hall Report were presented as an answer to the crisis by Brooke himself, but he hesitated in acting out the recommendations or securing the necessary support from the Treasury to implement them. In reaction to the questionable efforts by the government at Stormont, the NILP organized a petition signed by 100,000 people, demanding that action be taken. By the time the Hall Report was eventually made public the shipyards were announcing that there would be thousands more redundancies. The inability to manage the crisis inadvertently facilitated alterations to the local economic base by permitting multinationals to access the local labour market. It also brought down Brooke as the leader of the Unionist Party (26 March 1963), to be replaced by O'Neill. This

seat-changing exercise was to bring about a more critical understanding of the capacity of the local economy, and a realization that
it could not go back. Essentially, O'Neill acknowledged the need
for economic planning. It was also the start of a reassertion of the
Unionist hegemony against NILP support, which had peaked at 26
per cent of the electorate by 1962 and was evidently threatening the
Unionist Party itself (O'Leary and McGarry 1996: 162).

O'Neill's view of the north was influenced heavily by the changes
that were affecting economic policy in London. The attempt by the
UK government to get into the European Community had resulted in
more scrutiny of solutions to the silted-up northern economic base,
with all its reliance on heavy industry and resistance to modernization. Furthermore, the lesson to be communicated from London
in relation to export-driven economic growth was that political
dogmas might have to be forsaken in order to integrate the economy
with regional markets. In London's case it meant approaching
both France and West Germany; in the case of Stormont it would
mean looking towards Dublin as a potential economic partner. The
transfer of policies may have provided an incentive to adapt the
region to more cross-border integration and business stimulation,
but incoming investment was not targeted in a way that would
secure the internal stability of the state itself. This showed through
in the planned changes to the regional infrastructure – in a manner
that would cause controversy. Motorways were built from Belfast
towards Enniskillen and Coleraine, not to Newry or Derry as would
be expected if they were to enhance arterial routes for economic
access; a new university was located in a rural area outside Coleraine
and not, as expected, in Derry city; a new city of Craigavon was
planned, named after the former leader of the Unionist Party; and
new social housing estates were located in politically advantageous
locations. While there was a rhetorical battle that resembled the
debates that were occurring across the water on the need to change
for modernity and technological innovation, the Stormont administration still very obviously had political and communitarian interests
to placate.

Three additional reports weighed in to encourage the Stormont
government to shift strategic priorities towards openness. The
Matthew Report sought regional economic balance, and the Wilson
Report, entitled *Economic Development in Northern Ireland*,
continued in the vein of promoting modernization and providing
recommendations for the Stormont administration. Building on the
previous academic interventions, this report defined the region as a

peripheral economy in need of capital investment and job creation. On advocating regional planning Wilson outlined the priorities as, first, ' a general rise in the standard of living based on higher output per head and, second, a rise in employment sufficiently large to cope with the growth in population and to reduce unemployment with some decline in the net outflow of people from Northern Ireland' (Wilson 1965: 134). Specific locations were designated as areas in need of investment, while arterial routes and the diversification of service industries could encourage alternative means of growth. In specifying targets for growth, the need for job creation gave some indication of the problems faced by the region, with 30,000 new jobs being necessary in manufacturing alone after 1965. Another pressing issue that was brought up in the report was to become one of the most controversial civil rights issues of the period – 64,000 additional houses were urgently required by 1970.

Academically, the Matthew Report and its follow-up by Wilson were harshly criticized for their level of economic rigour, ideological bias and the skewed recommendations, as noted by Bew, Gibbon and Patterson in *Northern Ireland 1921–1996*: 'In fact both the Matthew and the consequent "Wilson plan" were a sham. References to "natural properties" in Matthew's report suggest its inspiration to have been classical rather than technocratic' (Bew et al. 1996: 135). The main criticism of these Stormont strategies was that they had a tendency to focus on infrastructural and capital initiatives as opposed to financial arrangements for change. Furthermore, there remained resistance within the Unionist cabinet to even these flawed initiatives. Modernization was considered important by a minority within the Unionist Party, but for an increasingly influential sectarian lobby outside the party, change was viewed to be too disruptive to the traditional religious and regional power balance. O'Neill attempted to address the criticisms with a vision for 'New Ulster', with its conventional hegemony intact, but with the option of dipping into the technological modernity that had brought Harold Wilson's Labour government to power in the United Kingdom on 15 October 1964. The building of the new city of Craigavon and the locating of a second higher-level educational institution in Coleraine (based on the Lockwood Report), both in Unionist heartlands, sent out signals to traditionalists about the nature of modernization in the north. In effect economic policies were transparently political and prejudiced in favour of the Protestant population, and by implication against the Irish Catholic population. It was also notable that no Irish nationalists were consulted on the modernization process, or worked on the various reports. When prominent professionals from the Catholic community wrote to O'Neill questioning the logic of his policies, his refusal to respond to their enquiries was matched with an attack on the Catholic Church and the Catholic community for continuing to educate their children outside the Unionist state system. O'Neill, even as a liberal within the Unionist Party, still remained wedded to opinions that predated the 1960s:

> It is frightfully hard to explain to a Protestant that if you give Roman Catholics a good job and a good house they will live like Protestants, because they will see neighbours with cars and TV sets. They will refuse to have eighteen children, but if the Roman Catholic is jobless and lives in a most ghastly hovel he will rear eighteen children on national assistance. It is impossible to explain this to a Protestant …. He cannot understand, in fact, that if you treat Roman Catholics with due consideration and kindness they will live like Protestants, in spite of the authoritarian nature of their church. (quoted in Buckland 1981: 112; and O'Leary and McGarry 1996: 163)

The sentiment was interchangeable with 'negro' or 'Jew'; the message remained the same in an apartheid-like society.

O'Neill, and indeed 'O'Neillism', recognized the problems of an antiquated economy and the implications for the Unionist hegemony and throughout his time in office attempted to manage decline through an awkward engagement with modernization. Irrespective of in-house party sentiments, sectarian, classical or conservative, there were also tentative overtures to the Irish Catholic community north and south, marking a departure from the 'staunch' positions taken by his predecessors. In June 1963, O'Neill passed on his condolences to the Irish Catholic Church on the death of Pope John XXIII, arranged to meet with the Taoiseach Lemass and with great media attention actually visited Catholic school children. This bipolar approach to sectarianism, however, left the often-touted aspiration of 'bridge-building' shallow. In reaction to these mixed messages, the increasingly assertive Catholic middle class – influenced by the civil rights movement in the United States of America – began to organize to demand basic rights. The National Democratic Party, the Campaign for Social Justice (CSJ), Republican Labour, Republican Clubs, Wolfe Tone Societies, the Campaign for Democracy in Ulster, and by 1967 the Northern Ireland Civil Rights Association (NICRA), emerged to campaign for equal rights. By all accounts, the IRA, the organization that had represented militant republicanism until the failed 1950s campaign, did not exist in any meaningful form at this point. Tellingly, the emergency Public Order Act, which was first put in place to restrict Catholic political activity, and the Flags and Emblems legislation which forbad the flying of the Irish national flag, were still in place. The insistence by extremist Protestant leader Ian Paisley on 28 September 1964 that the RUC should remove a tricolour, and the resulting sectarian riots, signalled that something had changed in Ulster society and that economic contraction was being matched by political destabilization. Between February and April 1966 the Unionist Ulster Volunteer Force (UVF) bombed Catholic shops, schools and houses, and in June of that year murdered two Catholics and one Protestant woman, Matilda Gould (whom they thought was a Catholic), in what were to become the first offensive acts of the modern Irish 'Troubles' (McKittrick et al. 1999: 25–9). The economy was to be relegated as a secondary issue for almost 30 years, as the north descended into virtual civil war.

INTO THE EUROPEAN ECONOMIC COMMUNITY

By the late 1950s the economic and political relationships between the Dublin and Belfast administrations had reached a low point. The position of the south on the issue of the unification of the island and an uncompromising sectarianism within unionism meant contact between the two states was a sensitive issue. Events in the north, such as the re-emergence of Unionist violence against Catholics, an assertive and uncompromising Protestant lobby and a Unionist Party that was caught between liberalizing and traditional Orange positions, were juxtaposed to the developing anti-partition rhetoric of the southern political establishment and the re-emergence of militant republicanism. In April 1964 Lemass reasserted his republican credentials in a widely reported statement on Irish unity which was picked up angrily in Unionist circles. After meeting with Alec Douglas-Home and Harold Wilson in London, Lemass stated that:

> I do not believe that there now exists in Britain either amongst its political leaders or the mass of its people any desire to maintain partition or any belief that it serves British interests .... I am sure there would be a general and sincere welcome for any move to bring [it] to an end by agreement amongst Irishmen .... I believe it is only a matter of time. (*Newsletter*, 14 April 1964)

Behind the scenes, however, and with specific relevance to the island's economic development, the two premiers from the north and south were in dialogue over business links and foreign investment. This dialogue led to the first meeting of the political leaders of republicanism and unionism since 1925, when Lemass arrived at Stormont in January 1965.

The divergence between the north and south meant that both regions had taken on differing and often competing economic paths. The problems of peripherality, a dislocation from larger markets and the legacy of political division had left the island economy constantly attempting to catch up with other regions of Europe and with the British economy. One peculiar and ongoing aspect of northern economic life, however, enabled the outward appearance of sustainability, and that was the inter-regional financial transfers between London and Belfast. By the mid-1960s this had reached an annual total of £126 million, without which the economy of the north would not be viable (FitzGerald 1972: 54–7, 180–7). The products of this transfer were that the old industries continued to be propped up, the public sector was expanded, and northern social services were to become the envy of the population of the south. The starkness of the difference was conveyed by F. S. L. Lyons, in *Ireland Since the Famine*, with reference to education and social security:

> Northern Ireland, with a population less than half of that of the Republic, had 95,000 children in secondary school in 1964 compared with 85,000 in the south, while expenditure on university education in 1963 was 17 shillings (85p) per head in the Republic and 48/9d (£2.44) in the six counties ... unemployment benefit [1969] for a single man was £3.25 per week in the Republic as against £4.50 in Northern Ireland. An unemployed man with two children drew £7.42½ per week in the south compared with £9.20 in the north. (Lyons 1963: 741–2)

The provision of health care and housing presented an island of two halves, with the south lacking many services that – because of the investment from London – were taken for granted in the north by the 1960s. Before a reversal of fortunes was to take place between the north and south, the measure of the difficulties faced by the politicians in the south was this statistic – the lowest point in the history of the state with regard to emigration was in 1961 when the population had declined to only 2.8 million.

The situation of the south in relation to the expansive alternative markets of the continent was given a boost when Lemass reduced tariffs by 20 per cent (in January 1964) and signed (in December 1965) the Anglo-Irish Free Trade Area Agreement (AIFTAA), operational from mid-1966. This permitted increased access to the British market, particularly for agricultural goods, but also encouraged the export of industrial produce from Ireland. The Irish side was adamant that they should be treated as equals in the negotiations around trade, but were disadvantaged through being grossly underendowed as a trading partner. That meant that Ireland needed access to the UK market more than the United Kingdom needed access to Ireland's. The detail of the Agreement provided for a more integrated sector-specific engagement between agriculture and industry across the Irish Sea, but it also revealed the determination of the Irish Government under Lemass to adjust to stimulate export growth and target areas that could actively participate in the new technologically driven economies of the European Community. When Lemass resigned in November 1966, he left a legacy of transformation and a vision that the future of the south should reside in a European common market.

By February 1968 the government in the south was engaged in an advanced support mechanism for the development of industries suited for entering new markets on the continent. The Committee on Industrial Organization was designing grants, loans and modernization schemes to look at product locating and marketing, and manufactured exports were registering a phenomenal rate of growth through this period. By the time the south was to enter the EEC in 1973 the growth rate of this section of the economy was averaging 23 per cent per annum (Kennedy et al. 1988: 68). Another aspect of the advanced growth economy was also starting to take shape in the south. What had become noticeable was the way in which foreign firms were able to access the continental market by relying on foreign direct investment (FDI).

Agricultural output assisted in the increased buoyancy of Irish produce internationally, showing year-in year-out growth rates and reflecting both returns on the Anglo-Irish Agreement and the strategic repositioning of the economy. Towards the close of the 1960s this was backed up with favourable market conditions for farmers, who in turn were able to invest in farming equipment. The 'agricultural price index' doubled and prices of livestock went up by two and a quarter times in the six years up to EEC membership. The readjustment of the economy of the south had, through its redesign, permitted a balance between agricultural and manufacturing industries, giving the export side the diversification needed and the markets for expansion.

In 1966 the National Industrial and Economic Council (NIEC) anticipated the possibilities of full employment for the first time in the south. What was notable about the changes to the Irish economy in the 1960s was the rapid nature of growth; it was quicker than at any stage since the formation of the state. Living standards rose by 50 per cent between the years 1961 and 1971 – the population of the region rose by over 100,000 to the highest level since 1921 (Walsh 1979: 34). Adjusting towards a Jean Monnet-type 'social market' model of economic development seemed to be paying dividends for the south, by balancing investment and job creation with strategies to enhance the general standard of living.

The Department of Finance was given the task of reviewing the government's economic programme and its objectives, and in this certain discrepancies could be seen in the management of the strategy. Perhaps the most noticeable difficulty faced by the Department was a disconnection between the stated aspirations and the outcomes. This could be read as political aptitude taking precedence over economic reality, and an erratic engagement by politicians with the economic strategies. The Second Programme for Economic Expansion was closed in 1967 and the Third Programme, which was supposed to run from 1969–72, was abandoned without any debate or comment by the government.

The only significant and long-term intervention in strategic planning for the economy in the south came with the Buchanan report of 1968, *Regional Studies in Ireland*, which proposed that there should be investment in growth areas, and that: '75 per cent of new industrial employment over a twenty-year period should be concentrated into a limited number of urban areas' (Bradley 1993: 59). This would entail development strategies and investment being concentrated in growth centres such as Cork, Limerick and – of course – Dublin among others. This generated heated debate and was resisted largely by those Teachtaí Dala (members of the Dáil, TDs) representing areas outside the proposed centres. Aspects of the Buchanan initiative could be seen to take effect, but by and large it was stifled by political contingency. It did however lead to the establishment of the regional development organizations (RDOs) which brought nine regions into a regional planning and investment structure. The report also led to the Industrial Development Authority being given formal statutory obligations in the regions and to the 1973–77 regional industrial plans.

Together with the attempts to join the EEC, quantifiable evidence suggests that there was potential through further adaptation, but that the growth patterns of the mid-1960s were vulnerable to external influences and a reliance on taxation. Upwards of half the investment coming through to the economy came directly from the government, with substantial additional investment emanating from companies that had their origins in other countries. Thus it left the Republic susceptible to fluctuations in the global market and systemic shocks that might occur elsewhere but would invariably impact onto the southern economy in general. It was a pattern of development that was to leave the fortunes of the south under the continual pull of external economic forces. After the 1969 Hague summit on the enlargement of the EEC, the Irish government again decided that integration was the only option to stabilize the Irish economy going into an uncertain period. The deliberations of this period were laid out in the April 1970 White Paper, *Membership of the European Communities: Implications for Ireland*. This document flagged up the fact that changes to the legal, political and economic system of the Republic could be so pervasive that a referendum would be necessary to complete the process of Irish integration into the EEC. Central to the objective was to generate the support needed to realign towards the continent, and this was articulated very strongly throughout the White Paper. It was made quite clear that the south would become a 'net beneficiary' of the EEC budget and, given the need for capital investment in the economy, this could act as a catalyst for further growth:

> because of its small scale, the domestic market does not in itself afford a sufficient basis for the expansion of the economy at a pace and to an extent that will enable the country to achieve its principal economic objectives, namely full employment, the cessation of involuntary emigration and a standard of living comparable with that of other Western European countries. (Government of the Irish Republic 1970: 106)

Negotiations on membership of the EEC ran until 18 January 1972 and worked extensively to position key aspects of the Irish economy, such as agriculture and the Anglo-Irish relationship, at the heart of the pitch. The outcome of the negotiations was a series of adjustment agreements where, over a five-year period, the south would be permitted to work outside the remit of the Treaty of Rome in regard to certain manufacturing industries and the uncompetitive granting of financial support, and allowed for safeguards on a number of agricultural concerns. The full terms of accession for the Republic to join the EEC were specified in *The Accession of Ireland to the European Communities* and with this document as a government proposal there began a referendum debate (Government of the Irish Republic 1972). The government's case was straightforward in that it saw no option for the Irish economy except to join. The *Irish Times* on 24 January 1972 presented the dilemma that the Irish were faced with going into the vote, that an Irish economy outside the Community would continue to be supine to a dominant British economy. The reality of the situation was that Ireland needed to be part of the greater continental market.

> Inside the Common Market, it is true, the whole nature of nationality will be revised. The rules of the EEC lay down a framework for economic development. These may be good or bad for Ireland in particular instances, but as they come into effect, they will remove one real disadvantage under which we labour: the unpredictable influences which govern our economy now, which would be bound to persist, because they are international. There is no panacea in strict internal control, or a declaration of total economic independence. (*Irish Times*, 24 January 1972: 11)

The result of the referendum on 10 May 1972 was that 71 per cent of the eligible voting population went to the polls and 83 per cent approved of joining the collection of treaties that made up the EEC, the European Economic Community, the European Atomic Energy Community and the European Coal and Steel Community. Ultimately, the weight of support for the south's participation in the Community came down to the strength of Fianna Fáil and Fine Gael, and their pro-Community stance. This political leadership was enhanced in the run-up to the poll by farmers' organizations and a number of diverse non-governmental organizations who felt that integration within the European project would help liberalize Irish society. The opposing camp was led by the Irish Congress of Trade Unions and the Labour Party, which cautioned about the loss of Irish economic sovereignty and job losses. Also influencing support for the European option for economic development were issues such as the volatile northern situation and the belief that interdependence with other states could assist in stabilizing the island as a whole. From the outset there was a notable sense of relief at being included in the European integration process, as reflected in the first five-year plan of the Industrial Development Authority (IDA), which highlighted foreign investment and an export drive as means of fully exploring the European market.

On entering the EEC the economy of the island was hit by a series of shocks that brought the two respective economies, north and south, to a point of isolation that had been unforeseen. The conflict in the north had escalated beyond Stormont's control and led to a breakdown in economic activity unseen since the war of independence. At the start of a decade of alternating governments in the south, Fine Gael and the Labour Party formed a new coalition administration in the face of unprecedented external pressures. Economic activity had all but ground to a halt in the north at this stage and the society was bracing itself for mass emigration and the possibility of all-out civil war between the two communities. As the border economy collapsed, the flood of northerners to the south was putting strains on housing and social services. This was compli- cated by the global oil crisis of 1973, which increased production costs and domestic costs, debilitated transport and caused inflation to rise sharply. The cost of fuel imports rose continually after this year for almost ten years and forced the governments, north and south, to look to the importation of coal from the north of England as a way of offsetting the demand. The impact of this was that demand for Irish produce went down due to inflation and there was a corresponding rise in unemployment. In response to the crisis the government of the south entered into a policy cycle that would come to be the standard method in the south for managing the balance of payments. This revolved around government borrowing.

By 1975 the budget deficit for the south as a percentage of the GNP was 6.9 per cent, up from 0.4 per cent on entering the EEC. In order to discipline the budget deficit the government resorted to a functional method of balancing the economy by seeking to reduce the amount of borrowing required through cuts to public spending. The budget deficit 'as a proportion of GNP was reduced from 6.9 per cent in 1975 to 4.4 per cent in 1976 and 3.8 per cent in 1977; while the Exchequer borrowing requirement fell from 16 per cent in 1975 to 11.1 per cent in 1976 and 10 per cent in 1977' (Kennedy et al. 1988: 76–7). The impact of the global recession refined the Irish engagement with the EEC and changed the attitude to borrowing which had been historically resisted by Irish governments. It took a period of three to four years before the borrowing rate stabilized. Only by the time of election of the Fianna Fáil administration in June 1977 was the south in a position to reduce borrowing and to invest in public services again. As the economy opened up, demand increased together with employment and within the context of a 'deepening' and 'widening' EEC, there arose optimism and the confidence to raise income tax to 25 per cent (in mid 1979).

During the 1977–87 period there were signs of recovery, with expansionary fiscal policies contributing to a growth rate that was comparable with the body of EEC member states. The adoption of a more conventional mixed economy led to a noticeable improvement in public sector provision and assets, while consumer confidence continued to rise with the expansion of the economic base. The increase in the cost of goods and tax hikes was to an extent offset by a greater provision of services but, significantly, the impact on disposable income led to a situation where unemployment remained a stubborn feature of this adapting economy. Emigration continued at an estimated 10,000 per year due to the decrease in the real GNP income per capita. This was compounded by a doubling of the number of unemployed over the course of the 1970s in the south and a process of shedding staff in the public sector and construction industry that was to continue well into the 1980s. This mix led to a profile of the south of Ireland within the EEC as a region with perennially high levels of unemployment and endemic emigration. Decline seemed to be cyclical, periodically expected, unstable and more often than not extreme.

> It is immediately clear just how great were the fluctuations in the terms of trade. Four periods of substantial decline in terms of trade stand out: 1931–5, 1939–42, 1954–7 and 1973–81. The extent of the decline experienced during these periods was 26 per cent, 19 per cent, 13 per cent and 25 per cent respectively. In all four periods the impact was severe, but it was particularly so in the period 1973–1981, given that by 1981 merchandise exports amounted to 44 per cent of GNP at market prices. (Kennedy et al. 1988: 182)

THE CONFLICT ECONOMY IN THE NORTH

The north in the late 1960s was a melting-pot of political and social upheaval. The collapse of the linen and shipbuilding industries, coupled with an inability of the Stormont government to shift the economy towards an alternative economic base, meant that sectarian tensions and political dysfunction were aggravated by economic contraction and the unemployment that it brought with it. Poverty remained high, incomes were significantly lower than the UK average and consumption per head by 1970 was three-quarters of the average consumption in the United Kingdom (Rowthorn and Wayne 1988: 73). While through the 1960s there had been improvement in employment opportunities in new growth industries such as mechanical engineering and electronics, the overall labour force was still less than it was immediately after the war. Furthermore, the sectarian make-up of the economy came to light when statistics exposing the extent of systemic discrimination against the Catholic population in the north were released in the 1971 census.

> According to the 1971 Census of Population, the overall (male and female) rate of unemployment for Catholics was 14 per cent compared with 6 per cent for Protestants. There were two key reasons for this ... discrimination by employers in their recruitment and training practices was a major problem which Catholics faced. The other main obstacle was the very location of industry itself. (Rowthorn and Wayne 1988: 74)

Since the war, companies locating in the north had been tacitly directed toward predominantly Unionist areas. Where Catholics were residing in large numbers there was also a concentration of the unemployed and a lack of investment. Belfast for example, which in 1971 had a significant Unionist Protestant majority, had an average unemployment rate of 12.1 per cent. Belfast Catholics, who were mostly resident in and around the Falls area of the city, in this same year and in this ward suffered an unemployment rate of 23.8 per cent. Investment was not only siphoned into the Unionist areas, but was also restricted from going into 'Catholic' areas. The whole economy of the north was fragmenting as the intensification of the conflict came to dominate life in the region. With the 'Troubles' frustrating economic growth, the population became increasingly dependent on subsidies or conflict-linked employment. From 1966 until 1978 the extent of Treasury support went up from £245 to £480 per capita. While the political structures were in a state of turmoil, the society went into meltdown and the economy had to be artificially supported (Rowthorn 1981: 23). Furthermore, this UK financial commitment cloaked a historical lack of interest in the province by successive Westminster administrations, with only one visit to the north by a UK minister (home secretary Frank Soskice) between 1964 and the outbreak of widespread violence in August 1969.

The civil rights movement that had arisen to lobby for equality of treatment for the Catholic population in the north represented a breaking point for that community and, inspired by the African-American rights organizations in the United States, presented the Unionist establishment with demands for wholesale reform of the state of Northern Ireland. The decision to mobilize the nationalist population through a series of popular demonstrations from late 1968 onward brought the focus of reform onto a more confrontational plain. It also signalled the emergence of a rights-focused nationalist community in direct opposition to the state and the almost exclusively Protestant and completely Unionist security forces. The Northern Ireland Civil Rights Association (NICRA) was founded in January 1967 and very quickly became the nemesis of the O'Neill regime. Its central demand was for 'one man one vote', the reform of an electoral system in local government that had been systematically engineered to discriminate against the Catholic population. By the time O'Neill resigned in April 1969, not only was the political form of the northern state being questioned regionally and internationally, but northern society was on the verge of sectarian disintegration. O'Neill resigned less than one week after his party narrowly agreed to permit an equal voting system for local government. He was replaced by James Chichester Clark – another pillar of the modernizing wing of the Unionist Party. In the tinderbox of Northern Ireland at this period economic interests were negated under a breakdown that was to engulf the north for a generation, only avoiding all-out civil war between the two communities through the work of the trade unions, community groups, education and health sectors that collectively held onto the fabric of normality. It is interesting that at this period the representatives of the nationalist community and the NICRA were calling for the British government to intervene directly in the crisis, for constitutional reform in Northern Ireland, and for the Special Powers and Public Order acts to be suspended.

It was only after the formation of the provisional republican movement in December 1969 that the idea of British government withdrawal was revisited. Their 'national liberation strategy' was to make the north ungovernable and was clandestinely bankrolled to the tune of an estimated £100,000 by the Fianna Fáil government in Dublin (English 2003: 119). The Labour government of Wilson had been increasingly vexed by the mounting violence in the north and introduced the option of direct rule from London. On 22 August 1969 the *Irish Times*, on the verge of some of the most violent clashes between the unionist and nationalist communities, outlined the scenario that would result after the return to direct British government control over the north. It highlighted the impact of such integration on the divergence of economies and living standards between the populations north and south:

> a decade of direct rule by Westminster might change the North so much that, ideologically the Nationalist portion of the population might drop out of the tradition of Irish nationalism .... If Westminster were to use the North as an example of a new federal system of government, money, ideas and energy would be poured in such an extent, the standard of living for everyone could rise so high that the rest of Ireland would be left behind. (*Irish Times*, 22 August 1969; Bew and Patterson 1985: 21–2)

The intensity of the sectarian violence in the north, followed by calls from the Irish government to have some form of British government intervention to manage the crisis, brought British troops onto Irish streets in a security role for the first time since the 1920s. The visit of James Callaghan to nationalist areas in October 1969 – representing the British government – carried with it economic incentives and the logic that sectarian violence was linked to economic disintegration. His proposal of a 'new deal' entailed £2 million worth of job creation initiatives, a 5 per cent increase in investment grants directed towards companies that would consider establishing in the north, housing reform and fair employment legislation. After this intervention there was a period of calm as the NICRA requests were being processed. It was however a short period of relative stability as the north spiralled into an inter-communal contest of blood-letting. In reaction, the south recoiled in the fear that it would get entangled in an all-island conflict. The lack of governance and resort to violence had horrendous consequences – as catalogued in the written monument to the casualties of the conflict, *Lost Lives*: between John Patrick Scullion's murder off the Falls Road on 11 June 1966 and Charles Bennett's murder, again, off the Falls Road on 29 July 1999, a total of 3637 people were killed. Various estimates of non-fatal casualties put that figure at as much as ten times the number killed. In some areas the casualty rate was as high a one in twelve of the population (McKittrick et al. 1999: 25, 1472).

As the severity of the conflict in the north developed with daily bombings and gun battles being fought out in numerous towns throughout Ulster, the economy of the region came to rely on the Treasury's subvention. Dependence on London by the north rose from £87 million to £1280 million by 1983. As Kieran Kennedy and his colleagues pointed out in *The Economic Development of Ireland in the Twentieth Century*, one result of the conflict was that there was a loss of around 20,000 manufacturing jobs between 1971 and 1981 (Kennedy et al. 1988: 98–9, 103). The embedded nature of the state apparatus and the inability to manage the economy during such a protracted conflict meant that through the core years of conflict there was an obvious transfer of interests from the traditional manufacturing industries to public sector employment, often conflict related:

> Since 1974 there has been a continuous and rapid decline in manufacturing employment from 172,000 to 105,000 in 1986. The decline in manufacturing was offset by a massive rise in services employment, which increased by two-thirds from 1958–1980. Most of this was in the public sector and depended heavily on the extension to Northern Ireland of the British welfare state. (Kennedy et al. 1988: 98)

The impact of such a catastrophic collapse in the manufacturing industries across the north, coupled with the corresponding need for public services to deal with the extent of social disintegration, meant that the north, with almost double the average unemployment rates of the various other regions of the United Kingdom (at 21 per cent in 1985), had evolved complications that were unique in the European context at that time. Only the former Yugoslavia was to present the European Union with a similar dilemma in its war of the 1990s. With the level of emigration rising steadily in the north, for a period in the 1970s and into the 1980s there was a reversal in the patterns of unemployment on the island when the north's levels went up at a period of relative decline in the south. While the south was able to attract increasing levels of external investment through the 1970s and diversify its target markets, the north bunkered down to try to stabilize its economic base in the middle of a war-like environment. The north's economy in the 1980s was to be shaped by the inability of the government to provide answers to seemingly intractable political issues. The companies that had set up in the 1950s and 1960s – Goodyear, ICI, Courtaulds, Enkalon, Dupont, Monsanto, Baird, Molins, ITT and Hoechst – were vulnerable to the extremes of the campaigns of both republicans (now marshalled under the largest group, the Provisional Irish Republican Army) and loyalists (under a number of banners, the largest being the Ulster

Defence Association and the Ulster Volunteer Force). The government's 'protection' of industry meant pound-for-pound matched funding on investment, where it could be found. The examples are striking: Dupont got £13 million, Courtaulds £13 million, and Hoechst £110 million to locate to the relative safety of Limavady. Apart from the 250 'new' firms that received government funding, there was additional support going to established firms, with the shipyards alone receiving £70 million with more on the way (Bew et al. 1996: 172–3).

In the chaos that ensued through the 1970s, the darkest moments coming with Bloody Friday, Bloody Sunday, the Abercorn and McGurk's bombs, the Ballymurphy massacre, the Monaghan and Dublin bombings, internment without trial, the Ulster workers' stoppage, Operation Motorman and the rapid militarization of the whole north of the island – with over 21,000 British troops deployed – economic activity in its usual sense seemed to break down. Solutions to the crisis were elusive and included the suggestion by the UK government of the Republic rejoining the British Commonwealth, and the Fianna Fáil and Fine Gael leadership retorting with the mantra of a united Ireland. One comment from Dublin, cited in the *Economist* in 1972, particularly incensed Unionist politicians:

> Ministers have made little secret of their belief that the most satisfactory solution in the end would be if a political solution were created over the years in which the Protestant majority in the north could come to recognize a future for itself in a united Ireland. (*Economist*, 12 January 1972)

The depth of the crisis became evident in 1973 when violence across the island was at its zenith. On 28 March 1973, under the terms of the Northern Ireland (Temporary Provisions) Act 1972, direct rule from Westminster was introduced, ending 52 years of one party Unionist rule in the north. Parliament was suspended on 30 March 1973, and abolished under the Northern Ireland Constitution Act of 1973. Devolved government was not to be returned for another 29 years. With the effects of such a dislocation of power, social disintegration and widespread violence, the economy went into abeyance.

> The volume of manufacturing investment fell by 9 per cent per annum between 1973 and 1978, while output dropped by 11 per cent in the two years 1973–5 and was stagnant thereafter up to 1979. In the wake of the second oil shock in 1979, the volume

of output fell by a further 16 per cent to the trough in the fourth quarter of 1982. (Kennedy et al. 1988: 109)

In 1970 the government in the north had allocated £2 million to new initiatives, and in 1972, with the realization that small business start-ups would be the only realistic way of encouraging growth, the Local Enterprise Development Unit (LEDU) was created. What marked the period was the lack of investment in the region, the inability of the established private sector to secure contracts that would allow for independence from government support, and the volatile state of the economy vis-à-vis the conflict. In the 1970s the impact of global competition had also caught up with the stalwarts of Ulster industry, as Japanese shipyards were emerging as world leaders, synthetic fibre was replacing natural fibre for clothing, and other, smaller manufacturing concerns – such as shirt-making – were shifting production to the Far East.

The early 1980s carried the whole island to a new low in terms of the effect of the conflict on Irish society. The political machinations around the republican hunger strikes of 1980 and 1981, together with the spiralling of inter-communal violence, brought the island – again – to a state of virtual civil war. The death of the republican Member of Parliament for Fermanagh and South Tyrone, Bobby Sands, and of his fellow hunger strikers in the H-Blocks of Long Kesh/Maze prison, saw an increase in violence across the province, registering another marker in the long war on the island – and became the catalyst for renewed politicization by the republican community. Within the intensity of this period a new generation of economically aware and community-based activists began to discuss the possibilities of a post-conflict scenario, a scenario which would eventually lead to the ceasefires of the early 1990s.

Three governmental interventions that emerged in the intervening period give a sobering review of the way in which the regional economy had adapted or contorted to the adverse circumstances. The first attempt to stabilize the north was the establishment of the Northern Ireland Assembly in 1982. With little regional support and having no effect on the levels of conflict, it collapsed by 1986. The second initiative was the New Ireland Forum which, between 1983 and 1984, brought the Irish government into a position where it could engage with the full complexities of the conflict. The Forum was established by Fine Gael taoiseach Garret FitzGerald in the face of resistance from both the Unionist parties, republicans and eventually the British prime minister Margaret Thatcher, who cynically recited her 'out, out, out' answer to its recommendations (press conference, Downing Street, 19 November 1984).

The New Ireland Forum's debates and reports surveyed the north's economy in stark light, with recognition that the conflict had created problems that had shaped a peculiar type of economic formation more pertinent to an unstable, even developing, country. *The Cost of Violence Arising from the Northern Ireland Crisis Since 1969* (New Ireland Forum 1983) and *The Macroeconomic Consequences of Integrated Economic Policy, Planning and Co-ordination in Ireland* (New Ireland Forum 1984) supplied evidence of how the unresolved cycle of violence was debilitating economic activity on the island as a whole. The conflict in 1982 alone had cost the north 23 per cent of its gross domestic product and the south 3 per cent. While not accounting for the social and community impact of the conflict, its cumulative effects were obviously devastating for the long-term development of economic relations and growth on the island as a whole. 'The estimated impact of the violence on manufacturing employment was very severe, involving a loss of 40,000 jobs from 1971 to 1983, or nearly a quarter of total manufacturing employment' (Kennedy et al. 1988: 112). As a consequence, the opening up of employment opportunities in the security sectors had led to an estimated 24,000 additional jobs, but skewed public sector spending and employment towards the conflict economy. What had emerged was dependence on conflict for economic stability – something that seemed to be lost on the politicians of the day. In comparative terms it also meant that, while the GDP per capita in the north was 70 per cent of that of the population in Britain, government expenditure per capita was in fact 125 per cent. Economically the north could not survive without the subvention, and this seemed set to increase as the violence increased (Canning et al. 1987: 23). Rowthorn and Wayne were to comment on the state of the northern Irish economy in the mid-1980s:

A large part of its population is unemployed. Those who are not are chiefly engaged in servicing or controlling each other, through the provision of health, education, retail distribution, construction, security and social services .... Like a typical workhouse, it is supported by taxes levied on the external community, while providing very little in return. If forced to live within its means, Northern Ireland would experience a catastrophic fall in living standards. (Rowthorn and Wayne 1988: 98–99)

The decrease in investment in the region was particularly damaging, and gave an indication of the impact of the conflict for business interests and jobs in the north. Paul Teague, in *The Economy of Northern Ireland*, catalogued the economic reality of the north:

> in 1990 there were 207 plants in Northern Ireland which were externally owned, a decrease of 144 or 41 per cent since 1973 ... the 207 externally-owned plants in Northern Ireland in 1990 employed just over 41,000 people. This represents a fall of almost 600 since 1986, but a huge fall of over 46,000 or 53 per cent since 1973. (Teague 1993: 196–7)

The third major intervention by both governments in trying to stabilize the region during this period was the Anglo-Irish Agreement of 15 November 1985. Born out of deliberations by the Anglo-Irish Inter-governmental Conference, this initiative sought to create the framework for an agreed agenda for peaceful transition towards consensus governance. Its ultimate objective was power sharing between the two political blocs in the north, Unionist and Irish nationalist. It also entailed an economic subtext which included 'the promotion of cross-border co-operation', putting in place a structure which would expand into the 1990s to define a distinct policy regarding the border economy and development therein. Power sharing, with the involvement of the Irish government under Fine Gael, however, would be a step too far for the Unionist hegemony and led to some of the bitterest confrontations between the British government and the Unionist community since the formation of the state. The Ulster Unionist Party, at this point under the leadership of James Molyneaux, and Ian Paisley's Democratic Unionist Party, organized street demonstrations against the agreement, culminating in a mass rally at Belfast City Hall on 23 November where the *Sunday Times* reckoned 100,000 attended. That was one in ten of the Unionist population. It ended in a night of widespread and bitter street violence. Molyneaux talked of 'hypocrisy', 'treachery' and 'fury', while Paisley railed against Thatcher in particular as a 'Jezebel' who had sought to 'destroy Israel', and against the Dublin government for being 'bedfellows' of the IRA. Republicans in turn rejected the agreement for legitimizing partition, and their war continued (Owen 1994: 41; Aughey 1989: 86). The agreement was, however, to be a precursor to the Downing Street Declaration of 1993 and the Belfast, or 'Good Friday', Agreement of 1998 which facilitated ceasefires from all the main protagonist organizations in the conflict.

THE BLEAK 1980S

In his first major speech on the Irish economy as taoiseach, Charles Haughey (in one of his three terms in power: 1979–81, 1982, 1987–92) summed up the state of the economy of the south in the year after the global recession of 1979. The terms of reference reflect the topicality of monetarism at the time, giving an ideological impulse to some of the policies that were subsequently to emerge under Haughey's guidance:

> As a community we are living away beyond our means. I don't mean that everyone in the community is living too well, clearly many are not and have barely enough to get by, but taking us all together we have been living at a rate which is simply not justified by the amount of goods and services we are producing. To make up the difference we have been borrowing enormous amounts of money, borrowing at a rate which just cannot continue ... we will just have to reorganize government spending so that we can only undertake those things we can afford. (*Irish Times*, 10 January 1980)

During the 1970s the levels of economic investment to the south from various sources had increased, and with the link to the European Community providing structural funding there were other moves at the core of the Irish economy that seemed to be encouraging dividends. A focus on international markets and attracting industries that could stimulate growth was cultivated by the government as a means of job creation and a solution to the reliance on small-to-medium indigenous industries producing for the local market. With membership of the European Monetary System (EMS) granted in 1978, the dependence on the Bank of England – which had been there since 1826 – was broken, leading the way for the south to eventually participate in a single European currency. Movement could be seen in certain aspects of the Irish economy, but it came at a cost. In the 1977–80 National Development Programme, there was the stated aim of stimulating growth in certain sectors, while restricting state planning initiatives. It was an adjustment process that was to gain momentum under Haughey.

Between joining the EEC and the mid-1980s, expenditure by the south's government had risen by 25 per cent, with the proportion of people employed on the government's payroll rising to a third of the working population (Breen et al. 1990: 45). The fiscal policies of the period constrained industrial growth, and emigration was again reaching proportions where it was adversely affecting the country as a whole. One enduring response by the southern government was to enhance spending on further and higher education courses which would feed directly into economic development. This included the building of institutes for higher education and regional technical colleges under direction from the Higher Education Authority. While giving school leavers an alternative option initially, the real impact of this intervention would only be seen a decade later when new industries started to rely on these graduates for a steady supply of skilled employees.

Another intervention by the government that changed the landscape for the south was the outworking of the 1979 budget and the restricting of the public sector borrowing requirement to 13 per cent of GDP (down from 17.3 per cent). This brought the national debt to a staggering 81 per cent of GNP (Ó Gráda 1997: 70–1). While the chief architect of the Fianna Fáil strategy, Martin O'Donoghue from Trinity College Dublin, struggled to get a handle on the debt crisis, an alternative from the right was plotting its engagement with fiscal policy. The 'Doheny and Nesbitt's School of Economics' (largely Brendan Walsh, Colm McCarthy and Paul Tansey), founded in a pub by Dublin economists and analysts, introduced an Irish variant of monetarism. Initially criticized, their address to O'Donoghue was in the form of a model of economic development that was to alter the direction of the southern Irish economy.

Another significant change that would lead to the reshaping of the southern economy was in labour relations, where the government was able to introduce a strategy for industrial development which accepted trade union interests under the awkwardly titled 'National Understanding' of 1979. Due to a government and business agreement against the unions this initial attempt at social partnership collapsed twice in 1980–81, and was not visited again until 1987. Partnership only came into full effect after this point with a German model type of social dialogue. Finally, in the late 1980s the National Economic and Social Council (NESC) came to the fore in economic policy, providing a forum for debate on managing the economy out of recession.

In *The Republic of Ireland* Barry Brunt, reflecting on the changes that occurred in the 1980s, noted that this period ignited something different in the formation of the economy. Building on the momentum for innovation, or gambling with economic strategies, became

symptomatic of the period (Brunt 1988: 28–40). Cutting employment across the public sector was perhaps the most visible aspect of
the Fine Gael and Labour coalition administrations in particular, but
this tactic was not exclusive to their governments at the time. This
can be seen from the fact the between 1982 and 1987 expenditure
on social housing alone was reduced by more than 50 per cent;
between 1981 and 1990 the number employed in the civil service was
reduced from 30,800 to 25,000; and as the government attempted to
offload health care into the private sector, spending and employment
in hospitals also declined significantly (Smith 2005: 111).

Four aspects of economic development led to the adjustments that
facilitated the emergence of the Celtic Tiger model of the 1990s
– and something new in the nature of political economy in the
south. First, the Industrial Development Authority (IDA) brought
forward its strategic plan for 1982–92 and altered its conventional
drive for the maximization of employment opportunities towards
investing in technological innovation and computer, pharmaceutical
and chemical industries. Twelve sectors were primed for support, to
highlight and facilitate growth in the service and new technology
sectors. This is where the supply of young skilled workers from the
colleges could revitalize these growth areas of the economy. Second,
the White Paper on *Industrial Policy* in 1984 profiled the form of
indigenous companies that could be targeted for investment and
support, and emphasized those products and services that could
have an international reach. Out of this emerged the Company
Development Scheme and National Linkage Programme, and the
National Development Corporation, both bringing international
attention to Irish innovation.

Third, 1986 saw the most trade-focused piece of legislation from
the European Community since the Treaty of Rome itself, with
the ratification of the Single European Act (SEA). The south had
pinned its corporation tax in 1981 to 10 per cent at the insistence of
Brussels; the SEA in turn brought a pro-business framework forcefully to the fore of EEC policies. Since the beginning of the 1980s
the EEC had been trying to encourage the member states to align
more closely. The Republic of Ireland had been considered one of
the more loyal members and the push from Brussels was expected to
be received favourably in Dublin. At the September 1985–January
1986 Intergovernmental Conference (IGC) in Luxembourg, policy
co-ordination was agreed to the extent of changing the mechanism
for market integration from being on a 'common' footing to a
'single' platform. The unification of the internal market would

mean in practice 'an area without internal frontiers in which the free movement of goods, persons, services and capital is ensured' (Dinan 2010: 81). It would also mean more economic management from the institutions of the EEC towards the policies of the member states.

The fourth intervention was a national plan that carried the rather pessimistic title *Building on Reality*. It attempted to return to a basic comprehension of the nature of the southern economic system. This plan took on board the relative position of the Irish economy both in geographical terms and in relation to the sectors that existed there. The era was marked by the instability of Irish governments and an erratic approach to economic planning, where in one 18-month period it endured three changes of government. The reality of the situation also entailed an acceptance by both main parties that poverty would be an enduring feature of the Irish economy, and consequently funding was directed towards a dedicated poverty alleviation agency, the Combat Poverty Agency (CPA) in 1986 (Brunt 1988: 28–9). The extent of the difficulties faced by the various governments in the south forced the minority Fianna Fáil administration in 1987 to work with what became known as the 'Tallaght strategy'. Articulated by the then opposition Fine Gael leader Alan Dukes, it signalled the beginning of an economic strategy aimed at co-ordinating the major parties' policies: to prioritize tax cuts, rationalize public spending, reduce borrowing and increase investment to open up competitiveness for Irish companies and companies willing to set up in the south. Dukes saw market restructuring and policy compliance as a priority over party interests. Commenting to the Tallaght Chamber of Commerce on 2 September, he stated that:

> When the Government is moving in the right direction, I will not oppose the central thrust of its policy. If it is going in the right direction, I do not believe that it should be deviated from its course, or tripped up on macro-economic issues. (www.finegael.ie)

While the strategy became the starting gun for the Celtic Tiger model of economic development, it also marked the further rationalization and privatization of public services.

Overall, until the 1987 national plan, government resistance to public spending and economic liberalism remained dominant features of policy design in the context of increased borrowing requirements and crises. The framework for subsequent growth, based on policy coherence to enhance foreign direct investment, could be recognized as early as 1986 as the central plank for change, subject only to favourable macroeconomic conditions. In *Showcasing Globalization?* Nicola Smith presented this period of Irish economic history succinctly:

> While the state made ad hoc attempts to reduce public sector pay and occasionally called for reductions in private sector pay, its broad stance was that of non-interventionism. It sought both to distance the unions from policy-making and to uphold the traditions and institutions of free collective bargaining. While various 'rounds' of pay increases occurred during this period, this was quite different from the previous system due to the growing disparities between wage levels and termination dates .... If the 1980s can be characterized as a period of transition, it was in 1987 that a radical change in approach occurred. (Smith 2005: 112–13; also see Kirby 2002: 42)

6 THE PEACE DIVIDEND (1988–2001)

Economic development in Ireland has been unique in the European Community because of its peripheral location, the conflict and the uneven development process that had separated the north from the south. The constitutional arrangements that had consolidated partition had evolved in a way that, by default, systematically under-developed the counties closest to the border. This was reflected in the way in which the respective local economies failed to connect throughout the concurrent policy shifts of the Stormont/London and Dublin governments. Geographically the counties contiguous to the border cover about a third of the island of Ireland, but economi-cally they were a microcosm of the problems faced by the island as a whole. To complicate this further the disparate policy initia-tives aimed at border county development had been inadvertently influenced by the ebbs and flows of the conflict:

> Every way one turns in the North, politics and economics are inter-twined. Thus, in order to explore the full range of possible economic implications of a permanent peace, it is necessary to examine a variety of North–South economic policy configurations. (Bradley 1993: 70)

(For a comprehensive list of documentation on the Irish border, visit www.borderireland.com.)

As a consequence, the border in the 1990s came to be portrayed as a key element in rebalancing the island economy as an integrated, peaceful, sustainable entity.

In the late 1980s, stalemate in the conflict between republicans, the British government, unionists and loyalists necessitated a change of political direction. This led to a protracted peace process and an eventual settlement between all the main protagonist groups, concluding with agreed inclusive government structures representing north–south and east–west interests. Informal talks between the constitutional nationalists and militant republicans, led respectively by John Hume of the Social Democratic and Labour Party (SDLP) and Gerry Adams, the president of Sinn Féin, began in January 1988.

Parallel to this process, on 14 October of that year the other main parties (Alliance Party, Democratic Unionist Party, SDLP and Ulster Unionist Party) began talks in Duisburg, West Germany, on possible post-conflict political arrangements. These bilateral talks, encouraged and financed by the British and Irish governments, facilitated a breakthrough on 9 November 1990 when the British secretary of state, Peter Brooke, announced that Britain had no 'strategic or economic interest' in Ireland. This led to negotiations over a lasting peace settlement. However, change in the economy had always been hostage to constitutional change, and only when this could be settled could alternative options for development appear. As James Goodman pointed out in *Single Europe, Single Ireland*:

> In the two parts of Ireland, the 1970s and 1980s saw a marked divergence in patterns of development and dependency. The end of the post-War boom in Western Europe had disrupted the process of economic 'modernization' in the two economies. With intensified conflict against a background of sharp economic recession, the North reverted to deepened deindustrialization and to sharpened dependency on Britain; the South, for its part, sustained a programme of industrialization with a temporary surge in transnational investment, becoming more dependent on non-British product markets and sources of capital. (Goodman 2000: 28)

Up until the 1990s, the spatial division had had a profoundly destabilizing effect on development across the border region. This divergence was manifested through the competitive tensions that existed between border towns and cities – Newry and Dundalk, Letterkenny and Derry, Enniskillen and Monaghan. In this scenario, the conflict, in which the border remained a contended region, had a quantifiable effect on the socio-economic fortunes of the whole northern half of the island. To be sustainable, north–south economic development would have to begin with the integration of the border regions. The problems were systemic, as Douglas Hamilton noted: 'hard economic examination of the current extent of north–south links, the degree of complementarity and divergence between the two economies and the actual opportunities and barriers that exist in realizing greater north–south integration have been largely absent' (2001: 13).

Uneven development between the north and south had become routine by the 1990s, and exposed facets of the border economy that were contributing to local depression and instability. They included the type and extent of investment by government agencies in the key towns adjacent to the border; the history of intervention in the locality and the impact on renewal; the effects of two diverging economic development strategies; the lack of investment in indigenous/traditional industries – particularly manufacturing; the extent of long-term unemployment and the patterns of poverty and community disintegration; the lack of vocational training initiatives; the perennial problem of migration; regional trade deficits; diverging fiscal policies; the effects of having separate currencies; EU regional policy and investment; the role of foreign direct investment; governmental prioritization on high-technology sectors; changing demographics; trade convergence in cross-border partnerships; the effects of the north's subvention on the border areas; differences in corporation tax rates; the role of the public sector in regional economics, with specific reference to targeting social need/combating poverty; a lack of investment in the social economy; and the divergence of agricultural, tourist, hi-technology and manufacturing industries between the two regions (Harvey 2005: 18–19). Collectively, these factors left the border region – covering ten of the 32 counties – impoverished and prone to depression.

Throughout the conflict the border region had been affected in a distinct manner, not only breaking economic links that existed prior to 1969, but also adversely impacting on community relations. Every town and village on the northern side at some stage had businesses destroyed or workers killed, and on the southern side bomb attacks were to become a regular feature of life. The southern towns of Belturbet in County Cavan in December 1972, Dundalk in County Louth in December 1975, and Castleblayney in county Monaghan in March 1976, suffered particularly damaging bomb attacks. Furthermore: 'For most of the conflict, the Irish border was the most militarized area of the European Union and the most militarized part of Europe west of the Berlin wall and the iron curtain' (Harvey 2005: 60). The border had become a symptom of the greater problem of regional conflict.

As the violence intensified the divergence became more entrenched; as the exchanges between combatants got more sophisticated, so too the economy contorted to accommodate the extreme circumstances. Most of the north had become engulfed in the cycle of violence as it again impacted onto the island's development in total. In May 1981, for instance, one bullet or baton round was being fired every seven seconds (Police Service of Northern Ireland (PSNI) figures, www.psni.police.uk, February 2010). Mike Tomlinson's research on the cost of the conflict gives some insight into the conflict economy as it emerged. In *The Northern Ireland Conflict: Legacies and Impacts*, he estimated that between 1968 and 1993 the direct cost of the conflict was in the region of £23.5 billion (€34.5 billion) – borne by the Northern Ireland purse to the extent of 80.5 per cent, the south by 12 per cent (or £2.82 billion; €4 billion) and Great Britain by 7.5 per cent. As if to show the complexity or ridiculousness of the conflict economy, Tomlinson also noted that by 1994 British military intelligence had 40 per cent of its 2235 staff working on the Irish conflict (Tomlinson 1995: 4, 1–22). The statistics on the conflict provided solid evidence of the link between political instability and the all-island economy, and how embedded the conflict actually was within the fabric of that economy. Chris Brazier, in a *New Internationalist* special on the north, placed the Irish conflict into a global context:

> Despite all I've read and viewed over the years about Northern Ireland, I was still profoundly shocked by the extent of the military presence on the streets of Belfast – it was more intrusive than anything I have seen in the Third World, South Africa included. (Brazier, *New Internationalist*, May 1994: 4)

In human terms, from a northern population of 1.7 million, at the time of the ceasefires, over '25 years of violence in northern Ireland, a total of 3163 people have died .... Another 36,603 have been injured, many maimed for life' (*Irish News*, 8 August 1994). John Reid, a former British secretary of state for Northern Ireland, noted that:

> [I]f the equivalent number of deaths had occurred in the rest of the United Kingdom, the total recorded number of deaths in Northern Ireland has to be multiplied by 40. That gives a total of between 120,000 and 140,000 people. If the same number of deaths had occurred in the United States, it would be equivalent to 480,000 people. (quoted in Hillyard et al. 2005: 7)

The latter is roughly the same number of deaths that occurred during the American Civil War. Statistics confirmed the burden that this conflict levied on a war-weary northern population and its society: 88,000 households were affected by conflict-related deaths, 28,000 had been intimidated from work, 350,000 British troops served there, 80,000 had been imprisoned for politically motivated crimes, and hundreds of thousands had engaged as combatants on both the republican and unionist/loyalist sides (Hillyard et al. 2005: 6–8). Peace and economic development were synonymous.

The sectarian composition of the economy also accentuated north–south divisions and in terms of community relations presented an almost intractable situation:

> In 1971, Catholics accounted for twenty-eight per cent of the 'economically active' workforce and forty-five per cent of Northern Ireland's male unemployment; by 1991, thirty-five per cent of the Northern Ireland workforce was Catholic and Catholic males comprised fifty-two per cent of total male unemployment ... the differential between Catholic male unemployment and non-Catholic male unemployment widened from 9.7 per cent to 14.4 per cent, while for Catholic and non-Catholic women the differential widened from 3.1 per cent to 5.7 per cent. (Goodman 2000: 23)

A further complication of this peculiarly Irish problem was highlighted by the *New Internationalist*: 'Northern Ireland is now heavily dependent on direct British subsidy for its employment, with an extraordinarily high proportion of jobs being in security fields like prisons, probation, the police etc. One in ten Protestant men now works in these fields' (May 1994: 19; also see Rowthorn and Wayne 1988: 104–19). The *Belfast Telegraph*, in its 1994 audit of the cost of the conflict, quantified its overall impact on public expenditure: 12,000 British soldiers stationed across the north; 5500 Royal Irish Regiment soldiers; 13,500 members of the Royal Ulster Constabulary; the loss of 77,000 manufacturing jobs through conflict and recession; and ongoing expenditure of £902 million on law and order alone (15 August 1994). The evidence suggested that the economy of the north in total and the southern border region had become not only defined by but also sustained by the conflict.

INTEGRATING THE BORDER AS AN ANSWER

It was not until the mid-1980s that the border region was designated an economic entity in its own right. A 1983 report by the Economic and Social Committee of the European Community first registered the implications of the border for the overall development of the island's economy. It surveyed the difficulties faced by these counties and defined them as 'serious', with a dependence on agriculture, dominated by small farm-holdings, low incomes, high unemployment levels, emigration and a conflict to deal with (Harvey 2005: 18). In this report there was a recognizable attempt to *strategize* the spatial and sectoral opportunities which existed in the region to try to develop an integrated developmental cross-border model. Furthermore, it argued that there existed an opportunity at this point to create converging sectors, a social economy, community development initiatives and investment in policy adaptation – all of which would be relevant to economic renewal within the context of an all-island economy. This Telesis Report complemented the idea of an integrated economy with the recommendation of an 'integrated indigenous Development Charter' based on the premise that: 'successful indigenously owned industry is, in the long run, essential for a high income economy' (NESC 1983: 185). At governmental level the need for the integration of the two economies was formally recognized in the Anglo-Irish Agreement of 15 November 1985. Article ten, the only clause on economic aspects of north–south co-operation, stated:

(a) The two Governments shall co-operate to promote the economic and social development of those areas of both parts of Ireland which have suffered most severely from the consequences of the instability of recent years, and shall consider the possibility of securing international support for this work.

(b) If it should prove impossible to achieve and sustain devolution on a basis which secures widespread acceptance in Northern Ireland, the (intergovernmental) Conference shall be a framework for the promotion of co-operation between the two parts of Ireland concerning cross border aspects of economic, social and cultural matters in relation to which the Secretary of State for Northern Ireland continues to exercise authority.

(c) If responsibility is devolved in respect of certain matters in the economic, social or cultural areas currently within the responsibility of the Secretary of State for Northern Ireland, machinery will need to be established by the responsible authorities in the North and South for practical co-operation in respect of cross-border aspects of these issues. (Government of the Republic of Ireland, Hillsborough, 15 November 1985, no. 1, 9678; HMSO, Treaty Series no. 62, 1985)

From this period onward economic development could be viewed in terms of sectoral networking – where the range of industries, community development organizations and the social economy could be invested in to stimulate enterprise and growth. For the first time border communities came to be recognized as possible hubs for economic renewal. Economic activity in the region was also surveyed in terms of the possibilities for informal and social economies. Indeed, the social economy was mapped in a manner which attempted to enhance its potential within an overall regeneration process and set within the context of EU-sponsored opportunities for local and indigenous businesses. In 1998 the Triskele and Holywell Trust investigated active integrative aspects of the economy on the island and specified a number of areas that were suitable for linkage. This report, entitled *Along the Borderline: A Review of the Impact of Funding on Community Development along the Border Counties*, became one of the few analytic reports on the potential of border integration at the time. The areas that were designated as having the potential to overcome the divisions of the north–south divide were: the Derry–Letterkenny corridor, the Belfast–Dublin corridor where it impacted on the border region, and the rural network running from Forkhill to Strabane. In this report, economic integration of the border region was presented as an agreed solution to political and economic instability.

The Triskele and Holywell plan entailed a review of inter-state policy pre and post-1992 and in the aftermath of the eradication of internal economic borders within the European Union. A first step that was suggested was that consensus on cross-border initiatives should be encouraged, as well as isolating areas of non-cooperation. There was also the ongoing question of administrative compliance and policy coherence in confronting disadvantage and community renewal. At this stage, going into relative peace and a process of Europeanization, there emerged scope for comparative analysis with other regions of the European Union which had trans-border disparities and similar obstacles to integrated and developmental economies (the Basque region, Southern France, Northern Spain, the German border regions, South Tyrol and the Belgian–Dutch border). This intra-EU comparative analysis offered insight into the potential for the immediate to long-term future of economic convergence. The European Union also had the authority to step in to finance such strategies.

Total EU Peace funds (funding dedicated to peace building) allocated between 1995 and 1999 were €503 million. This was distributed in three tranches: €300 million for the period 1995–97 and €100 million in both 1998 and 1999. Northern Ireland accounted for 80 per cent of the allocation with the remainder going to the border counties. Cross-border actions accounted for approximately 15 per cent of approved funds. The Northern Ireland Statistics and Research Agency (NISRA), in its *EU Support Programme for Peace and Reconciliation: Analysis of Community Uptake*, noted that 'By September 1998, about 18,000 applications had been received and more than 7500 projects had received funding, the grants allocated ranging between £100 and £1m.' By June 2001 the European Union reported that almost 13,000 projects had been supported (Haase 1999: 1). While the other EU programmes were primarily intended to promote economic and infrastructural development, with an implicit assumption that there would be positive social outcomes, the Peace Programme was primarily intended to have political and social impact. Increasingly, it had an economic renewal aspect which was intended to stimulate indigenous business and social economic growth within those areas which had been most affected by the conflict – but its primary role was to assist in building sustainable peace on the island.

The EU Special Support Programme for Peace and Reconciliation (SSPPR) was for many organizations the first funding which targeted social inclusion in any meaningful way, providing funding for core staff and investing in significant revenue intensive projects. For example one objective was, as pointed out in the Proteus review document 'Lessons of Peace I', to target areas such as North Belfast and West Belfast which together had seen up to 40 per cent of 'all deaths associated with the Troubles' (Proteus 2000: 5). It also aimed to address the complications of poverty with many conflict-prone areas being 'concentrations of deprivation' (Proteus 2000: 5; also see McCann 2001b: 1–2). For many grassroots organizations working in communities adversely affected by the conflict, the European support was the first sustained attempt at encouraging their services as a facet of regeneration. For them the commitment of the EU member states to underpinning the peace process was a welcome addition to the efforts of the local politicians, British and Irish governments to build a socio-economic infrastructure.

European Commission president Jacques Santer noted on 25 July 1997 that 'Through its actions and in particular the work of the Peace Programme, the European Commission can assure the citizens of Northern Ireland that the European Union will continue to show its solidarity with their hopes for peace and reconciliation' (*Irish News*, 26 July 1997). In April 1998 the then Northern Ireland secretary of state, Mo Mowlam, commented in the European Parliament in response to Santer, on the effects of the peace process as implemented through the Belfast Agreement and the EU programmes:

The agreement reached in Belfast marks an opportunity for a fresh start. It is the foundation on which a new society can be built based on the fundamental principles of fairness, consent and co-operation. It is about co-operation across the community within Northern Ireland, between north and south and between the peoples of the UK and Ireland. There is still a long way to go and many obstacles before us. Support from the international community will continue to play a vital role helping the region's economy adapt to peace. That is why I attach particular priority to the special support for peace and reconciliation. Its aim is to aid sustainable economic and social projects which underpin peace and reconciliation, promoting both cross-community and cross-border development. Its impact in Northern Ireland has been remarkable. (*Irish News*, 28 April 1998)

The 1990s brought community development into economic policy for the first time, and from this a recalibration and better understanding of the economy in general emerged. Community development organizations across the north and the border counties had been working to locate the weaknesses of the regional economy and obstacles to growth by monitoring the impact of policies on microeconomies and local communities, avoiding the usual governmental method of registering development by listing business activity. Their work revealed persistent poverty, the limited capacity of businesses in the region, the extent of cross-border market development, rural deprivation, the sustainable development of small-to-medium sized enterprises and social economy initiatives, restricted investment to indigenous firms, contradicting governmental policies towards investment, relative and fluctuating investment, the problems for new industries setting up in rural environments, and the important influence of the areas in question in relation to the demands of an island economy. All these questions loomed large.

A further formative element of the debate around regeneration and the possibilities of the post-conflict society in Ireland came with the emergence of a women's lobby, largely out of this community development sector. In 1990 Mary Robinson had been elected president of Ireland, bringing a woman to the fore of Irish politics. It was the first time in any significant way across the country that a definitive gender focus had been brought to economic and political development (Rooney 1995: 51–56). The culmination of gender politics at this period was the formation of the Women's Coalition (founded by Monica McWilliams and Pearl Sagar in 1996), which went on to have full participation in the peace process, fight successive elections and, importantly, highlight the role of women in Irish society. It was a precedent that was to lead to women having a more assertive role in politics across the island, with Mary McAleese succeeding Robinson as president in 1997 (and again in 2004), Inez McCormack becoming the first woman president of the Irish Congress of Trade Unions in 1999, and Sinn Féin's Bairbre de Brún gaining the highest number of votes in the north's European elections of 14 May 2009 and becoming the first female Member of the European Parliament to represent the north.

REGIONALIZATION AS DEVELOPMENT

With the Maastricht Treaty of 1992 being assimilated into regional legislation, the process of European integration brought a settling atmosphere into economic and political life across the region. The EU influence was operating on a number of levels, acting as a major source of funding for a wide range of cross-border and cross-community economic projects. The border counties had been typical areas of economic disadvantage and had been the beneficiaries of significant funding from the European Union for many years, principally through the mainstream structural funds and the Common Agricultural Policy, targeting regional development, social inclusion and agriculture. In theory the 'Objective 1' support should have been a catalyst for the progressive convergence of the policies and economies north and south. Much of this funding either had an integrating element – a principle increasingly promoted by the European Union – or had implications for cross-border development, whether intended or not.

The continuing legacy of partition was that, through the process of consolidating the two jurisdictions, the economic infrastructures of the north and south had developed in relative isolation from each other and with little account taken of how development could be best co-ordinated to address specific social and economic needs. Moreover, the border had created areas of internal peripherality, cut off from their natural economic hinterlands. A key issue in this regard had been the lack of priority given, both north and south, to improving links. On both sides of the border, economic networks were largely to do with intra-regional priorities rather than economic harmonization. The impact of this dislocation was evident:

The districts of the northern border corridor are characterized by lower levels of educational attainment, a lower density of public services, under-representation of service industries and an overrepresentation of declining sectors ... violence had a differential impact on the border areas, creating high levels of tension in those areas adjacent to the border, but others living in more distant parts of the border counties 45km away were comparatively unaffected. (Harvey 2005: 25)

From the point that the United Kingdom and Republic of Ireland joined the EEC in 1973, Ireland had been designated as a special region for investment. Structural fund investment increased steadily throughout the 1970s and 1980s to become component parts of the two economies. Prior to the EEC 1988 reform of the structural funds and from 1973 onwards, Northern Ireland alone was in receipt of £870 million, and between 1973 and 1999 a staggering £2547 million was committed to its economy. Between joining the EEC in 1973 and 2003 the south's economy received €17 billion. Apart from the United Kingdom's often-begrudged subvention, as an external influence the European Union's intervention had been unprecedented in Irish economic history. The European Commission, Council and Parliament (EP) had concerns regarding the economic stability of Ireland going back to the earliest days of the discussions on membership, where the problems of the island were discussed as a pan-European issue and not just regional. Indeed, as early as 1981, a EP briefing paper noted that 'the desire for peace is closely linked to living conditions and employment'. In 1983 the Commission called the region 'a blot on the Community', and committed itself to working on the practicalities of investment. Regulation 1739/83, on 21 June 1983 allocated €100 million for an 'integrated operations' programme which would be additional to existing public funding (EC, *Official Journal*, L171 29–26). This laid out the terms of a strategy to assist peace building as well as to encourage economic development. This qualification was attached to most EC funding coming through to Ireland thereafter. The Objective 1 structural funds lasted from the approval by the European Commission decision of 29 July 1994 until its closure on 31 December 2000. The allocation for the north and border region alone was €1233 million, or £956 million. This was matched with €511 million of national public spending to bring the total to €2658 million, or £2060 million. Until the end of structural funding in its most involved sense in the early 2000s, economic development on the island had arguably been underwritten by the European Union.

EU regional policies emphasized border economies and, through a Brussels-based categorization, it became possible to overcome a historical difficulty over a disputed definition of the border region. Its definition included all local authority areas contiguous to the land boundary, but was flexible enough to go beyond this. Indeed, the EU's 1983 INTERREG initiative included the whole of Northern Ireland except Belfast. O'Dowd defined it as all local authority areas contiguous to the land border, plus Down District Council area given that it was a member of the Eastern Border Region Committee (O'Dowd et al. 1995: 62–4). The allocation of EU funding enabled local government, community development interests and politicians to focus on the differentiation and the extent of dislocation. In the run-up to the IRA ceasefire of August 1994, the Confederation of British Industry (CBI), the Belfast and Dublin Chambers of Commerce and the Institute of Directors came together to advocate all-island economic integration, where 'corridors' between both jurisdictions could be created to enhance the potential of partnership. George Quigley, the Chair of the Ulster Bank, labelled this process 'synergy'. Four hundred and fifty companies rallied behind the idea, with the CBI arguing that the 1994–99 tranche of EU structural funds should prioritize north–south partnership. Quigley commented: 'it would be ludicrous to be part of a single European market post-1992 and fail to transform the island of Ireland into a single market, not simply to raise cross-border trade, but also to develop all-island economic, "synergies"' (1992: 128–9).

Key economic indicators for the south showed that the border regions were experiencing multiple disadvantages. With regard to population growth between 1991 and 1996, for example, the border region had the slowest rate of growth at just 1 per cent (at a time of historic and unprecedented growth for the island), while the mid-east and Dublin were growing the fastest at 6.7 per cent. In terms of unemployment, the border region retained the highest rate of overall unemployment at 14.7 per cent in 1997 and, when rounded up, the highest rate of long-term unemployment at 59 per cent of the total. However, in terms of gross value added per head (the nearest indicator to the average standard of living) the border region had the third lowest level at 77 per cent of the southern state average, with only the midlands and western regions lower. The latter regions were in an inclusive sense 'border' also. In terms of personal disposable income per head, the border region had the second lowest level (Harvey 2005: 60). What this suggested was that by the mid-1990s, as the Celtic Tiger rolled out, its benefits were largely concentrating in the south-east. This underdevelopment continued to be vexing and frustrating for regional economic growth. Furthermore, with the governments, north and south, disinvesting in local companies and privileging foreign firms, they could be seen to be reshaping the nature of the Irish economy in a manner that would have adverse consequences through to the 2000s. Indigenous businesses suffered as a consequence across the island. As James Goodman observed in *Single Europe, Single Ireland*:

> there was little indigenous development in the key sectors of auto, steel, electrical goods or consumer goods: Irish indigenous production in these sectors stood at fifteen per cent of industrial employment in 1978 while in the EU as a whole it stood at fifty-six per cent. Employment in foreign owned manufacturing grew by some twenty-two per cent in the period from 1973 to 1980 (to 80,000), while employment in indigenously owned sectors declined by some seven per cent over the same period (to 102,000). (Goodman 2000: 24)

In one of the analyses of the border region, Liam O'Dowd et al., in 'Borders, National Sovereignty and European Integration', examined the political, economic and social experiences of the counties involved. Their research was revealing in the admission that from the outset they struggled to find appropriate data: 'limited by non-availability of statistics, lack of comparability across time and place and by lack of information on the "unofficial economy"' (1995: 67). The conclusion that they arrived at was that the border region was far from homogeneous, and in fact would be better understood as being made up of three parts – the western, eastern and middle sections – although the west and east have many similar characteristics despite the physical distance separating them. With regards to the indicators that were discernible, the border as it stood going into the Celtic Tiger contained a number of debilitating facets. Population growth in the border region over the period 1981 to 1991 was below that in the rest of the island. In the northern border area, emigration was much the same as in the rest of the north, but in the southern border area, while there had been marginal net immigration between 1971 and 1981 due to families from the north escaping the conflict, there was significant emigration in the following ten years. Importantly, it revealed that the experiences along the border differed considerably from other parts of the island, with larger numbers moving out and higher dependency ratios (proportions of the population who are elderly, young or long-term unemployed). Levels of unemployment were also significantly higher in these counties – 19 per cent in the northern border area compared with 14 per cent for the rest of the north in 1991. The differences were particularly pronounced for males and Catholics. The southern border region had the highest rate of unemployment in 1997 (14.7 per cent) compared with the overall southern average of 11.6 per cent. The border areas had higher levels of long-term unemployment, with one-third of the unemployed being out of work for more than one year in both the northern and southern border counties. Indeed, the southern border region and the south-west region shared the highest long-term unemployment (at 59 per cent of the total in 1997) (Hillyard et al. 2005: 92–6).

Most people in the ten border counties worked in the agri-economy and services, with a relatively higher proportion of public sector jobs and a lower proportion in the private sector. Not surprisingly, agriculture was a far more important source of employment in the border region, with noticeably lower numbers in manufacturing. This made it all the more important in the mid-1990s when the region suffered a fall in agricultural employment, while missing out on the more general increase in financial services jobs. All these indicators suggested that the policy response had been historically negligent and to a large extent ignorant of spatial specific policies. O'Dowd summarized the socio-economic structure of the border region and highlighted some of the persistent problems:

> It lacks good access to markets, centres of innovation and large centres of population (unlike central border regions of the EU). It has few large towns which might provide a focus for development, suffers from relatively low income levels, high levels of out-migration, poor land and infrastructure. (O'Dowd 1995: 28)

The disadvantages that came with the poor economic structure were complicated by the negative historical legacy of divided policies, communities and economies. There also remained the problem that city-based policy making was ill informed – defined and managed by urban civil servants and not by border-based policy makers. As a consequence there had been little formal contact between local authorities on either side of the border and little or no opportunity for a co-ordinated regional response to development challenges. This was made worse by the highly centralized nature of governments in Dublin and Belfast, and the different economic agendas followed by the two states. These factors exacerbated the extremes of the economic divide. Many of the possible cross-border links had also been greatly affected over the years by the closure of all but a few cross-border roads and the intense militarization of the region, frequently causing long delays and a disjointed arterial route system. Links were also impeded by an ongoing republican campaign to blow up the train lines between the north and south. After the announcement of a 'complete cessation of military activities' in Ireland by the IRA on 31 August 1994, ten sealed border roads were reopened, providing greater access across the midlands. This move suggested that the British and Irish governments were using economic integration as a bargaining chip in the conflict, and this was far from conducive to effective economic and social development for the region. More progressively, some were arguing for a rewriting of the north–south relationship to overcome the problems of divergence and uneven development. George Quigley, in a ground-breaking speech to the Confederation of Irish Industry in February 1992, proposed one way forward: 'Ireland, North and South, should become one integrated "island economy" in the context of the Single European Market', advocating 'nothing short of a sea-change in economic relationships within the island' (Quigley 1992: 4).

Arguably both governments – at least since the 1960s – had been avoiding greater socio-economic integration designed to overcome the economic problems associated with the border. Only after January 1994 did the southern government designate the border counties as a region for the purposes of planning, made possible through the Local Government Act of 1991 which set up eight regional bodies to co-ordinate the 1994–98 structural funds. The southern border was designated as a region covering Donegal, Leitrim, Cavan, Monaghan, Louth and Sligo. In 2000 these eight regions were rationalized into two: the Border, Midland and Western (BMW) and the Southern and Eastern (S&E). What was clear by the mid-1990s was that the physical presence of the border appeared to have had a significant and adverse impact on economic development policy. Furthermore, the north had a different set of compliances to overcome than the south, as explained by Will Hutton in *Fortnight*:

> Northern Ireland is locked into a downward economic spiral. It has not only all the problems of a peripheral region, but is a region of a wider British economy, itself in trouble. It neither controls its own affairs, nor does it benefit from a wider set of economic institutions which generate growth and employment. (Hutton, *Fortnight*, November 1994)

The conflict economy in the north had reached a point where it was embedded into the economic fabric and carried the effects of contagion. This was borne out by the amounts being pumped into the region with little or no economic movement. 'In 1992–3 the subvention – public spending in the province not covered by tax raised there – amounted to £3.3 billion ($4.8 billion)' (*New Internationalist*, May 1994: 19). Ending the conflict without an all-island economic agenda would have proved to be immensely destabilizing for both states.

Throughout the other regions of the European Union there had been evolving regional and social partnerships which placed small-to-medium enterprises and the social economy on a complementary set of relationships with the large private and public sectors – with the common objective of supporting more equitable, balanced structures of development. This was recognized by the European Union in policies targeting conditions that were leading to the break-up of communities and the run-down of local economies. Implicit in this was the social economy. Attitudes to the involvement and capacity of the third sector (the social economy, women's groups, church groups, youth initiatives and so on), however, led to some confusion about the type of sustainable development strategies that this sector could get involved in. There had also been a tense relationship between certain governmental departments and the third sector, causing recurrent funding difficulties and a rationalization process for agencies working in some of the most difficult aspects of economic and rural regeneration. Indeed, the commitment of the regional governments north and south to social partnership, social inclusion and the very concept of investing in communities was often cynically manipulated as a budgeting exercise, which did not necessarily enhance socio-economic development. On occasion social economy initiatives were linked to paramilitary activity by government representatives, thus delegitimizing the work. The outcome of this disconnection, together with the residual effects of 'black-spots' in the economy, was a breakdown in communication between government departments and many voluntary and community organizations throughout the late 1990s. This resulted in the loss of indigenous businesses, community services, and an underdeveloped and dispersed local economy; which all magnified the effects of socio-economic disadvantage. Stripped back, it was clear that the government bodies did not trust many of the communities they were obligated to support, and the distrust was mutual.

Additionality was another ongoing problem with funding coming to Ireland to assist political and economic stability, as indeed was the civil servants' interpretation of what 'peace' actually meant. Many had come to understand investing in peace as enterprise support or a budget backup, as opposed to community capacity building. Additionality was where certain government departments attempted to supplement their own existing social and community services with EU funding. Skewing funds had become common practice among Irish civil servants, and in effect, meant that in some areas there had been negligible additional support for deprived communities, undermining the services which were being provided. Blame was laid at the door of the senior civil servants who by the late 1990s – with the local politicians dedicating their time to maintaining the peace process – were running the north. An *Irish Times* article of 12 November 1997 relayed the problem, 'Government stands accused of siphoning off peace funds'. The report stated:

> But with the money now spent, and a second allocation pending, it's emerged that around half of the £190 million that went to Northern Ireland was grabbed by government departments and no-one – except those departments – knows how that money was spent. It's a situation which has enraged community organizations who have had to account for and justify every penny received and spent, while central government has swallowed nearly £100 million and accounted for almost nothing.

Many groups were forced to apply for peace funding when other funding was lost through cutbacks or had disappeared into entrepreneurial activity. For social economy representatives, the voluntary and community sector and the indigenous business sectors in areas which were susceptible to political violence, social inclusion and sustainable renewal did not remain at the core of the regeneration or the European Union's contribution. It caused a disintegration of services in many of the interface areas. Evidence of questionable decisions on the commitment to peace and reconciliation from government departments, north and south, could be seen from a number of questionable examples of the allocation of peace funding – such as the £5.14 million that had been allocated to the National Roads Authority for the Aghalane–Belturbet bypass, or £1.275 million for the construction of the approach road to Aghalane Bridge, £1.152 million to the N16 improvements, £1.3 million to LEDU for its 'Information Strategy' and a further £1.5 million for their development scheme, £1.003 million to the Industrial Development Board (IDB) for a Trade Advisor Programme, £1.1716 million to the IDB for factory development costs, and a further £370,000 to the IDB for a 'sectoral marketing campaign'. The examples suggested that governmental managers were looking for market solutions to the conflict and social exclusion.

The ideologically informed market preference for funding that was taken by many civil servants in Belfast and Dublin was in stark comparison with the monies allocated to the Central Community Relations Unit working to eradicate sectarianism. In their figures to May 1999 for areas most affected by the conflict, they stated that 'The total amount of approved funding to the parliamentary constituency of West Belfast totalled £6,746,758' (CCRU, information request, 28 May 1999). This can be compared with the £31.59 million of EU funding that was committed to the Laganside Corporation public-private partnership and £9.5 million to the Odyssey leisure complex (Mark Durkan, *NI Hansard*, AQW 83/00, 27 Sept 2000). In terms of Peace I, only 1.7 per cent of the fund went on social inclusion which promoted 'pathways to reconciliation', whereas 14.8 per cent went on 'industrial development, seed capital and trade development'.

Those most affected by the breakdown in this support system worked within the community sector itself and at the coalface of the conflict. In 1998 an NIVT report on EU funding, 'Taking Risks for Peace', outlined how important directing funds to projects in disadvantaged areas and supporting the social inclusion of marginalized groups actually was, and how it contributed to the peace process. It was clear that many community-based organizations did not receive a commensurate share of the funds. 'With the exception of Sub Programme 5 on productive investment, 83 per cent of applications were submitted from community based voluntary groups, yet they tended to receive relatively small awards in comparison to private-enterprise-driven projects promoted by government departments' (NIVT 1998: 4). A neoliberal reference had come to prominence among the senior civil service in Ireland. In the north its controlling mechanism could be located in the quango established to manage the economy, the Strategic Investment Board (SIB) – comprised of finance, banking, accounting, law and management specialists with no political, trade union or community development input. In the south, government policies were increasingly being driven by the needs of multinational corporations.

THE AGREEMENT

With the Good Friday (or Belfast) Agreement – signed by the majority of parties on 10 April 1998 – the public and civic sectors involved in regenerating areas of socio-economic disadvantage were given a mandate to build north–south links. They were working in a transformed political and policy context. In the first all-island poll since the 1918 general election, 94.4 per cent of the southern electorate and 71.1 per cent of the northern electorate voted for the Agreement's implementation (McCann 2001b: 1). Institutional and policy changes carried on apace and policy commitments relevant to socio-economic regeneration went through a phase of rapid transition – not only in terms of the funding structures – but also in terms of the political environment in which they were developing. The Agreement specified twelve areas for north–south cooperation, with operations equally divided between newly created bodies and the enhancement of existing ones (government departments and agencies). Economic development and synergy were to be central to this structure. The range of policies covered:

(i)   Agriculture – animal and plant health.
(ii)   Education – teacher qualifications and exchanges.
(iii)   Transport – strategic transport planning.
(iv)   Environment – environmental protection, pollution, water quality and waste management.
(v)   Waterways – inland waterways.
(vi)   Social security/social welfare – entitlements of cross-border workers and fraud control.
(vii)   Tourism – promotion, marketing, research and product development.
(viii) Relevant EU programmes – SPPR, INTERREG, Leader II and their successors.
(ix)   Inland fisheries.
(x)   Aquaculture and marine matters.
(xi)   Health – accident and emergency services and other related cross-border issues.
(xii)   Urban and rural development.

In taking this approach the governments were acknowledging that the north–south economy had been uneven in character and divided along policy boundaries which had compounded the divisions. Ultimately, the Agreement confirmed the theory that the integration of the respective economies was implicit to peace and reconciliation (Anderson and Goodman 1994: 49–62). To achieve effective and meaningful reconciliation of communities north and south, socio-economic barriers to development needed to be lifted. In practice this meant building the economic corridors linking Dundalk to Letterkenny, tying in communities, businesses and social economy initiatives. This needed investment and political encouragement, and this came with the David Trimble–Seamus Mallon statement of 1998 on 'Joint Work'. This contained a list of six areas for north–south co-operation through the offices of existing policy-making structures north and south. These were:

(i)   Transport – cross-border issues in the areas of road and rail planning, as well as ports and airports.
(ii) Agriculture – issues related to the Common Agricultural Policy, animal health and rural development.
(iii) Education – education for children with special needs, under-achievement, teacher qualifications and exchanges.
(iv) Health – accident and emergency planning, co-operation on the use of high-technology equipment and health promotion.
(v)   Environment – research into environmental protection, water quality and waste management.
(vi) Tourism.

Tourism as a policy area was given a unique role in the economic development of the island post-conflict. A publicly owned limited company was set up by the existing tourist boards, north and south – the Northern Ireland Tourist Board (NITB) and Bord Fáilte respectively. This new company would provide a range of services in the areas of planning, marketing and market research, with an emphasis on overseas marketing and a special remit to address the problems that the conflict had created for this growing industry. The operations of the company would be monitored by the existing tourist boards, as well as by the north–south Ministerial Council. Tourism was to be used as an agent of north–south integration, with a proposed growth rate of upwards of 7 per cent per year, and the island of Ireland being marketed as a single destination. It was one strategy that had been anticipated and was paying dividends, as Bill Rolston pointed out:

> NITB chairperson Hugh O'Neill announced that five years of sustained peace could bring about at least 20,000 additional tourism-related jobs ... for the first time in two and a half decades, the North of Ireland has an absence of manifest political violence. There would thus seem to be a realism involved in the assessment that tourism will benefit as a result. (Rolston 1995: 37–8)

The role of government agencies was also reassessed, in the clear under-standing that the renewal of the regional economy would depend on the convergence of policy initiatives. It was an aspect of integration that Richard Kearney had flagged up in *Across the Frontiers: Ireland in the 1990s* with the view that economic development and peace could be frustrated by the extent of statutory indifference (Kearney 1988; also see Tomlinson 1995: 8–14). The Irish Trade Board, Invest Northern Ireland and the Industrial Development Authority in the south, along with a number of profiled projects from the Irish Business and Employer's Confederation, provided investment for programmes which emphasized the cross-border dimension. By the end of the 1990s there were precedents and examples of initia-tives which were showing success – areas where the strength of the programmes and policies could be quantified, highlighting areas which could generate cross-border socio-economic development on a long-term basis within different sectors and taking account of area specificity. This came to be crystallized in the work of the North/South Co-operation Implementation Bodies which were established by the Northern Ireland Order 1999. These bodies covered:

(i)   Inland waterways – with responsibility mainly for the Shannon–Erne waterway, development and restoration of the Ulster Canal, and associated promotional activities.

(ii) Food safety – with responsibility for a range of activities in the areas of research and promotion of food safety and scientific co-operation.

(iii) Trade and business development – with a remit to exchange information and co-ordinate work on trade, business develop-ment and related matters, in areas where the two administra-tions specifically agreed that it would be in their mutual interest to do so. Specific areas of implementation were considered under the two headings of business and trade development:

– *Business development issues*: cooperation on business development opportunities, north and south; devising new approaches to business development in a cross-border context in such areas as research, training, marketing and quality improvement; supporting business by making recommendations to increase enterprise competitiveness in a north–south context in areas such as skills availability, telecoms, IT and electronic commerce.

– *Trade development issues*: promotion of north–south supply chains, including business linkages and partnerships;

promoting cross-border trade events and marketing initiatives; identifying new areas of trade between north and
south; promoting market awareness and trade development
in a north–south context; undertaking specific projects and
events in relation to trade promotion, when asked jointly
on a project-by-project basis; providing advice on specific
aspects of trade promotion when tasked jointly to do so.
It was also noted that existing economic agencies would
continue to be funded by and operate under the direction of
their respective administrations.

(iv) Special EU programmes – with responsibility to monitor,
research and give technical assistance in relation to certain existing north–south EU programmes such as INTERREG and the
Special Support Programme for Peace and Reconciliation, as
well as an advisory role in connection with the negotiation with
the EU Commission of post-1999 Community Initiatives and of
the common chapter of the Community Support Framework.

(v) Irish language – with responsibility for activities in promoting
the Irish language and Ulster Scots.

(vi) Aquaculture and marine matters – with responsibilities for
Lough Foyle, Carlingford Lough and lighthouses.

At the beginning of the 1990s the vast majority of cross-border
economic development links were dependent on two specific sectors
– food/retail and manufactured goods. By the end of the 1990s there
was in principle a mechanism for a fuller process of integration. This
gave a regional pattern for convergence and provided the architecture
for more practical engagement within governmental policy frameworks than had existed since partition. The potential of this network
had already existed, but had yet to be fully explored by diversifying
and investing with a view to bringing various sectors, including
the social economy, into a more competitive all-island system for
sustainable economic development (Loughlin 1991: 183–5). What
is also noticeable about the north–south integration strategy of the
late 1990s and early 2000s was that, unlike the hub of Celtic Tiger
activity around Dublin, it was primarily indigenous businesses that
were operating at a cross-border level, small-to-medium-sized enterprises and social economy initiatives that could be seen to be the
backbone of a long-term strategy for development. These aspects
of regional development could then match the influence of other
more conventional forms of economic development – such as foreign
direct investment and government agency enterprise initiatives.

The impact of the sequence of regionally specific initiatives, as well as the Special Support Programme for Peace and Reconciliation, the emergence of the Lottery Funds (Community Fund), the International Fund for Ireland, the EU's Objective One in Transition status and changes to urban renewal agencies, altered the island's economic environment significantly and for a time facilitated the progressive integration of the economies north and south. There was also a general recognition that something was giving in the command-like northern economy, as explained by Will Hutton: 'The budgetary transfer from Great Britain is too high and because of the underlying deterioration in Northern Ireland – which without major political and economic change can only get worse – the cost is set to rise' (*Irish News*, 11 June 1994). All-island economic integration offered a way out of this dependency. With peace the economic benefits could start to accrue:

> If the conflict-related elements of policing are excluded, the Northern six counties would need a police force of approximately 3750 (including civilian staff), that is a mere 23 per cent of its current size. By withdrawing troops, Britain would immediately save £500 million per year. (Tomlinson 1995: 10)

The establishment of a devolved administration in the north, notwithstanding its 'stop–start' form and periodic violent shocks – such as the annual Drumcree protests – nevertheless brought forward policy changes which continued to benefit regeneration.

The relative peace was shattered on 15 August 1998 with a no-warning bomb in Omagh, Country Tyrone, planted by opponents of the peace process. Twenty-nine civilians and two unborn children were killed, and 220 were injured while shopping on a Saturday afternoon. The slaughter shocked the Irish and international communities and was the biggest single loss of life in the history of the Troubles. It served to re-emphasize the urgency of the ongoing process. While the vast majority of the population in the north had settled into an uneasy peace, interfaith and sporadic violence was cited by Superintendent Alan McQuillan of the Police Service as the worst in 20 years. With the administration at Stormont caught in a seemingly perennial stutter from crisis to collapse in disagreements over which parties were eligible to participate, from the viewpoint of those working in areas which had been the primary target of a peace process, community relations had become more difficult than at any time since the early 1980s. Figures and reports coming through in 2001 from the community representatives and organizations in interface areas gave some indication of the scale of the problem (Fisher and McVeigh 2002: 12). Up to 100 people had been killed in conflict-related incidents since Good Friday 1998, with up to 3000 people being forced from their homes by intimidation between 1994 and 2001. Tony Kennedy in the *Irish Times* outlined one particularly difficult night in the north on 5 September 2001:

> The RUC said that 45 officers and two soldiers had been injured in trouble since early yesterday morning, which has seen some 250 petrol bombs and 15 blast bombs thrown and four cars set on fire and burned out. Last night petrol bombs, nail bombs and blast bombs were thrown at police lines during disturbances close to the Ardoyne Road. In the Glenbryn area, a large crowd of loyalists threw bottles, bricks, fireworks and ball bearings at the security forces. There were also reports of clashes between rival mobs in the North Queen Street, Limestone Road and Westland Road areas. Yesterday one RUC officer needed treatment for a broken collarbone after loyalists threw a pipebomb just yards away from Holy Cross Primary school. The Newry bypass in Co Down was closed in the early hours of this morning after an articulated lorry was hijacked and set on fire. Two gunmen flagged the lorry down at 12.16 a.m., ordered the driver to place the vehicle across the road. They then set it on fire with petrol bombs. Meanwhile a house in Larne Co Antrim was shot at overnight. (*Irish Times*, 12 September 2001)

While the peace process was evolving slowly and was paying dividends in regards to relative peace and political stability there continued to be flare-ups, a legacy of generational conflict. It meant that while the politicians of the north began dedicating their work to creating consensus politics, the civil servants were still effectively managing the economy. The major strategies affecting socio-economic development, north and south, going into the new century were:

- New Targeting Social Need (north specific)
- the European Union's Special Support Programme for Peace and Reconciliation (cross-border)
- the European Union's Objective One Status (all-island)
- the Programme for Government (north specific)
- equality legislation (all-island)

- Strategy 2010 (north specific)
- human rights legislation and the Bill of Rights (all-island)
- the Harbinson Report on Funding for the Community and Voluntary Sectors (north specific)
- the Promoting Social Inclusion initiative (north specific)
- Partners for Change (north specific)
- education and training policies (all-island)
- the National Development Plan 2000–2006 (south specific)
- NUTS II (south specific)
- National Anti Poverty Strategy (south specific).

Although the six northern counties did not experience the rapid economic growth and inward investment that characterized the Celtic Tiger economy, there were determined efforts to attract private capital to the north in the wake of the Agreement. The northern administration openly sought to mimic the neoliberal model in the south and to play off the perceived successes of the Celtic Tiger. The new era also reflected an opportunity to change priories away from constitutional issues – which were eventually settled by the Agreement and its renewal at St Andrews on 13 October 2006 – towards economic recovery. The economic emphasis of the new northern executive created the relative political stability necessary to instil confidence in foreign investors to consider locating in the north. Although economic development was increasingly being directed by the Strategic Investment Board, the upturn in the economy was evident, suggesting an economic 'peace dividend'.

The northern economy continued to be sustained through the annual subvention from Britain by up to 20 per cent of GDP, attended by the heavily layered and subsidized public and security sectors, and the service industry (Ruddock 2006). The manufacturing base in the north, particularly textiles, was deliberately run down, to be superseded by more globally competitive information and communications technology (ICT) industries. Ulster's traditional industries were, by the 1990s, virtually non-existent or specializing, and even with government-sponsored efforts to introduce new niche market products, they struggled to survive. The aerospace industry (Canadian company Bombardier) located at Belfast docks became the largest private sector employer in the whole of the north, followed by chemical and electrical engineering multinationals DuPont, Nortel and Seagate. By far the biggest employer remained the state. In 1992, the public sector in Northern Ireland accounted for 37 per cent of the total workforce; by 2008 it was still 30.8 per cent, even after successive initiatives to transfer – 'rebalance' – government investment towards 'enterprise' and downsize the public sector (Northern Ireland Government 2009). This was the economic context that was inherited by the new northern institutions created under the Belfast Agreement. In contrast, whereas the Celtic Tiger was to only partially migrate northward, in the south, the administration had created something different in the shape of an enterprise-driven model of economic development, with a monetarist import.

7 NEOLIBERAL IRELAND

Until the 1990s the Irish economy was developing in an erratic manner, disjointed in terms of sectors collapsing, with significant regions going into virtual underdevelopment. The entry of the south into the European Community's exchange rate mechanism (ERM) in 1979, the Single European Act (SEA) of 1986 and investment coming through from foreign corporations all helped create a dynamic for growth. These shifts in the macroeconomy permitted the revitalization of other types of multinational activity and, with the repositioning of compliant elements of Irish economic policy to assist foreign direct investment (FDI), it opened up opportunities to explore emerging global markets. The results of the changes were extraordinary. The development of the southern Irish economy after the introduction of the Programme for National Recovery in 1987 – within the context of the EEC, concentrating on multinational corporations with global outreach and with a social partnership in place between labour, government and business – meant that the government was able to engineer one of the most prominent globalized neoliberal economies on earth.

One long-standing critic of this model, Denis O'Hearn, introduced the Irish application of this method of economic development as a nuanced 'showpiece of globalization' (2000: 73). From another perspective, the International Monetary Fund (IMF) – which later moved in to manage the dysfunction that resulted – presented the Irish model as a remarkable example of structural adjustment that should be copied globally. 'No other OECD country has been able to match its outstanding outcomes' (IMF 2001: 4; OECD 1999: 9). Irish neoliberalism, with its global influence and reach, for one moment in time seemed to have provided an answer to the problem of the boom-and-slump cycle in advanced market economies. It was seen as an exemplary driver of the process of globalization.

Prior to the 1990s the chaos of Irish economic history was evident in the manner in which other countries, academics and the international financial institutions (IFIs) viewed the island. For the European Union the north was a 'blot on the community', whereas the south repeatedly appeared with the lowest average income per capita in the European Union; domestic production had fallen through most of the 1980s and employment in manufacturing had dropped by

20 per cent. Indeed, the Organisation for Economic Cooperation and Development (OECD) at different times registered the Irish economy as 'underdeveloped' in 1976, and 'stagnant' and 'sliding' by 1999 (OECD 1976: 60, 68; 1999: 10). Joseph Lee commented that 'No other European country, east or west, north or south, for which remotely reliable evidence exists, has recorded so slow a rate of growth of national income in the twentieth century' (Lee 1989: 515; Smith 2005: 37). The question in the mid-1980s had been: was Ireland a third world county?

Between 1979 and 1985 unemployment was the main concern in southern economic planning, registering a continual rise from 7.8 per cent to 18.2 per cent. Domestic consumption levels had remained static during that period, as consumers simply had little to spend. Signs of change and policy shifts, however, could be seen mid-way through the decade. While indigenous industry went into decline, foreign firms – with their labour-intensive production largely founded on high-technological commodities, chemicals or information and communication technology (ICT) – offered a quick fix for the unemployment problem. Investment was arriving, jobs were being created and growth was apparent (Hamilton 1993: 190–217). An unusual pattern of economic development was evident even prior to the boom that was to occur. In 1985, over 80 per cent of all non-food exports, 50 per cent of this being electronics and chemicals, was coming from foreign direct investment. The OECD recognized that 'the Republic had become the "export platform" for multinational trade into the EEC' (1985: 47). Furthermore, profit repatriation represented 50 per cent of total industrial profits, meaning that the wealth of the produce, beyond job creation, was being largely siphoned out of the country. By 1990, multinational corporations in the south were employing 45 per cent of the manufacturing workforce. This trend had been evident previously, but its acceleration after 1990 resulted from a series of government interventions on behalf of multinational firms.

The Fianna Fáil election victory of February 1987, under the leadership of Charles Haughey and finance minister Ray MacSharry, signalled a new direction for the economy and the ideological underpinnings of that party at that time. Fiscal austerity was rebranded as an innovative and disciplining approach to economic management and, with pay cuts for public servants being brought in almost immediately, the theory of 'expansionary fiscal contraction' was put into practice. Their *Programme for National Recovery* marked a new approach to the management of the southern economy. Running from 1987 to

1990, it brought forward a series of schemes that had the primary objective of stimulating investment. While the actual programme itself had a measured impact on employment during its own timeline – with the numbers employed in the manufacturing sector in 1990 remaining the same as in 1973, at just over 19 per cent – formative changes could be seen with the foreign companies: 'Inward investment increased and manufacturing employment rose by some 15,000; but only 2000 of the new jobs were based in indigenous industry' (Goodman 2000: 25). The figures were set against the recession of the early 1980s when manufacturing jobs (particularly indigenous jobs) were being lost and investment was reserved. What was notable in the programme and encouraged foreign firms was its framework of tax exemptions for exporting companies, as the government tried to imaginatively adjust public revenue and expenditure to support enterprising, even risk-prone, aspects of economic growth. Enhanced foreign direct investment was the outcome of this intervention, with profit repatriation going up to over 60 per cent of total industrial profit by the early 1990s.

Early in this adjustment process, O'Hearn was to notice something distinctly problematic about the system that was being rolled out across the Irish economy – the gap between gross domestic product (GDP) and gross national product (GNP) was rising at a rate of 1.5 per cent per year. It was eventually to go up to 14.3 per cent by 2000 (O'Hearn 2000: 74–5). The problem was that the Irish model seemed to be focusing on GDP growth without taking the GNP into account, GDP being the main indicator of total economic activity, representing growth in an economy: 'consumer spending, plus business investment, plus government purchases, plus net exports' (McCann and McCloskey 2009: 268). Crucially, GDP included the profits from multinationals that were being repatriated, which skewed the figures on the actual wealth of the county. In effect the wealth being created was being transferred out of the country, leaving it susceptible to fluctuations within the global market and possible collapse in the manner that the Asian economies collapsed in the 1990s. Furthermore, as James Goodman noted:

> there was a dramatic increase in net outflows of property income from 1980 to 1990, which was only partially offset by EU subsidies. As a result, GNP fell as a percentage of GDP, from 101 per cent in 1970 to eighty-eight per cent in 1990. (Goodman 2000: 27; also see Bradley 1993)

The most visible effect was in public spending where, for example, by the start of the 2000s the government of Ireland was spending less on the country's biggest killer, heart disease, than any other member of the European Union.

For the population of the south the changes were not immediately apparent, and people were still feeling the squeeze on personal finance since the austerity measures of the mid-1980s. With taxes at up to 60 per cent of income, unemployment levels reached 20 per cent in 1991 – yet the Fianna Fáil programme sought to cut public expenditure further, sell off public assets and bring private sector expansion to the centre of government spending plans. Another element of the policy was a preference by the government to rebalance the foundations of the Irish economy away from agriculture and towards manufacturing for export – with multinational corporations central to this recalibration. For once in the history of the Irish economy, opposition to agricultural reform was muted. Furthermore, the introduction and apparent feasibility of social partnership 'pay-pacts', which could restrain and better manage public sector wages, integrated the trade union movement into economic policy making. The objective of a knowledge-focused economy would, in theory, place the workforce in a globally competitive position and attract new industries in much the same way that Ireland did in the early 1960s. Over 50 per cent of the government's commitment to industrial growth was to be directed towards drawing down and retaining multinational companies in target sectors.

The warnings started early. The *Culliton Report* of 1992, the administration's enquiry into industrial policy, picked up on the disproportionate influence of multinationals on economic policy, arguing for the need to invest in Irish-based companies for the long-term sustainability of jobs and growth (Government of the Irish Republic 1992). Cautionary voices were however not being listened to by the Dublin government. At this point, favourable external circumstances and changes to the macroeconomy had created the trajectory necessary for the Irish economy to leapfrog into a model compatible with the ongoing process of globalization.

The European Union had its role in the reconfiguration. Ratification of the Maastricht Treaty in 1992 brought with it a myriad of policies that would help direct southern-based corporations' exports towards the continental market. Identification with the new European Union was not only a departure in terms of policy making, but also provided an opportunity to confirm the Europeanization of Ireland. Consensus in the Irish business sector was that this was the best direction in which to turn, and the government readily complied, opting for additional integration into the full spectrum of EU governance and economic structures. This single European market could locate Irish industry and its multinationals within new markets. With entry into the ERM, the south, unlike the United Kingdom – and the north by default – had committed itself to the full implications of its long-term strategy for economic and monetary union. While this had the effect of devaluing the punt, resulting in an inability to meet the convergence criteria set out in Maastricht, it nevertheless enhanced the avowed commitment by both government and business sectors to integrate further into the continental economy in whatever way possible.

Significant change in the macroeconomic policies of the south at this time came with the introduction of the National Development Plan for 1994–99 and its attendant policy document, the *Programme for Competitiveness and Work*. The programme's remit covered 1994–97, and the initiatives included defining and enhancing entrepreneurial activity and the enterprise culture as catalysts for accelerated economic development. This was matched with a corporation tax rate of 10 per cent (later 12.5 per cent), thus positioning the south of Ireland as the most competitive location for foreign companies in the European Union at that time. Multinationals, particularly from the United States, saw the region as a prime stepping stone for the lucrative European market.

This was backed up by the continued injection of billions of punts in structural funding from the European Union (€10 billion between 1989 and 1999), which in turn was used by the government to take the pressure off its social obligations, rationalize public expenditure and enhance the business environment to make it more appealing to investors (Finn 2011: 9). EU funding was also increasingly becoming a life support for public services. By 1993 EU financial support, principally through structural and cohesion funds, represented over 10 per cent of public expenditure in the south and 3 per cent in the north. In that year, EU financial support stood at 2.7 per cent of the south's GDP (Northern Ireland Office, press release, 27 July 1993). Relative peace in the north and border counties gave a positive spin for the Irish economy, where the image and violence of the 1970s and 1980s could be replaced by an apparently open and welcoming society. Indeed, the Irish economy was moving through the 1990s to match the self-fulfilling globalized image of a corporate-friendly ideal location.

With this evolving neoliberal model, one facet was becoming patently obvious: that the GDP growth rates did not seem to influence key development indicators. Going into the first phase of adjustment in 1994, Eurostat statistics showed that there were three times (18.7 per cent) as many unemployed in the south as there were in 1970; and in the north, with all its subvention, there were double the number of unemployed (at 14 per cent) than in 1970 (Finn 2011: 9–11).

Of the variants of classical liberalism that resurfaced through governmental and academic circles in the 1990s, and as its contemporary application for the globalized market came to prominence in the United States and most European states, the Celtic Tiger rose to become the most elevated example of this economic theory in modern times. Of this dominant theory David Harvey, in *A Brief History of Neoliberalism,* commented:

> Neoliberalism is in the first instance a theory of political economic practices that proposes that human well-being can best be advanced by liberating individual entrepreneurial freedoms and skills within an institutional framework characterized by strong private property rights, free markets, and free trade. (Harvey 2005: 2)

Through this model the pattern of governmental action became similar the world over – emphasizing commercial freedom and individuality as rights, dismantling unionized labour relations, cutting taxes, deregulating corporate operations, prioritizing financial interaction in policy design, privatizing public utilities, and attempting to dissolve welfare provision into market forces. Curiously, the Irish variant seemed to develop in a more zealous manner than in any other western European country, due possibly to a lack of a concerted left alternative on the island to check the extremes of this model for economic growth, or due to the historical connections with the United States and its economy (Brown 2004: 10). The politicians of the main parties, together with their Machiavellian civil servants, north and south, took up the challenge of integrating liberalization policies with gusto as quick-fix market solutions.

Doheny and Nesbitt's pub in Dublin has the unenviable credit of being the bear-pit of neoliberalism in Ireland, where economists, bankers, property developers and politicians socialized in the late 1980s and early 1990s, and where they formed common ground on pushing through an aggressive adjustment programme which would force up the Irish GDP. The methods that were suggested by the most vocal of this 'school' – Brendan Walsh, Colm McCarthy and

Paul Tansey – were based around a menu of policies that would, in theory, drive Irish exports onto the world stage while attracting privileged types of foreign investment. Their ideas included drastic cuts to taxes, the reduction of import duties to enhance competition, providing an open and flexible environment for direct foreign investment, joining the single European currency when it was created, low interest rates and searching out large capital markets. It would technically be bankrolled by borrowing, EU funding, a credit drive and FDI, all managed by a business-biased government.

The risks of this type of economy were evident from the outset. As well as the realignment of the purpose of government to become compliant with corporate financial strategies, a symptom of this economic model would be vulnerability to systemic crises that would periodically shock the global economy. In its process of readjusting to rapidly changing global markets, its exposure to the open chaos of globalization would increasingly become apparent. An adverse event in one area of commercial or financial life, in New York for example, would see effects ripple out across the globe, impacting on microeconomies and the macroeconomy alike. Through favourable geographical positioning, shrewd management of the economy and a large element of luck, the Celtic Tiger was able to navigate through a number of these shocks.

The series of initiatives and mechanisms set in place by the Irish government in the 1990s, together with its international reach, underpinned this distinctly European version of an enterprise-driven economy. It was hinged on the free circulation of finance, direct foreign investment through the targeting and enhancement of specific sectors (finance, service, chemicals and computers) and government-sponsored marketing of Irish goods. Kevin Gardiner, from the US bank Morgan Stanley, commented in 1994 about the growth rate and potential of the Irish economy, comparing it with the frantic activity of the Asian economies of the 1980s. The international understanding of the Irish adaptation of this model brought its form of networked growth into the European arena for the first time. Consequently, the rate of GDP growth and the capacity for global outreach for the southern Irish economy led to a sea-change in the way in which the island was viewed by others. The ripple-effect and apparent success gave the model a dynamic that seemed to be self-replicating. Nicola Smith's survey of the international reaction to the early Celtic Tiger is perhaps the most comprehensive:

The Economist described Ireland as 'Europe's shining light', remarking that growth was at 'positively East Asian pace'. The *Financial Times*, too, congratulated Ireland on its 'exceptional growth' and argued 'Ireland fully deserves to be called the "Celtic Tiger"'. *The Times* labelled Ireland's economic performance as 'nothing short of remarkable' and the *Wall Street Journal* described the Republic as the 'envy' of its European neighbours. (Smith 2005: 37)

In this first phase of the Celtic Tiger, growth rates were revealing evidence of an unprecedented success story. The GDP growth rate reached a steady level of 6 per cent by 2001, and from OECD ranking, this placed the south along with some of the most developed (wealthiest) countries on earth. Indeed, it had gone very quickly from being one of the least developed regions of the European Union, in constant need of structural funding, to being statistically on a par with Japan and the United States in per capita GDP terms. The World Bank presented the country as the 'most globalized' on earth. The *Economist* listed the Republic of Ireland as providing the best 'quality of life' in the world (Forfas 2008; *Economist* 2005; www. Stats.oecd.org). Its success was contagious. The Celtic Tiger model was taken up with vigour by emerging economies across the world, with the Polish Eagle, the Scottish Lion and even the Zambian Lynx being examples of the exploitation of national symbols for a mechanism of achieving high GDP rates and an apparent exponential increase in the standard of living. Philip Lane, from Trinity College in Dublin, commented on the first phase of the boom: 'There was a genuine Irish economic miracle, with very rapid output, employment and productivity growth during the 1994–2000 period' (quoted in Wolf 2011: 11).

The methods used to create the policy matrix that was to become the Celtic Tiger depended on a number of facets. The first was geo-economic circumstances, where the 1990s provided a particularly favourable environment for foreign companies. Ireland's location – within the European Union yet with historical links with the United States – gave it a unique role in acting as a foothold for US multinationals looking to get established in the European market. Second, a flat rate of corporation tax became the marker of the model and gave Ireland a competitive advantage over other EU regions. Third, the use of the monetarist method of delivering on GDP growth provided a 'success generating success' dynamic. Fourth, the government adapted the education system, and particularly the technical colleges and universities, to provide a steady supply of qualified white-collar professionals willing to work at competitive rates. Ireland also had a well-educated young population, and indeed 'We are the young Europeans' became the Industrial Development Agency's (formerly Authority's: IDA's) campaigning message to attract foreign corporations. Fifth, with the social partnership arrangement, wage levels could be negotiated through pay deals and union compliance. Finally, the silver bullet of the whole system was the government's ability to attract foreign direct investment in such an aggressive manner that the economy came to be promoted globally as a brand in itself. 'Ireland PLC' was picked up particularly well by multinationals from the United States. 'The US share of industrial investment in the local economy rose from 32 per cent in 1990 to 68 per cent in 1997' (Finn 2011: 9). They also targeted high-growth, high-tech sectors and key companies in those sectors, the arrival of Intel and Dell leading to others being attracted. The IDA became crucial in meeting corporate needs, and its influence on government policy became paramount.

Padraic White, the managing director of the IDA between 1981 and 1990, and considered to be one of the architects of this model, asserted that the rate of corporation tax 'remains ... the unique and essential foundation stone of Ireland's investment boom' (MacSharry and White 2000: 250). In MacSharry and White's early analysis of the model, *The Making of the Celtic Tiger*, they lauded its successes, presenting the attracting and holding of investment from large foreign companies as the key to the model. In comparison with the Irish corporation tax rate, which stood at 12.5 per cent in 2003, the average across the European Union was 35 per cent (with some countries having rates as high as 40 per cent), making the south of Ireland a tax haven within the European Union. Meanwhile, the United Kingdom's rate stood at 28 per cent, leaving the north of Ireland caught in the hinterland and struggling to attract investment against unfair southern competition. Coupled with low relocation costs and a selection of government 'sweeteners' (incentives) to the multinationals, the south of Ireland – and particularly the south east – had built an enterprise-friendly competitive opportunity to exploit the European markets.

Tax rules became almost fluid in order to entice direct foreign investment, bringing in or enhancing the commitment of multinationals such as Google, Dell, Microsoft and Intel, along with a stream of call centres, financial services organizations and pharmaceutical companies. Changes to tax law under Section 23 meant that construction costs could be offset against tax. This opened up the property market and, with banks expanding their operations after the 1995 deregulation of banking activities by the World Bank, they could now provide high-risk low-interest mortgages, with customers encouraged by having to make little or no down-payment. After this date credit and consumer spending converged to become drivers of the model, with increasing beneficiaries of the new economy spending excessively and living lavishly. With these changes the three pillars of the economic 'miracle' were in place: property development, financial services and foreign investment.

To further nurture this system, in December 1999 Charlie McCreevey, the finance minister who was overseeing the tax regime, introduced Section 71 of the Finance Act (1999) which brought in a 12.5 per cent tax band for corporation trading income and 25 per cent for non-trading income. The objective was to make it even easier to attract foreign investment. With new businesses moving in throughout the 1990s and the Irish economy reaping evident dividends from the process of globalization, the neoliberal model could be seen to be creating jobs and pushing up incomes. As O'Hearn pointed out in *The End of Irish History? Critical Reflections on the Celtic Tiger*, between 1995 and 1999, 85 per cent of total economic growth in the Republic of Ireland had resulted from multinational operations (2003: 38).

> From 1987 to 2003, gross domestic product per person rose from 70 per cent of the EU average to 136 per cent, while unemployment sank to 4 per cent from 17 per cent. GDP growth regularly touched an astonishing 10 per cent a year – three times the EU average. (Arlidge 2009: 23)

Between 1990 and 1999 the southern Irish GDP rose by 75 per cent, of which 30 per cent was a direct result of multinational income. With GDP as the measure, it propelled the Republic of Ireland to the fore as an international economy, marked by the creation of hundreds of new property-rich (heavily mortgaged) millionaires.

Within governmental circles the rebalancing of the economy brought about an unflinching euphoria, and the pub-school of economics was celebrated for discovering alchemy as the public entered into an unprecedented credit-driven spending spree. The management of this economy manifested itself in other ways also. Of over 600 civil servants coordinating economic and financial policy for the southern government, only a handful were qualified economists and few knew the theory they were promoting or its philosophical lineage; Keynesian and development economists and analysts were shunned or removed from governmental and academic positions, and journalists who flagged up warnings of overheating within the economy were criticized for trying to depress the miracle. Antoin Murphy, from Trinity College Dublin, cynically referred to this form of economic development as 'the three Cs', reflecting on a system based on computers, chemicals and cola. Jim O'Leary, commenting on the 1993 trade statistics, noted that they had 'about the same empirical status as moving statues, flying saucers and the statue-of-Elvis-found-on-Mars stories'. Ó Gráda likened the 1990–93 national accounts to: 'children's fairy-tales, science-fiction or horror stories' (1997: 33). In 1998, O'Hearn highlighted the rawness of this globalized Irish model:

> Foreign capital is the main beneficiary of such dependent growth, but host countries like Ireland benefit somewhat less (speaking purely in terms of average income). The real global losers in the medium term are regions which lose foreign investment and become marginalized within global commodity chains. In terms of long-run growth, however, regions like the south of Ireland are still seriously endangered by sectoral overspecialization and geographical overdependence on a small range of foreign investors. (O'Hearn 1998: 128–9)

At this stage of the Tiger economy, the implications of global economic stress and contagion were registered. The possible effects of dislocation were foreseen – including the possibility of the European Union withdrawing structural funding – but the short-term fix that was the Celtic Tiger had created its own dynamic which kept people spending, jobs available, investment stable although dependent on the stability of international markets, and political buoyancy for the government. The south was even overtaking the north and Britain in terms of per capita income for the first time. The figures were, however, warped by the concentration of wealth in and around Dublin and within Tiger-privileged sectors. Dublin came to have the highest property prices on earth and the richest property developers. The statistics hid something else in the Irish model – they covered up the growth of relative poverty and gross inequalities when it came to access to health services, job opportunities and education. It exposed the skewed distribution of wealth towards the 'richest' sections of society:

> In the mid 1990s the bottom 10 per cent of households had about 2 per cent of total income whereas the top 1 per cent had 20 per cent. However, between 1994 and 1998 there was a redistribution of over 1 per cent of total income away from

the bottom 30 per cent of income distribution – representing a substantial shift in a short period. The increasing inequality reflects a shift from the bottom half of the distribution to the top half, rather than to those right at the top. (Nolan et al. 2000: xix)

There were also suspicions that inequality and poverty were implicit to the system, built into the Celtic Tiger itself – given that someone had to pay for the wealth being created:

McCreevy made sure that the boom would preserve the deep inequalities in Irish society by using his budgets to redistribute income upwards. His budget for the year 2000, for example, made the incomes of the poorest 20 per cent of the population rise by less than 1 per cent, those of the middle-income groups rise by 2–3 per cent, and those in the top 30 per cent by about 4 per cent. (O'Toole 2010: 23)

Even with the introduction of the southern government's National Anti-Poverty Strategy – as with Targeting Social Need in the north – relative poverty remained persistent. By 1998, 150,000 were estimated to be in serious housing need, with a 60 per cent rise in homeless people having to sleep rough in Dublin between 1997 and 2000 (Drudy and Punch 2001: 245; Kirby 2002: 62). Poverty was becoming a visible outcome of the Celtic Tiger.

Opinions on the effects of the Tiger economy came from both sides of the ideological divide. Undoubtedly, the 2002 budget brought the social partnership some returns, with lower-paid workers being removed from the tax net and benefits increasing. With unemployment going down to under 4 per cent by the end of 2000, it opened a unique situation on the island of Ireland where immigration for the first time in its history became an aspect of economic development. Members of Ireland's new communities – mostly from Poland and Lithuania – came to represent up to half the growth of the labour force (Clinch et al. 2002: 45–7). Indeed, immigration to the island was so forceful that in 2001 the government announced that the population had finally recovered from the loss of the famine years. Immediately after the 2004 EU enlargement process, an estimated 12 per cent of employees in the south of Ireland were immigrant labour, the vast majority from eastern Europe. In the biggest replacement of people since the famine, Ireland was being portrayed as 'Little Poland' on the continent. Curiously, Polish government maps started to position the island of Ireland at the top left-hand corner of Poland, substituting the geographic location of

Denmark with the economic location of Ireland. Benefits were quantifiable for a number of sections of the society and this was registered with wins in successive elections for Fianna Fáil, the key sponsors of the model, from Charles Haughey's departure as taoiseach on 11 February1992 until Brian Cowen's 7 May 2008 general election victory (with Albert Reynolds and Bertie Ahern in between).

The influx of multinational businesses and the redirection of governmental energy and resources towards supporting the globalizing aspects of the economy brought some highly visual benefits to favoured sections of the economy. In 1997 the Economic and Social Research Institute (ESRI) anticipated a growth rate of 4.9 per cent up until 2000 and suggested a further adjustment process which would demand substantial policy changes and prioritization towards the new entrepreneurial base. By 1998 over 60 per cent of southern grants to businesses were going to foreign companies. Indigenous activity seemed to be in terminal decline, matched by job losses in these sectors and the demise of manufacturing on the island of Ireland. The effects could be seen in areas and communities that had been dependent on indigenous industry and the way the Celtic Tiger depreciated their role in the economy. Fintan O'Toole, in *After the Ball*, commented:

> The great difference between the foreign and indigenously owned sectors is that the level of gross value added per employee is more than five times greater in the former than the latter. In 2001 gross value added per employee in Irish-owned firms stood at €44,700, an increase in nominal terms of 10 per cent. Despite this strong growth, the gap widened, as value added per employee in foreign firms increased by 12 per cent to €226,000 per employee. (O'Toole 2003: 162)

Of the indigenous Irish firms that did survive, being sold off became the norm. Two renowned and successful Irish breweries, Beamish and Murphys, were sold to Heineken and Carling; Ballygowan went to Budweiser; the largest indigenous Irish electronics firm, Lake Electronics, was sold to a Swiss company; and Guinness, the stalwart of the Irish economy since the Union itself, ended up in a merger in 1997 with the Spanish company Diageo.

FROM MODEL TO MIRACLE

In the summer of 2001 a series of transatlantic financial shocks gave some indication of the vulnerability of the Irish model. Extreme fluctuations could be monitored through the activities of the multi-national corporations. An oil price hike in the United States had put pressures on indigenous American companies and multinationals alike, acting as a check on over-stretched capacity and globalization. This was compounded by the collapse of the so-called 'dot-com' boom which would directly affect the numerous computer companies that had set up in Ireland, including Intel with its 5000 employees, Dell with 4300, Microsoft with 1200, Hewlett-Packard with 2500 and IBM with 3500. It resulted in corporations seeking to restrict operations outside the United States, with companies that had become stalwarts of the Tiger economy starting to withdraw or downsize. As the computer industry contracted, so did the Irish economic base. 'Annual growth in exports, which had averaged over 17 per cent between 1995 and 2000, struggled to reach 5 per cent over the next five years' (Finn 2011: 10; also see Kirby 2010: 35; Allen 2009: 36). Without urgent adaptation or market shifts, this collapse could have been terminal for the Celtic Tiger at this point. As chance took effect, the system was to benefit from a number of macroeconomic gambles orchestrated by the government in the hope that sheer luck (market forces, the 'invisible hand') would turn things around. This came in the form of a staged property boom, the introduction of the euro to the south and the influx of financial service industries. So began the second phase of the Celtic Tiger.

For the population of the south, and to a lesser extent the north – which was more comparable to the growth and policy patterns in Britain and still cushioned by upwards of 25 per cent of its GDP coming from the UK Treasury and the European Union – jobs were still available for those who were equipped to work in the new industries. Income was rising, credit was available and mortgages were being approved at will by lenders. For the first time since the land war of the 1870s and the land grabbing of the 1920s, land and property owning, or more correctly mortgage securing, became a national pastime. The Thatcherite dream of having a property-owning general public could be seen to be taking effect across Ireland. Critically, the population followed the government and its financial advisers into a property 'bubble' with borrowing at its core. In this second phase of the Tiger economy, a quarter of the southern Irish economy was to consist of an artificially sustained, debt-dependent property market. As the banks lent more, the public borrowed and spent more, and as the property prices inflated so did the spiral of debt.

Bank lending, mainly to developers and homeowners, was rising by 30 per cent annually. Anglo-Irish [Bank] ended up lending an amount equivalent to twice the national debt. House prices, quadrupling every 10 years, were outpacing incomes and rents by more than five to one. Household debt as a percentage of GDP had jumped from 60 per cent to almost 200 per cent, the highest figure in the developed world. (Arlidge 2009: 23)

Relief came in the form of changes to the monetary system of the European Union and the conclusion to a 50-year plan to introduce a single currency across the continent. Introduced on 1 January 2002, the euro was used as an opportunity to refresh the economy of the south. The region was ideally placed for building on the European financial markets and immediately went into overdrive to secure its position in the global banking system. The aim was to establish a Hong Kong-style base for banks working through to the eurozone. The euro was also used as a means of exploiting the new-found wealth across the island, with prices rising by an average of 25 per cent across the retail and service sectors. Instantly, Dublin became one of the most expensive places on earth to live, and the inflation brought accusations that the business community was profiteering on the changes without acknowledging the effects it would have on the population. The national television station RTÉ caught the mood of the population at the time with its series on *Rip-off Ireland*. Fintan O'Toole, in his *Ship of Fools*, commented:

> Inflation under McCreevy rose at twice the rate of Ireland's EU partners. Prices in Ireland in 2004 were 28 per cent above what they were when McCreevy took office in 1997; the corresponding figure for the EU was 14 per cent. (O'Toole 2010: 23)

Banking and financial services came into their own at this point, as these sectors gained prominence over industry for the first time in terms of job creation. By 2008, 14 per cent of the workforce would be employed in financial services. The completion of the International Financial Services Centre in Dublin marked a highpoint for this sector and led to the creation of 14,000 high-value jobs in accounting, legal and financial management. Likewise construction was catapulted to the fore of the Celtic Tiger, creating private sector employment in the building of hundreds of new housing estates and institutional bases for the emerging city of Dublin. Between 2000 and 2008, employment in construction rose by almost 60 per cent (Allen 2009: 44; Finn 2011: 11). Other elements of the economy were moving in tandem. In a resurgence of certain industrial sectors in the second phase, pharmaceuticals became the south's fastest growing sector, hosting 13 of the top 20 drug companies. By 2006 it was producing six of the top ten selling drugs in the world and was given the accolade of being the biggest supplier of Viagra. In terms of employment the drug sector was able to retain 24,000 jobs and was exporting €34 billion worth of products per year. Across the board FDI picked up. As the *Financial Times* noted of the pre-2008 period:

> The contribution of FDI to GDP growth is 10 times the rate in Germany, five times that of France, and four times the UK rate. The total value of investments by US companies in Ireland has grown from $36bn (€26bn) in 2000 to $87bn in 2008. (*Financial Times*, 9 January 2009)

The Celtic Tiger appeared to have survived its first major test.

From the northern perspective, the introduction of the euro brought about an unusual situation where two global currencies were operating side by side and in direct competition with each other. The immediate effect was that the border divisions and the economic differences therein were further accentuated. *Strategy 2010*, which was introduced by the Stormont civil servants as a response to the Celtic Tiger, attempted to create a parallel system in the north, but inevitably suffered due to the ongoing instability of government, the reluctance of companies to locate north of the border, a corporation tax rate twice that of the south, and financial dependence on London and Brussels. The strategy's vision was for: 'A fast growing, competitive, innovative, knowledge-based economy where there are plentiful opportunities and a population equipped to grasp them'. The closest the north was to come to its southern role model was in the building of iconic public–private partnership entertainment facilities, promoted as part peace dividend and part 'Ulster Tiger' (the Waterfront Hall, Odyssey Complex, Bangor Marina and Derry's Riverside).

Throughout the Celtic Tiger period, political stability and peace remained the central priority for the northern politicians, who only achieved inclusive and sustainable consensus government in May 2007 when the Democratic Unionist Party under the leadership of Ian Paisley – who became First Minister of Northern Ireland – went into a coalition with Sinn Féin, the UUP, the SDLP and Alliance Party. When it completed its term of government in May 2011 it

had achieved the feat of being the first ever cross-community administration in the history of the state of Northern Ireland to complete
a term. While the politicians navigated the complexities of the St
Andrews and Belfast agreements, the economic management of the
north resided principally with senior civil servants and their advisers.
Where the Celtic Tiger did, however, impact on the northern economy
was in the speculative buy-up of properties by developers from the
south, in the hope that the southern boom would eventually spread
northward.

In the quarterly national accounts of the southern government for
the year 2005, GNP and GDP growth were 5.4 per cent and 4.7 per
cent respectively. While growth was increasingly relying on domestic
consumption, the property boom and credit-based spending, the
system seemed to be holding up. Some statistics stand out in the
review of the second phase of the Celtic Tiger:

> We forecast an improvement in Ireland's export performance with
> growth rates of 3.5 per cent in 2006 and 4 per cent in 2007.
> These forecasts are based on a favourable external context, in
> particular a pick up in the Euro Area ... On employment, we
> expect 2006 and 2007 to produce increases of 67,000 and 60,000
> respectively. Accounting for new labour market entrants and a
> marginal increase in participation, these employment increases
> imply gross immigrant inflows of 53,000 in 2006 and 48,000
> in 2007. (Irish Government, *Quarterly National Accounts* 2005,
> summary)

This was the height of the second phase, when the south could
claim more personal helicopters per capita than anywhere else, the
highest property prices, the highest levels of holidays taken by its
population and a consumer frenzy that seemed to be never ending.
Caution was, however, flagged up by a number of government
agencies and economists, warning that there had been 'poor export
performance', 'declining competitiveness' and 'concern regarding
ongoing developments in the housing market'. Critically, economic
activity was increasingly revolving around the property bubble and
reckless banking practices. This overheating was registered in 2005
on a number of fronts, but largely ignored. As late as 2007, the
Republic's politicians and media were celebrating the fact that it
had unprecedented property prices, the most costly places to live
and the largest numbers of people living off credit – all contributing to a spending 'binge' managed by the government, facilitated

by the banks and based on credit. In the 'Globalization Index' the economy of the south was listed as the most globalized country on earth for three consecutive years; its form of neoliberal adjustment was presented by the World Bank and the European Union as the model that others, particularly emerging economies, should follow. Ireland, so the argument went, had finally caught up with the rest of Europe as a properly growth-focused, developed country. For the developers and the bankers the 'goldrush' was complete, revealing the real *modus operandi* of the model:

> The findings of a Revenue study of 400 top earners (defined, it is important to remember, by their declared income rather than their actual wealth) in 2002 were stark. Six had an effective tax rate of zero – they had quite lawfully managed to pay no tax at all. Forty-three paid less than 5 per cent. Seventy-nine paid tax at less than 15 per cent. Conversely, just 83 paid more than 40 per cent, and none paid more than 45 per cent. To put this in perspective, the top tax rate for PAYE [ordinary] workers in the same year was 42 per cent. (O'Toole 2010: 88)

Growth rates were getting stretched through to 2007, but when the American subprime mortgage sector collapsed at the beginning of 2008 the contagion to Ireland was almost immediate.

THE COLLAPSE

In the mid-2000s Irish banking had changed substantially and, with little government regulation and irresponsible lending, Irish banks began to borrow on international markets to provide property developers with loans that were at the very least high risk. In a return to classical liberal theory, the assumption was that property would be safe and would continue to sell, and that profits would be assured. Trusting the property market, the banks gambled the borrowed capital. Net foreign borrowing between 2003 and 2008 by Irish banks went up from 10 per cent to 60 per cent to feed the property boom. Irish banks, principal among them Anglo Irish and the Bank of Ireland, followed the new markets in high-risk loans on property, to 'subprime' borrowers, giving billions of euros to developers in particular to speculate on property. Being globally linked to the American banking system, its collapse in this type of business meant that Irish banking and the property development markets fell into an uncontrolled and virtually unregulated spiral of borrowing, credit and debt. Bank lending to private individuals went up from 60 per cent of GDP in 2003 to 200 per cent in 2008. Even before the crash in the subprime markets in the United States and the crisis that this caused globally, the Irish economy was unsustainable in this form.

The warning signs did not stop the Irish property frenzy. From 1995 until 2008, in a state populated by less than 4.5 million people, 1.1 million mortgages were approved. In the ten years up to 2006, 597,000 new houses were built; towns on the commuting zone to the cities were redesigned by developers: Stamullen had a 726 per cent increase in its housing, Ratoath 651 per cent, Sallins, 417; 64,000 new holiday homes were constructed to encourage the market in second properties. 'Between 1994 and 2006, the average second-hand house price in Dublin increased from €82,773 to €512,461 – a rise of 519 per cent' (O'Toole 2010: 101, 111, 174, 226). Average prices for new builds went up from €67,000 in 1991 to €334,000 in 2007 (Finn 2011: 11). With opportunistic practices from the property agents of Ireland, dysfunction in the housing and construction sectors, bankrolled by dubious methods, this market came to represent the very essence of neoliberal enterprise culture.

Through this fault line, the global recession delivered the fatal blow to the Irish model of economic development, by stemming capital inflow. Many multinational companies pulled out as the American economy contracted, government borrowing was exposed and increasing unemployment levels could be sourced to a dissolving mortgage industry. Like a deck of cards, the line-up of Celtic Tiger industries folded. The south officially fell into recession in September 2008 as its economy shrank for two consecutive quarters. The famed Irish GDP declined by 3 per cent in 2008, 10 per cent in 2009 and over 13 per cent in 2010.

The Celtic Tiger came to an end with the crash of summer 2008, and when the recession hit Ireland it was pervasive and extreme. Property prices went down abruptly and with this construction and financial service industries folded, forcing the government to take control of mounting, unredeemable bank loans. The banks were propped up repeatedly with public finances before government action proved to be ineffectual. The response, going further into recession, was that the Fianna Fáil government introduced an austerity programme which was one of the harshest in its history – with the purpose of trying to release more finance into the Irish banking system. The reaction of the government was instinctively neoliberal and classically monetarist – it sought to bail the Irish banks out of debt and shore up finance. Pay cuts of 15 per cent were imposed on public sector workers as the government prepared to make 25,000 redundant – hitting front-line services such as the police, health workers, teachers and local government. On further advice from banking specialists, the government moved to support the banks with a series of financial bailouts and the creation of the National Asset Management Agency (NAMA), which would permit the public sector to take over the financial liabilities of banks and manage 'toxic' loans. NAMA planned to give the banks €57 billion for property loans that could not be repaid, most of it speculative – €40 billion of it to the Anglo Irish Bank and its subsidiaries. A Marshalsea for modern times, NAMA's books quickly filled with 1500 individual debtors and controlled up to 15,000 individual loans. The top 30 Irish property developers accounted for €27 billion of NAMA's transfers (McDonald 2011: 44–5). As the government tried to manage its way through the crisis things went from bad to worse, with the economy moving towards virtual bankruptcy.

> Everything, it seems, has grown worse …. The recession started earlier and its bite has been deeper. Housing prices have fallen by as much as 50 per cent. Bank shares have plummeted by more than 90 per cent. Unemployment is approaching 10 per cent. (*New York Times*, 4 January 2009)

According to the Central Statistics Office Ireland, the unemployment rate reached 6.7 per cent in September 2008, the highest since September 1998, and the number of people claiming unemployment benefits rose by 11,734 to a total of 251,951 – the most claimants since August 1997. House building, mortgage lending, external investment and government spending all went into abeyance. The first desperate attempts to stave off bankruptcy by taoiseach Brian Cowen continued. As Daniel Finn, in the *New Left Review*, noted:

> the Fianna Fáil-led administration moved to nationalize Anglo Irish, the third-largest bank in the state, and shore up its two main competitors with huge cash injections. Anglo Irish specialized in massive loans to a small body of customers; fifteen accumulated debts to the bank of at least €500m each. Its losses of over €12 billion for 2009 were the largest in Irish corporate history. Once the bank guarantee was put in place, the overriding goal of Cowen's government was to shore up the private financial system at any cost …. As the rotten foundations of Irish banking

gradually came into public view, the anticipated cost of the guarantee rose exponentially: realistic estimates ... lie somewhere between €50 and €70 billion (Irish GDP in 2008 was a little over €200 billion). (Finn 2011: 11)

The Economic Recovery Plan of 4 February 2009 gave some indication of the ideological import of the government's response to the recession. Savings were to be made through withdrawing €1.4 billion from the public service bill through pension-related payments; reductions in travelling and subsistence rates for public servants; €1 billion by deferring national wage agreement payments; €95 million by reducing overseas development aid; €75 million in cuts to the early childcare supplement; €140 million through 'general administrative efficiencies'; and €300 million cut from the 2009 budget exchequer capital allocations. Beyond this a forum was established by the government from 18 to 20 September 2009 to debate the collapse of the Irish economy. The effects of the forum were negligible as the crisis intensified. The Irish Republic, once the fastest-growing economy in Europe, by early 2010 was among the most heavily indebted in the 16-member eurozone, with a deficit amounting to 12 per cent of GDP. It had become one of the so-called 'PIIGS': peripheral EU countries with economies verging on insolvency, comprising Portugal, Italy, Ireland, Greece and Spain. The impact was accentuated by contraction across all sectors of the economy. The south was now suffering the highest unemployment in its history, with key economic sectors (construction, financial services, banking) effectively collapsing. In human terms the recession meant 100 people losing their jobs every day.

The collapse was not restricted to the south but was felt island-wide. In the north, the high levels of subvention and public sector involvement in the economy cushioned the region from the extremes of the economic shock, but the impact became very apparent with the closure or run-down of high-profile private sector companies that had been drivers of regional economic development (Visteon, Seagate, Zavvi, Shorts, Nortel, Woolworths and Adams). There were job losses averaging 1000 per month; between May 2008 and May 2009 there was a 159 per cent increase in redundancies with 49,000 people unemployed – an 11,000 increase on the previous year (*Belfast Telegraph*, 13 May 2009). This was exacerbated by a 10 per cent contraction within the public sector in 2010 and cuts anticipated to be worth £370 million. With this single sector of the northern economy employing 32 per cent (222,000) of the working population, an estimated 10,000 faced redundancy. Stephen Kingon, the chair of Invest Northern Ireland, commented, 'I do not think we will be spared any harsh realities. It is going to be a tight decade or two' (*Belfast Telegraph*, 16 June 2009).

In the autumn of 2010 the neoliberal strategies of shoring up finance failed monumentally. The effects were almost immediate for the people of the south: house prices declined by up to 60 per cent, leaving almost 70 new private sector housing estates unoccupied and abandoned; 100 jobs per day continued to be lost, with 400,000 people signing on to the live register for unemployment benefits, the highest number ever, and food queues were seen in the cities. The impact resonated throughout Irish society, with levels of emigration not been seen since the 1950s and social exclusion similar to that of the 1970s. Over 600 'ghost estates', where families can no longer afford to live, were vacated; homelessness went to a record high – yet 17.5 per cent of houses (all built by private developers) lay unoccupied; house repossessions reached a point where the banks struggled to administer the paperwork (Carey and Ashton 2010). The most tragic repercussions were that by early 2011, a thousand people per week were losing their jobs and a thousand people (mostly young) were haemorrhaging out of the country each week to seek employment opportunities elsewhere.

On 19 November 2010 a dozen representatives of the IMF, backed by the European Central Bank and the European Commission, arrived at Irish government offices in Dublin with a (€85 billion) plan to bail out the Irish economy from the debt crisis that had brought it to the verge of bankruptcy. The debt amounted to a staggering 54 per cent of the Irish GDP, and pushed the south into an economic category more often seen in Africa than in Europe. The mission's brief was to 'look at whatever measures might be needed' to clear the south's debt, Caroline Atkinson, the delegation's spokeswoman commented. The taoiseach, Brian Cowen, let the population know that there was no 'reason for the Irish people to be ashamed and humiliated'. The IMF, the European Commission and the European Central Bank (ECB) arrived in Dublin to take substantial control of the economy of the south of Ireland.

The collapse of significant sectors of the Irish economy since the boom and waste of the second phase of the Celtic Tiger had left the country in such a state of financial chaos that by February 2011 the Fianna Fáil government fell, after ruling for almost 60 of the previous 80 years. From the onset of the recession the standard of living had dropped so quickly for the population of the south that it created poverty levels not seen in a generation. The model of economic development that had been engineered for 15 years by Fianna Fáil and encouraged by Fine Gael – the 2011 electoral successors – had resulted in taxpayers having to underwrite banking failures amounting to 135 per cent of the country's GDP. Ireland's international credit rating lost its value, leaving the liability with the Irish people themselves. Andrew Clark of the *Observer*, highlighted some common wisdom on the government's economic management: 'We're being asked to rescue the richest people in the world – the people who bet on every horse in the race and lost' (2010). Instead of liquidating uncompetitive banks, the new government under Enda Kenny followed its ideological instincts and again turned on the taxpayers, referring to the 'pain' to come. The cost of the bailout represents one-third of the country's national income, leaving an impossible scenario. 'The regime being imposed on Ireland is utterly unrealistic. A depressed and deeply indebted economy with just 1.8 million people at work cannot underwrite private banking liabilities of 200bn (135 per cent of GDP)' (*Observer*, 27 February 2011: 34).

On the back of a banking frenzy that lasted six years, an artificially sustained property boom, a 230 per cent ratio of private credit to GDP, state investment in banks that amounted to 45 per cent of the country's GDP and 55 per cent of its GNP (at €75 billion), and a budget deficit of 32 per cent of the GDP by 2010, the Celtic Tiger – so lauded by the IFIs – had arrived at its logical conclusion. It was left to be picked over by the IFIs. There ended one of the most celebrated exhibitions of the neoliberal model of economic development that had ever been visited upon a European country. Its effects were devastating for communities across the island, which were subjected, first, to the risk and squander of the Celtic Tiger, and then to economic desolation in its wake. The unsustainable nature of this version of economic development could be seen in its outcome when, on closing the accounts for the Celtic Tiger, an emasculated Irish government could not afford to pay for its own people's public services, health or education, and has left Ireland indebted as a country for decades to come.

CONCLUSION

If anything has been learned from the demise of the Irish model of economic development, it is that this archetypal neoliberal economy – so celebrated by the organizations charged with managing its liquidation – is fundamentally flawed. The system created around global commercial networks and the primacy of the finance and property sectors, and lauded around the world as the most rapid method of economic development, turned out to be as destructive as it has been erratic. It reached its end in the most inauspicious manner, reducing the island to the role of being – in the words of one of the managers of this economic model, taoiseach Enda Kenny – a 'laughing stock'. Ireland, almost overnight, had returned to being the 'sick man of Europe'.

As a survey of some of the patterns of economic development on the island of Ireland, this polemic provides some evidence to suggest that the problems can be sourced to post-colonial mentalities and ideological dogmatism, but ultimately to bad governance. Decade after decade of debilitating decisions have been taken, north and south, on the basis of short-term fixes and patronage, without considering the needs or rights of the population. Essentially, evidence would suggest that what has been lacking have been the principles of inclusivity and social justice in economic management.

This remains a fundamental question. Throughout their history the Irish people have been subjected to extreme political and economic circumstances that few other European populations have had to suffer. After enduring long periods of recession and depression, extensive levels of poverty, ongoing and seemingly intractable political violence, and a form of market fundamentalism that was alien to the post-war social market consensus, the island has again been visited by flawed economic management through the Celtic Tiger. Cronyism, nepotism and patronage have been prominent features of Irish economic culture throughout its history, north and south, with references to the common good being cynically rhetorical rather than genuine and practical. In this culture the principles of subsidiarity and solidarity have been relegated as obstructions to wealth creation, while any concept of social responsibility has been downplayed as philanthropy that is beyond the role of government. Economic development without conscience seems to be the core legacy that the various administrations and their advisors have left the Irish people, north and south.

The result of this has been an estimated 100,000 people being forced to emigrate in 2011 for economic reasons. An overview of Irish economic history reveals a number of cold truths that do not often apply to other European regions. The scale of the crises and the intensity of uneven development have been unprecedented, mirroring the scale and scope of economic and political dysfunction. The facts that most Irish people live outside Ireland, that many continue to suffer shortages, and that the region has been involved in almost continual internal and external conflicts, give some indication of their endurance.

Three distinct features stand out in the economic history of the island, each of which has crippled economic development, but each of which also suggests answers to the malaise. First, there are the implications of the diverging border economy. This border arrangement had been created to placate state and communitarian interests, and was a construct of harsher political times. Covering a third of the island, the border counties have been subjected to the worst aspects of differentiation, while its townland communities have remained largely outside policy frameworks and investment programmes since the start of the last century. Economic theory from the Treaty of Rome onwards suggests that integrated borders can create a catalyst for improvement in the standards of living and opportunities for those living in border regions. Structurally, evidence exists to prove that regional linkage – 'synergy' – can work for developmental purposes and that integration pacifies. Economically, regionalization can stimulate growth and employment.

Second, peace has been elusive for the Irish people for centuries. A person born in 1935, residing in Ireland and living to the age of 75, would have been witness to the spectrum of political and sectarian violence stretching over 50 years in total. A culture of militarism, sectarianism and conflict was built into the fabric of Irish society and its political economy. It dehumanized the communities it affected and crippled their development. In contrast, countries which have peace building knitted into the national fabric, such as the Scandinavian countries, distil the ideal of peace throughout their policies and society in general. Irish society – as with other divided communities – if it is not investing in peace will be a society preparing for war. While history seems to repeat itself on a chillingly regular basis in this context, there have also been profound moments of change. The state visit by Queen Elizabeth II to the south of

Ireland in May 2011 at the request of President Mary McAleese (the first from a British monarch since July 1911) offered an insight into the potential of peace building between the islands and within Ireland itself. In her address to the State dinner in Dublin Castle on 18 May 2011, President McAleese outlined the status quo:

> The Good Friday Agreement represented a fresh start and committed us all to partnership, equality and mutual respect as the basis of future relationships. Under the Agreement, unionism and nationalism were accorded equal recognition as political aspirations and philosophies. Northern Ireland's present status within the United Kingdom was solemnly recognized, as was the option for a united Ireland if that secures the agreement and consent of a majority of the people of Northern Ireland.
>
> The collegial and cooperative relationship between the British and Irish Governments was crucial to the success of the Peace Process and we can thank the deepening engagement between us as equal partners in the European Union for the growth of friendship and trust. The Governments' collaborative efforts to bring peace and power-sharing to Northern Ireland have yielded huge dividends for the peoples of these two islands. W.B. Yeats once wrote in another context that 'peace comes dropping slow'.
>
> The journey to peace has been cruelly slow and arduous, but it has taken us to a place where hope thrives and the past no longer threatens to overwhelm our present and our future. The legacy of the Good Friday Agreement is already profound and encouraging. We all of us have a duty to protect, nurture and develop it.

Finally, the most formidable legacy of Irish economic history has arguably been the role of market fundamentalism in undermining the emergence of a balanced and equitable socio-economic environment. Classical liberalism originally evolved from schemes to maximize profit for specific commercial interests, based on the risk factors of the market, compliant or invisible governments, and enterprise driven by and for privileged elites. Historically, its vanguards were the landlords, marketeers and commercial agents who systematically exploited the natural and human resources of the island. Its modern incarnation in neoliberalism, working from the same ideological stem, adjusted the theories to fixate on profitability derived from financial management, aggressive entrepreneurialism, deregulation, property ownership, restricted government intervention in the economy, and extracting profit from public assets wherever

possible. In this the vanguards of the Celtic Tiger have striking simi-
larities with their landowning and mill-owning predecessors; their
philosophy of wealth has remained steadfastly the same.

In the final analysis the outworking of Irish economic history
compels the question of change and the possibility of alternatives. Its
more recent disposition demands a debate around political accountability and the appropriate (democratic) management of public assets.
Root and branch constitutional change is also an option, as articulated by the call for a second republic, with a socially informed,
inclusive constitution. The underdevelopment of the economies,
north and south, would suggest the need for renewal in a manner
that would be appropriate to the needs of the Irish people and not
the wants of economy. As an alternative to the failed economic
model of the past 20 years and the problems related to the peripheral
location of the island, answers could be drawn from other European
regions with more assertive social market models – regions that due
to careful democratic management of economic policies have been
able to navigate through recessions without too much pain for their
populations. The starting point, however, needs to be an acceptance
by the Irish political establishment that other models exist which
would be more appropriate to the Irish context and history. The
island's people – and particularly its young – deserve better.

BIBLIOGRAPHY

Allen, Kieran (2000) *The Celtic Tiger: The Myth of Social Partnership in Ireland*, Manchester University Press, Manchester.

Allen, Kieran (2009) *Ireland's Economic Crash*, Liffey Press, Dublin.

Anderson, J. (1994) 'Problems of Interstate Economic Integration: Northern Ireland and the Irish Republic in the Single European Market', *Political Geography*, Vol. 13, No. 1, pp. 53–73.

Anderson, J. and J. Goodman (1994) 'European and Irish Integration: Contradictions of Regionalism and Nationalism', *European Journal of Urban and Regional Studies*, Vol. 1, No. 1, pp. 49–62.

Arlidge, John (2009) 'Recession: The Bad Luck of the Irish', *Sunday Times Magazine*, 29 March, pp. 18–25.

Aughey, Arthur (1989) *Under Siege: Ulster Unionism and the Anglo-Irish Agreement*, Blackstaff, Belfast.

Barry, F. (ed.) (1999) *Understanding Ireland's Economic Growth*, Macmillan, Basingstoke.

Bew, Paul and Gordon Gillespie (2000) *Northern Ireland: A Chronology of the Troubles, 1968–1999*, Gill & Macmillan, London.

Bew, Paul and Henry Patterson (1979) *The State of Northern Ireland 1921–1972*, Manchester University Press, Manchester.

Bew, Paul and Henry Patterson (1985) *The British State and the Ulster Crisis*, Verso, London.

Bew, Paul, Peter Gibbon and Henry Patterson (1996) *Northern Ireland 1921–1996*, Serif, London.

Bicheno, J. (1830) *Ireland and its Economy*, Murray, London.

Black, R. D. C. (1960) *Economic Thought and the Irish Question*, Cambridge University Press, Cambridge.

Blake, J. W. (1956) *Northern Ireland in the Second World War*, Blackstaff, Belfast.

Bourke, Austin (1993) *The Visitation of God? The Potato and the Great Irish Famine*, Lilliput, Dublin.

Boylan, T. and T. Foley (1992) *Political Economy and Colonial Ireland*, Taylor & Francis, London.

Boyle, P. P. and Cormac Ó Gráda (1986) 'Fertility Trends, Excess Mortality, and the Great Irish Famine', *Demography*, No. 23, pp. 543–62.

Bradley, John (1993) *Stabilisation and Growth on the EC Periphery*, Avebury, Aldershot.

Breen, R., D. Hannan, D. Rottman and C. T. Whelan (1990) *Understanding Contemporary Ireland: State, Class and Development in the Republic of Ireland*, Gill & Macmillan, Dublin.

Bromage, Arthur (1938) 'Anglo-Irish Accord', *Political Science Quarterly*, Vol. 53, No. 4, December, pp. 516–32.

Brown, Terence (2004) *Ireland: A Social and Cultural History, 1922–2002*, Harper Perennial, London.

Brunt, Barry (1988) *The Republic of Ireland*, Paul Chapman, London.

Buckland, P. (1981) *A History of Northern Ireland*, Macmillan, London and New York.

Burns, John (2002) 'Ireland's Post-famine Boom Put it Ahead of Germany', *Sunday Times*, 27 October, p. 9.

Butt, Isaac (1837) *The Poor Law Bill for Ireland Examined*, B. Fellowes, London.

Byrne, Patrick (1984) 'Memories of the Republican Congress', *Irish Democrat*, Dublin. www.oocities.com/irelandscw/docs-RepCog.htm.

Caherty, Thérèse et al. (eds) (1992) *Is Ireland a Third World Country?*, Beyond the Pale, Belfast.

Canavan, Tony (ed.) (1991) *Every Stoney Acre Has a Name*, Federation for Local Ulster Studies, Belfast.

Canning, D., B. Moore and J. Rhodes (1987) 'Economic Growth in Northern Ireland: Problems and Prospects', Economic and Social Research Council paper, Belfast.

Capuchins (1940) *The Persecution of Catholics in Northern Ireland*, Capuchin Annual, Dublin.

Carey, Brian and James Ashton (2010) 'Drowning in Debt', *Sunday Times*, 3 October, p. 5.

Carson, William (1956) *Ulster and the Irish Republic*, William W. Cleland, Belfast.

Central Community Relations Unit (CCRU) (1999) Response to an information request from the West Belfast Economic Forum, Belfast, 28 May.

Chubb, F. B. and P. Lynch (eds) (1969) *Economic Development and Planning*, Institute of Public Administration, Dublin.

Clark, Samuel (1979) *Social Origins of the Irish Land War*, Princeton University Press, Princeton.

Clark, Andrew (2010) 'The Irish want to Punish Builders, Bankers and Politicians', *Observer*, 5 December, Business, p. 52.

Clarkson, L. E. and E. M. Crawford (2001) *Feast and Famine: Food and Nutrition in Ireland 1500–1920*, Oxford University Press, Oxford.

Clinch, Peter, Frank Convery and Brendan Walsh (2002) *After the Celtic Tiger*, O'Brien Press, Dublin.

Colin Stutt Consultancy (1997) 'NI Single Programme 1994–99, Mid Term Review – External Evaluation', Colin Stutt Consultancy, Belfast.

Combe, George (1847) *The Constitution of Man and Its Relation to External Objects*, Stewart & Co., Longman & Co., London. http://darwin-online. org.uk/content/frameset?viewtype=text&itemID=A33&pageseq=1.

Connolly S. J. (ed.) (1998) *Kingdoms United? Integration and Diversity*, Four Courts, Dublin.

Coopers & Lybrand (1997) 'Mid-Term Evaluation Draft Report', Coopers & Lybrand, Belfast.

Costello, Francis (2003) *The Irish Revolution and its Aftermath 1916–1923*, Irish Academic Press, Dublin.

Coyne, W. P. (ed.) (1901) *Ireland: Industrial and Agricultural*, Browne and Nolan, Dublin.

Crotty, R. D. (1966) *Irish Agricultural Production: Its Volume and Structure*, Cork University Press, Cork.

Cullen, L. M. (ed.) (1964) *The Formation of the Irish Economy*, RTÉ, Dublin.

Cullen, L. M. (1987) *An Economic History of Ireland Since 1660,* 2nd edn, Batsford, London.

Cullen, L. M. (1996) 'The Politics of the Famine and Famine Historiography', *Comhdháil an Chraoibh Án*, Roscommon, Ireland, pp. 9–31.

Curran, J. M. (1980) *The Birth of the Irish Free State 1921–1923*, University of Alabama Press, Alabama.

Curtis, Edmund (1952) *History of Ireland*, Methuen, London.

Dáil Éireann (1919) *Dáil Éireann Loan Prospectus*, SPO, Dublin.

Daly, Mary (1987) 'The Employment Gains from Industrial Protection in the Irish Free State during the 1930s', *Irish Economic and Social History*, Vol. 15, pp. 71–5.

Darby, John (ed.) (1983) *Northern Ireland: the Background to the Conflict*, Appletree Press, Belfast.

Davison, Robson (1979) *The Effects of the German Air Raids on Belfast,* PhD thesis, Queen's University Belfast, Belfast.

De Valera, E. (1928) *Fianna Fáil and its Economic Policy*, National Executive of Fianna Fáil, Dublin.

Department of Finance and Personnel (DFP) (1999) 'Consultation Conference: On EU Structural Funds 2000–2006', DFP, Belfast.

Desmond, Adrian and James Moore (1991) *Darwin*, Penguin, London.

Dinan, Desmond (2010) *Ever Closer Union*, Palgrave, Basingstoke.

Dixon, Paul (2008) *Northern Ireland: The Politics of War and Peace*, Palgrave, Basingstoke.

Doherty, Gillian and Tomás O'Riordan (2011) 'Dublin, 1913: Strike and Lockout', University College Cork, Cork. http://multitext.uuc.ie/d/Dublin_1913Strike_and_Lockout.

Donnelly, James (2000) *The Irish Potato Famine*, Sutton, London.

Donnelly, James (2005) *The Great Irish Potato Famine*, Sutton, London.

Drudy, P. J. and Michael Punch (2001) 'Housing and Inequality in Ireland', in Sara Cantillon et al. (eds) *Rich and Poor: Perspectives on Tackling Inequality in Ireland*, Oak Tree Press, Dublin.

Dudley Edwards, Ruth and T. Desmond Williams (eds) (1954) *The Great Famine*, Browne & Nolan, Dublin.

Dumont, Charles (1921) Report of US Consul, 23 April 1921, Records of US Legation, State Department Files, 841.00/351.

Economist (2005) 'The Economist Intelligence Unit's Quality-of-life Index', online.

Edwards, R. D. and T. D. Williams (1956) *The Great Famine: Studies in Irish History, 1845–52*, Browne & Nolan (new edn, Lilliput Press, 1994), Dublin.

Eiriksson, Andrés (1997) 'Food Supply and Food Riots', *Famine 150: The Teagasc/UCD Lectures*, edited by Cormac Ó Gráda, Teagasc, Dublin, pp. 67–93.

English, Richard (2003) *Armed Struggle: The History of the IRA*, Pan, London.

European Commission (1994) 'The Ireland Single Programming Document 1994–1999', Office for Official Publications of the European Communities, Luxemburg.

European Commission (1998a) *Northern Ireland in Europe*, EC, Brussels.

European Commission (1998b) 'Peace and Reconciliation: An Imaginative Approach to the European Programme for Northern Ireland and the Border Counties of Ireland', EC, Brussels.

European Commission (1998c) 'Driving Regional Development', EC, Brussels.

European Court of Auditors (2000) 'Special Report No7/2000 Concerning the International Fund for Ireland and the Special Support Programme for Peace and Reconciliation in Northern Ireland and the Border Counties of Ireland (1995–1999)', EU Court of Auditors, May, Brussels.

Evans, E. Estyn (1949) *Irish Heritage: The Landscape, the People and Their Work*, Dundalgan Press, Dundalk.

Fanning, Ronan (1983) *Independent Ireland*, Dublin.

Farrell, Michael (1976) *Northern Ireland, The Orange State*, Pluto, London.

Finn, Daniel (2011) 'Ireland on the Turn? Political and Economic Consequences of the Crash', *New Left Review*, No. 67, pp. 5–39.

Fisher, Charlie and Robbie McVeigh (2002) 'Chill Factor or Kill Factor: The Effects of Sectarian Intimidation on Employment in West Belfast', Confederation of British Industry, Belfast.

FitzGerald, Garret (1968) *Planning in Ireland*, Institute of Public Administration, Dublin.

FitzGerald, Garret (1972) *Towards a New Ireland*, Charles Knight, London.

Fitz Gerald, John (1998) 'An Irish Perspective on Structural Funds', *European Planning Studies*, Vol. 6, No. 6, pp. 677–94.

Fitzgerald, M. (2000) *Protectionism to Liberalisation: Ireland and the EEC, 1957 to 1966*, Ashgate, Aldershot.

Fitzpatrick, David (1977) *Politics and Irish Life, 1913–1921*, Gill & Macmillan, Dublin.

Fitzpatrick, David (1978) 'The Geography of Irish Nationalism', *Past and Present*, No. 78, February.

Fitzpatrick, David (1989) 'Emigration: 1801–70', in W.E. Vaughan (ed.) *A New History of Ireland, Vol. V: Ireland under the Union, 1801–1870*, Oxford University Press, Oxford.

Forfas (2008) 'Annual Competitiveness Report 2008, Vol. 1: Benchmarking Ireland's Performance', Forfas, Dublin.

Foster, R. (1988) *Modern Ireland 1600–1973*, Penguin, London.

Gibson, N. J. and J. E. Spencer (eds) (1977) *Economic Activity in Ireland: A Study of Two Open Economies*, Gill and Macmillan, Dublin.

Girvin, Brian (2006) *The Emergency: Neutral Ireland 1939–45*, Macmillan, London.

Goodman, James (2000) *Single Europe, Single Ireland*, Irish Academic Press, Dublin.

Government of the Irish Republic, Finance (Agreement with United Kingdom) Act (1938) No.12/1938. www.irishstatutebook.ie/1938/en/act/pub/0012/print.html.

Government of the Irish Republic, Department of Finance (1958a) *Economic Development*, Stationery Office, Dublin (Pr. 4803).

Government of the Irish Republic, Department of Finance (1958b) *Programme for Economic Expansion*, Stationery Office, November, Dublin (Pr. 4468).

Government of the Irish Republic (1961) *Census of Population*, Stationery Office, Dublin.

Government of the Irish Republic (1970) *Membership of the European Communities: Implications for Ireland*, Stationery Office, Dublin.

Government of the Irish Republic (1972) *The Accession of Ireland to the European Communities*, Stationery Office, Dublin.

Government of the Irish Republic (1992) *Culliton Report*, Stationery Office, Dublin.

Government of the United Kingdom, *Poor Laws*, Parliamentary Papers, Hansard, 44, XXVII.

Gray, Peter (1999) *Famine, Land, and Politics: British Government and Irish Society, 1843–50*, Irish Academic Press, Dublin.

Greaves, C. Desmond (1961) *The Life and Times of James Connolly*, Lawrence & Wishart, London.

Guinnane, Timothy W. (1997) *The Vanishing Irish: Households, Migration and the Rural Economy in Ireland, 1850–1914*, Princeton University Press, Princeton, N.J.

Guinnane, Timothy W. and Cormac Ó Gráda (2002) 'Workhouse Mortality and the Great Irish Famine', in Tim Dyson and Cormac Ó Gráda (eds), *Famine Demography*, Oxford University Press, Oxford, pp. 44–64.

Guinness (1939) *Guinness*, James's Gate, Dublin.

Haase, Trutz (1999) *EU Support Programme for Peace and Reconciliation: Analysis of Communty Uptake*, NISRA, Belfast.

Hall, F. G. (1949) *History of the Bank of Ireland*, Bank of Ireland, Dublin and Oxford.

Hall, Robert (1962) *Report of the Joint Working Party on the Economy of Northern Ireland*, HMSO, Belfast.

Hamilton, Douglas (1993) 'Foreign Investment and Industrial Development in Northern Ireland', in Paul Teague (ed.) *The Economy of Northern Ireland: Perspectives for Structural Change*, Lawrence & Wishart, London, pp. 190–216.

Hamilton, Douglas (2001) 'Economic Integration on the Island of Ireland', *Administration*, Vol. 49, No. 2, pp. 73–89.

Harkness, David (1983) *Northern Ireland Since 1920*, Criterion Press, Dublin.

Harvey, Brian (1997) 'Report on the Programme for Peace and Reconciliation', Joseph Rowntree Charitable Trust, York.

Harvey, Brian, Assumpta Kelly, Sean McGearty and Sonya Murray (2005) *The Emerald Curtain: The Social Impact of the Irish Border,* Triskele, Carrickmacross.

Harvey, David (2005) *A Brief History of Neoliberalism*, Oxford University Press, Oxford.

Hederman, Miriam (1983) *The Road to Europe: Irish Attitudes 1948–61*, Institute of Public Administration, Dublin.

Hensey, B. (1959) *The Health Services of Ireland*, Dublin.

Hillyard, Partick, Bill Rolston and Mike Tomlinson (2005) *Poverty and Conflict in Ireland*, Institute of Public Administration, Dublin.

Hooper, Glenn (2001) *The Tourist's Gaze: Travellers to Ireland*, Cork University Press, Cork.

Hopkinson, M. (1988) *Green Against Green: The Irish Civil War*, Gill & Macmillan, Dublin.

House of Commons (1824) Select Committee Inquiring into the Disturbances in Ireland, *Hansard*, 5 June, London.

Inglis, Henry (1834) *A Journey Through Ireland*, Whittaker & Co., London.

Institute of European Studies (2000) 'European Funding and the Voluntary Sector', Institute of European Studies, QUB, Belfast.

International Labour Review (November 1948) Vol. 58, No. 5.

International Monetary Fund (2001) *Ireland: Staff Report for the 2001 IV Consultation*, IMF, Washington DC.

Isles, K. S. and N. Cuthbert (1955) 'Ulster's Economic Structure', in T. Wilson (ed.), *Ulster under Home Rule*, Oxford University Press, Oxford.

Isles, K. S. and N. Cuthbert (1957) *An Economic Survey of Northern Ireland*, HMSO, Belfast.

Jacobson, David, Peadar Kirby and Deiric ÓBroin (2006) *Taming the Tiger: Social Exclusion in a Globalised Ireland*, Tacs, Dublin.

Jeffery, Keith (2000) *Ireland and the Great War*, Cambridge University Press, Cambridge.

Johnson, D. (1985) *The Inter-war Economy in Ireland*, Economic and Social History Society of Ireland, Dundalk.

Kearney, A.T. (2004) 'Measuring Globalisation: Economic Reversals, Forward Momentum', *Foreign Policy*, March–April, pp. 52–60.

Kearney, Richard (1988) *Across the Frontiers: Ireland in the 1990s*, Wolfhound, Dublin.

Kee, Robert (1976a) *The Most Distressful Country*, Quartet, London.

Kee, Robert (1976b) *The Bold Fenian Men*, Quartet, London.

Kee, Robert (1976c) *Ourselves Alone*, Quartet, London.

Kennedy, J. F. (1946) article in the *New York Journal*, quoted in the *Sunday Times*, 14 March 2010, p. 13.

Kennedy, K. A. (1971) *Productivity and Industrial Growth: The Irish Experience*, Oxford University Press, Oxford.

Kennedy, K. A. and B. R. Dowling (1975) *Economic Growth in Ireland: The Experience Since 1947*, Gill & Macmillan, Dublin.

Kennedy, Kieran, Thomas Giblin and Deirdre McHugh (1988) *The Economic Development of Ireland in the Twentieth Century*, Routledge, London.

Kennedy, Liam and P. Ollerenshaw (eds) (1985) *An Economic History of Ulster 1820–1939*, Manchester University Press, Manchester.

Kennedy, Liam et al. (1999) *Mapping the Great Irish Famine*, Four Courts Press, Dublin.

Kennedy, M. and E. O'Halpin (2000) *Ireland and the Council of Europe: From Isolation Towards Integration*, Council of Europe, Strasbourg.

Kennedy, Tony (2001) 'Community Relations the Key to NI Peace', *Irish Times*, 12 September.

Keogh, Dermot and Mervyn O'Driscoll (eds) (2004) *Ireland in World War Two: Diplomacy and Survival*, Mercier, Cork.

Keynes, John Maynard (1933) 'National Self-sufficiency', *Studies*, Vol. 22, June, pp. 177–93. Also in *Review of the International Statistical Institute*, Vol. 18, No. 1–2, pp. 1–20.

Kinealy, Christine (1994) *The Great Calamity: The Irish Famine 1845–52*, Gill & Macmillan, Dublin and London.

Kirby, Peadar (2002) *The Celtic Tiger in Distress: Growth and Inequality in Ireland*, Palgrave, Basingstoke.

Kirby, Peadar (2010) *Celtic Tiger in Collapse: Explaining the Weaknesses of the Irish Model*, Palgrave, Basingstoke.

Laffan, Brigid and Jane O'Mahony (2008) *Ireland and the European Union*, Palgrave, Basingstoke.

Lawlor, Sheila (1983) *Britain and Ireland 1914–1923*, Gill & Macmillan, New York and Dublin.

Lawrence, R. J. (1965) *The Government of Northern Ireland*, Clarendon Press, Oxford.

League of Nations (1940) *Statistical Year-Book*, League of Nations, Geneva.

Leddin, A. and B. Walsh (1998) *The Macro-Economy of Ireland*, Gill & Macmillan, Dublin.

Lee, Joseph (1989) *Ireland, 1912–85: Politics and Society*, Cambridge University Press, Cambridge.

Leibfried, Stephan and Pierson, Paul (1997) 'Social Policy', in Helen Wallace and William Wallace (eds), *Policy Making in the European Union*, Oxford University Press, Oxford, pp. 185–208.

Longfield, M. (1834) *Four Lectures on Poor Laws*, W. Curry, Dublin.

Loughlin, P. (1991) 'The Anglo-Irish Agreement: Federal Arrangement or Affirmation of the Nation-State?', *Federalisme*, Vol. 3, pp. 183–97.

Lyons, F. S. L. (1963, reprinted 1971) *Ireland Since the Famine*, Fontana, London.

MacDonagh, Oliver (1961) *A Pattern of Government Growth 1800–1860*, MacGibbon & Kee, London.

MacSharry, R. and P. White (2000) *The Making of the Celtic Tiger: The Inside Story of Ireland's Boom Economy*, Mercier Press, Cork.

Madden, R. R. (1846) *The United Irishmen: Vol. I*, James Duffy, Dublin.

Maguire, J. F. (1868) *The Irish in America*, London. www.libraryireland.com/Maguire/contents.php

Maguire, Orla (2006) *The Rise and Fall of the West Belfast Mills*, Beechmount Community Project, Belfast.

Maher, D. J. (1986) *The Tortuous Path: The Course of Ireland's Entry into the EEC, 1948–73*, IPA, Dublin.

Mandle, M. F. (1987) *The Gaelic Athletic Association and Irish Nationalist Politics, 1884–1924*, Gill & Macmillan, London.

Mansergh, N. (1934) *The Irish Free State: Its Government and Politics*, Allen & Unwin, London.

Martindale, Hilda (1944) *From One Generation to Another*, Allen & Unwin, London.

Marx, Karl (1867, repr. 1974) *Capital*, Vol. 1, Lawrence & Wishart, London.

Marx, Karl and Frederick Engels (1971) *Marx and Engels on Ireland*, Lawrence & Wishart, London and New York.

McCann, Gerard (2001a) *Navigating the Crisis*, South Belfast Partnership Board, Belfast.

McCann, Gerard (ed.) (2001b) *The Rights Debate*, West Belfast Economic Forum, Belfast.

McCann, Gerard and Stephen McCloskey (eds) (2009) *From the Local to the Global*, Pluto, London.

McCracken, J. C. (1958) *Representative Government in Ireland*, Oxford University Press, Oxford.

McDonald, Gary (2011) 'Nama and the North', *Agenda*, No. 45 (March), pp. 44–45.

McDonald, Henry (2010) 'Ireland on the Brink of Economic Abyss as Austerity Budgets Fail to Revive Celtic Tiger', *Observer*, 26 September, Business, p. 39.

McKeever, Gerald (1979) *Economic Policy in the Irish Free State*, McGill University, Montreal.

McKittrick, David, Seamus Kelters, Brian Feeney and Chris Thornton (1999) *Lost Lives*, Mainstream, Edinburgh and London.

Meenan, J. (1970) *The Irish Economy Since 1922*, Liverpool University Press, Liverpool.

Mill, John Stuart (1886, reprinted 2008) *England and Ireland*, Cosimo, New York.

Miller, Kerby (1985) *Emigrants and Exiles: Ireland and the Irish Exodus to North America*, Oxford University Press, New York.

Mitchel, John (1861, reprinted 2005) *The Last Conquest of Ireland*, University College Dublin Press, Dublin.

Mitchell, Arthur (1995) *Revolutionary Government in Ireland: Dáil Éireann 1919–22*, Gill & Macmillan, Dublin.

Mitchell, A. and P. O'Snodaigh, (1985) *Irish Political Documents 1916–1949*, Irish Academic Press, Dublin.

Mjøset, L. (1992) *The Irish Economy in a Comparative Institutional Perspective*, Report No. 93, National Economic and Social Council, Stationery Office, Dublin.

Mokyr, Joel (1983) *Why Ireland Starved: A Quantitative and Analytical History of the Irish Economy, 1800–1850*, Allen & Unwin, London.

Mokyr, Joel and C. O'Grada (1982) 'Emigration and Poverty in Pre-famine Ireland', in *Explorations in Economic History*, Vol. 19, No. 4, pp. 360–84.

Mokyr, Joel and Cormac Ó Gráda (2002) 'What Do People Die of During Famines? The Great Irish Famine in Comparative Perspective', *European Review of Economic History*, Vol. 6, No. 3, pp. 339–64.

Moody, T. W. and J. C. Beckett (eds) (1954) *Ulster Since 1800*, BBC, London.

Morgan, Austin (1991) *Labour and Partition: The Belfast Working Class 1905–23*, Pluto, London.

Munck, Ronnie (1993) *The Irish Economy: Results and Prospects*, Pluto, London.

Murphy, Antoin (1998) *The Celtic Tiger: The Great Misnomer*, Money and Markets International.

Murray, Alice Effie (1903) *A History of the Commercial and Financial Relations between England and Ireland from the Period of the Restoration*, P. S. King, London.

National Economic and Social Council (NESC) (1983) *Review of Industrial Policy (Telesis Report)*, Report 64, NESC, Dublin.

Neal, Frank (1998) *Black '47: Britain and the Famine Irish*, Macmillan, London.

Neary, J. P. and Cormas Ó Gráda (1986/1991) 'Protection, Economic War and Structural Change: The 1930s in Ireland', Centre for Economic Research, University College, Dublin, Working Paper No. 40. Repub. in *Irish Historical Studies* (May 1991), Vol. 27, No. 107, pp. 250–66.

New Ireland Forum (1983) *The Cost of Violence Arising from the Northern Ireland Crisis Since 1969*, Stationery Office, Dublin.

New Ireland Forum (1984) *The Macroeconomic Consequences of Integrated Economic Policy, Planning and Co-ordination in Ireland*, Stationery Office, Dublin.

New Jersey Commission on Holocaust Education (1998) *The Great Irish Famine*, New Jersey State, New Jersey.

Nolan, Brian, Bertrand Maître, Donal O'Neill and Olive Sweetman (2000) *The Distribution of Income in Ireland*, Oak Tree Press, Dublin.

Northern Ireland Council on Voluntary Action (NICVA) (March 2000) 'NICVA Response to Government Consultation Paper on Northern Ireland Structural Funds Plan 2000–2006', NICVA, Belfast.

Northern Ireland Government, Department of Finance and Personnel (DFP)

(2009) *2009–10 Northern Ireland Public Sector Pay and Workforce Technical Annex*, DFP, Belfast.

Northern Ireland Voluntary Trust (NIVT) (1998) 'Taking Risks for Peace', NIVT, Belfast.

Ó Broin, Eoin (2009) *Sinn Féin and the Politics of Left Republicanism*, Pluto, London.

Ó Gráda, Cormac (1993) *Ireland: Before and After the Famine*, Manchester University Press, Manchester.

Ó Gráda, Cormac (1994) *Ireland: A New Economic History 1780–1939*, Oxford University Press, Oxford.

Ó Gráda, Cormac (1997) *A Rocky Road*, Manchester University Press, Manchester.

Ó Gráda, Cormac (2001) 'Famine, Trauma, and Memory', *Béaloideas*, 69, pp. 121–43.

Ó Gráda, Cormac (2006) *Ireland's Great Famine*, University College Dublin Press, Dublin.

Ó Gráda, Cormac (2008) 'The Irish Economy Half a Century Ago', UCD Centre for Economic Research, Working Paper Series, August, Dublin.

Ó Gráda, Cormac and Kevin H. O'Rourke (1997) 'Mass Migration as Disaster Relief: Lessons from the Great Irish Famine', *European Review of Economic History*, Vol. 1, No. 1, pp. 3–25.

O'Brien, D. P. (1975) *The Classical Economists,* Oxford University Press, Oxford.

O'Brien, George (1936) 'Patrick Hogan', *Studies,* No. 25, pp. 360–1.

O'Connor, R. and C. Guiomard (1985) 'Agricultural Output in the Irish Free State Area before and after Independence', *Irish Economic and Social History,* Vol. 12, pp. 89–97.

O'Dowd, Liam et al. (1995) 'Borders, National Sovereignty and European Integration', *International Journal of Urban and Regional Research*, Vol. 19, No. 2, pp. 272–85.

O'Hagan, J. W. (2000) *The Economy of Ireland*, Gill, Dublin.

O'Hearn, Denis (1998) *Inside the Celtic Tiger*, Pluto, London.

O'Hearn, Denis (2000) 'Globalisation, "New Tigers," and the End of the Developmental State? The Case of the Celtic Tiger', *Politics and Society*, Vol. 28, No. 1, pp. 67–92.

O'Hearn, Denis (2003) 'Macroeconomic Policy in the Celtic Tiger: A Critical Reassessment', in Colin Coulter and Steve Coleman (eds), *The End of Irish History? Critical Reflections on the Celtic Tiger*, Manchester University Press, Manchester.

O'Leary, Brendan and McGarry, John (1996) *The Politics of Antagonism: Understanding Northern Ireland*, Athlone Press, London.

O'Rourke, Kevin (1991) 'Agricultural Change and Rural Depopulation, 1845–1876', *The Journal of Economic History*, Vol. 51, No. 2, June, pp. 464–66.

O'Rourke, Kevin (1994) 'The Economic Impact of the Famine in the Short and Long Run', *The American Economic Review*, Vol. 84, No. 2, May, pp. 309–13.

O'Toole, Fintan (2003) *After the Ball*, New Island Press, Dublin.

O'Toole, Fintan (2010 edition) *Ship of Fools: How Stupidity and Corruption Sank the Celtic Tiger*, Faber & Faber, London.

Observer (2011) 'Comment', 27 February, p. 34.

OECD (1976) *Regional Problems and Policies in OECD Countries: France, Italy, Ireland, Denmark, Sweden, Japan*, OECD, Paris.

OECD (1985) *Ireland, Economic Survey*, April, OECD, Paris.

OECD (1999) *Economic Surveys: Ireland 1999*, OECD, Paris.

Owen, Arwel Ellis (1994) *The Anglo-Irish Agreement: The First Three Years*, University of Wales Press, Cardiff.

Paseta, Senia (2010) 'Northern Ireland and the Second World War', from *Northern Ireland: A Divided Community, 1921–1972*, Gale Digital Collection, www.gale.com/DigitalCollections

Pomfret, J. E. (1930) *The Struggle for the Land in Ireland*, Princeton University, Princeton, N.J.

Póirtéir, Cathal (1995) *The Great Irish Famine*, RTÉ/Mercier, Dublin.

Press, Jon (1989) *The Footwear Industry in Ireland 1922–1973*, Irish Academic Press, Dublin.

PRONI (n.d.) http://www.proni.gov.uk/index/exhibitions_talks_and_events/from_north_to_south_online/the_workhouse_orphans.htm

Proteus (2000) 'Lessons of Peace I', Proteus, Belfast.

Public Accounts Committee of the House of Commons (2001) 'Northern Ireland Appropriation Accounts 1998–99, Vote 1 (NIA 6) and National Agriculture Support: Fraud', *Hansard*, London.

Quigley, George (1992) 'Ireland: An Island Economy', Speech to the Confederation of Irish Industry, February, Dublin.

Rees, Russell (1998) *Ireland 1905–25*, Vol. 1, Colourpoint Books, Newtownards.

Riordan, E. J. (1920) *Modern Irish Trade and Industry*, Dutton, London.

Robinson, Nugent (1862) 'The Condition of the Dwellings of the Poor in Dublin, with a Glance at the Model Lodging Houses', in *Transactions of the National Association for the Promotion of Social Science*, London.

Rogers, Nini (2009) *Ireland, Slavery and Anti-slavery*, Palgrave, Basingstoke.

Rolston, Bill (1995) 'Selling Tourism in a Country at War', *Race and Class*, Vol. 37, No. 1, pp. 41–50.

Rooney, Eilish (1995) 'Women in Political Conflict', *Race and Class*, Vol. 37, No. 1, pp. 51–6.

Rowthorn, Bob (1981) 'Northern Ireland: An Economy in Crisis', *Cambridge Journal of Economics*, Vol. 5, pp. 1–31.

Rowthorn, Bob and Naomi Wayne (1988) *Northern Ireland: The Political Economy of Conflict*, Polity, Cambridge.

Ruddock, Alan (2006) 'Addicted to State Subvention, North will Suffer When it's Gone', *The Times*, 8 January.

Ryan, W. J. L. (1949) *The Nature and Effects of Protective Policy in Ireland, 1922–1939*, unpublished, Trinity College, Dublin.

Sadler, M. T. (1828) *Ireland: Its Evils, and Their Remedies*, London, Murray.

Scally, Robert James (1995) *The End of Hidden Ireland*, Oxford University Press, Oxford.

Scrope, G. P. (1831) 'Poor Law for Ireland', *Quarterly Review,* No. 44, February, pp. 511–54.

Sexton, James (1936) *Sir James Sexton: Agitator*, Faber, London.

Simpson, J. (July 1971) 'Regional Analysis: The Northern Ireland Experience', *Economic and Social Review,* Vol. 2, No. 4.

Smiley, James (1955) *The Social and Historical Background of the Irish Linen Trade*, reading to a joint meeting with the A.I.M.O. of Ireland, Dublin, 12 July, http://occmed.oxfordjournals.org/cgi/reprint/5/4/103.pdf

Smith, Adam (1776) *The Wealth Of Nations*, Methuen, London. http://www.econlib.org/library/Smith/smWN.htm.

Smith, F. W. (1876) *The Irish Linen Trade Hand-book and Directory,* W. H. Greer, Dublin.

Smith, Nicola Jo-Anne (2005) *Showcasing Globalisation? The Political Economy of the Irish Republic*, Manchester University Press, Manchester.

Solar, Peter M. (1997) 'The Potato Famine in Europe', in Cormac Ó Gráda (ed.), *Famine 150: The Teagasc/UCD Lectures*, Teagasc, Dublin, pp. 113–27.

Spiegel, H. (1992) *The Growth of Economic Thought*, Duke University, Durham, N.C.

Sraffa, P. (ed.) (1951–1973) *The Works of David Ricardo*, Oxford University Press, Oxford.

Steed, Guy and Morgan Thomas (June 1971) 'Regional Industrial Change: Northern Ireland', *Annals of the Association of American Geographers*, Vol. 61, No. 2, pp. 344–60.

Sweeney, P. (1999) *The Celtic Tiger: Ireland's Continuing Economic Miracle*, Oak Tree Press, Dublin.

Swift MacNeill, J.G. (1886) *English Interference with Irish Industries*, Cassell, London.

Symposium on Economic Development (1958–1959) in the *Journal of the Statistical and Social Inquiry Society of Ireland* (1959), Vol. 20, Pt 2, pp. 112–48.

Taillon, Ruth (1997) 'The EU Peace Programme', West Belfast Economic Forum, Belfast.

Teague, Paul (ed.) (1993) *The Economy of Northern Ireland: Perspectives for Structural Change,* Lawrence & Wishart, London.

Teague, Paul (1998) 'Monetary Union and Social Europe', *Journal of European Social Policy*, Vol. 8, No. 2, pp. 117–37.

Thackeray, William Makepeace (1843) *The Irish Sketchbook*, Chapman, London.

Thompson, E. P. (1991) *Customs in Common*, Merlin, London.

Tocqueville, Alexis de (1968) *Journeys to England and Ireland*, Anchor, New York.

Tomlinson, Mike (1995) 'Can Britain leave Ireland? The Political Economy of War and Peace', *Race and Class*, Vol. 37, No. 1, pp. 1–22.

Tomlinson, Mike (2004) *The Northern Ireland Conflict: Legacies and Impacts*, Combat Poverty Agency, Monaghan.

Townshend, C. (1975) *The British Campaign in Ireland 1919–1921*, 2nd edn, Oxford University Press, Oxford.

Triskele and Holywell Trust (1998) *Along the Borderline: A Review of the Impact of Funding on Community Development along the Border Counties*, Holywell Trust, Derry.

Wakefield, Edward (1812) *An Account of Ireland, Statistical and Political*, Longman, Hurst, Rees, Orme & Brown, London.

Walsh, Brendan (1979) 'Economic Growth and Development 1945–70', *EconPapers*, University College Dublin, Dublin.

Weale, James (1834) *Revised Valuation Survey of 1821 of Bassington and Gale*, Quit Rent Office Papers, National Archives of Ireland, Dublin.

Whelan, Bernadette (1992) 'Ireland and the Marshall Plan', *Irish Economic and Social History*, Vol. 19.

Whelan, Karl (1999) 'Economic Geography and the Long-run Effects of the Great Irish Famine', *Economic and Social Review*, Vol. 30, No. 1, pp. 1–20.

Whitaker, T. K. (1973) 'From Protection to Free Trade – The Irish Experience', *Administration*, Vol. 21, No. 4, winter, pp. 405–23.

Williams, T. Desmond (ed.) (1995) *Ireland in the War Years and After, 1938–1951*, Gill & Macmillan, Dublin.

Williams, T. D. (ed.) (1969, reprinted 1995) *Ireland in the War Years and After, 1939–51*, Gill & Macmillan, Dublin.

Wilson, Robin (2000) 'Structurally Unsound: The Northern Ireland Bids for Further EU Monies', Democratic Dialogue, Belfast.

Wilson, Thomas, Government of Northern Ireland (1965) *Economic Development in Northern Ireland*, HMSO, Belfast.

Wolf, Martin (2011) 'Ireland Needs Help with its Debt', *Financial Times*, 23 February, p. 11.

Woodham-Smith, Cecil (1964, 2nd edn 1991) *The Great Hunger: Ireland 1845–1849*, Penguin, Harmondsworth.

Wrightson, W. B. (1837) 'The Workhouse System; the Irish Poor Bill', *Quarterly Review*, 66, October, pp. 186–208.

INDEX